New Directions in Career Planning and the Workplace

Jean M. Kummerow • EDITOR

SECOND EDITION

New Directions in Career Planning and the Workplace

practical strategies for career management professionals

DAVIES-BLACK PUBLISHING
PALO ALTO, CALIFORNIA

Published by Davies-Black Publishing, an imprint of Consulting Psychologists Press, Inc., 3803 East Bayshore Road, Palo Alto, CA 94303; 800-624-1765.

Special discounts on bulk quantities of Davies-Black books are available to corporations, professional associations, and other organizations. For details, contact the Director of Book Sales at Davies-Black Publishing, an imprint of Consulting Psychologists Press, Inc., 3803 East Bayshore Road, Palo Alto, CA 94303; 650-691-9123; fax 650-623-9271.

Visit the Davies-Black Publishing website at www.daviesblack.com.

04 03 02 01 00 10 9 8 7 6 5 4 3 2 1
Printed in the United States of America

Library of Congress Cataloging-in-Publication Data

New directions in career planning and the workplace : practical strategies for career management professionals / Jean M. Kummerow, editor.—2nd ed.
p. cm.
Previously published: Palo Alto, Calif.: Consulting Psychologists Press, c1991.
Includes bibliographical references and index.
ISBN 0-89106-145-2 (pbk.)
1. Career development. 2. Vocational guidance. I. Kummerow, Jean M.

HF5549.5.C35 N48 2000
658.3—dc20

00-030855

SECOND EDITION
First printing 2000

Contents

Introduction

New Directions in Career Planning and the Workplace was first published in 1991. While much of the content remained relevant at the end of the decade, albeit no longer "new," it seemed time to address more current issues. The search for those issues was an interesting one that led to writers who help assess the impact of globalization, diversity, technology, an expanding service economy, and change on the world of work, and to topics dealing with life quality, values, personal development, and more.

I've had an opportunity to "live" with these chapters for several months now. I've been able to discuss their contents with colleagues and, more important, to use them with my clients to help them in their career transitions. It's a paradox that the more my clients understand that the world (and their role in it) is rapidly changing, the easier it is for them to handle the changes even when the pace of change is accelerating. And it's also a paradox that the more we know, the more we know what we don't know. It is my wish that this book add to your understanding of the work world as well as the career counseling process and that we all keep searching for what we don't know.

To introduce you to the chapters, a description of each follows. You'll find more about the authors at the end of the book.

1 THE CHANGING WORLD OF WORK: Preparing Yourself for the Road Ahead

Wayne Cascio, an internationally renowned industrial psychologist, examines the new workplace realities and the business trends that are shaping them—globalization, technology, change, intellectual capital, speed of market change, and cost control. He identifies what a global marketplace means for workers, including its psychological side. He shows how restructuring, mergers, and acquisitions have redefined loyalty and career success. He suggests some roles for companies in this new world of work, but also highlights the necessity of individual workers taking charge of their own careers. This chapter succinctly captures what is happening in our work world.

2 PLANNING FOR THE 21st-CENTURY WORKFORCE: Key Trends That Will Shape the Employment and Career Landscape

Andrea Saveri and Rod Falcon of the Institute for the Future are masters at studying the labor market numbers and pointing out the exciting meanings in the trends they identify. They look at the next decade, in which the labor force will grow much more slowly than it has in recent years, and see these trends: intergenerational workforce creating challenges; demographic fragmentation leading to population niches; women pioneering work alternatives; youth culture transforming organizational work; labor mobility contributing to nonlinear career paths; and global work becoming a local experience. Saveri and Falcon also examine the nature of jobs in the next decade and foresee an expanding service economy. They identify communications management as a key work activity and discuss how young workers will shape the adoption of new tools at the office. Their data are compelling and their discussion of them fascinating. They offer unique practical exercises to help in the application of their ideas.

3 A NEW DEAL FOR A LEARNING ECONOMY: Jobs and Careers in Postindustrial Society

Stephen Herzenberg, John Alic, and Howard Wial are experts at labor market analysis and give us the benefit of their wisdom as they investigate the current service economy and explore possibilities for transforming it. They present a model of four work systems encompassing the jobs of the service sector and discuss current career paths for workers within each of those systems. They identify three major problems in the current service economy: many service jobs are "bad" jobs with low pay and limited opportunity for advancement; uncertainty and insecurity are part of even many good service jobs; and poor productivity performance exists in many service industries. They do not leave us hanging, however, instead offering solutions to these problems and suggesting ways to reorganize work to reduce the number of low-wage, dead-end jobs; create new pathways out of low-wage jobs within and across industries; and strengthen the infrastructure for career development for all service workers. The result is improved service products for us all, and higher-paid workers with more opportunities to advance into better jobs. The authors offer case studies of where their ideas have been put into practice. They are sure to get you thinking about jobs in a different way. Their chapter is based on their book, *New Rules for a New Economy: Employment and Opportunity in Postindustrial America,* and I recommend it to those who'd like to learn more.

4 INTEGRATIVE LIFE PLANNING: A New Worldview for Career Professionals

Sunny Hansen is a well-known career development educator. Her career psychology perspective focuses not only on the societal context of workplace changes and how these affect work and other life roles, but also on human development within the context of societal improvement. She suggests that career management professionals emphasize the needs of human beings, and encourages us to be change agents in our own organizations, in the lives of our clients, and in our own lives. She offers a framework, Integrative Life Planning, to help us focus on what's really important, and gives us an ideal to strive for in integrating our work and personal lives. This not only increases our self-satisfaction with work but also benefits our community and our society. The six critical tasks of her framework are (1) finding work that needs doing in changing global contexts, (2) weaving our lives into a meaningful whole, (3) connecting family and work, (4) valuing pluralism and inclusivity, (5) exploring spirituality and life purpose, and (6) managing personal transitions and organizational change. Hansen offers many exercises to help readers understand and apply the six critical tasks to their lives. Her chapter is based on her book *Integrative life Planning: A New Worldview for Career Professionals.* Those who want more depth are invited to read further.

5 INFORMED OPPORTUNISM: Career and Life Planning for the New Millennium

Judith Waterman contributes her considerable expertise as a career counselor and trend watcher to help us understand the new world of career counseling. While the fundamentals of career planning remain the same, the context has shifted. With our accelerated society facing rapid change on all fronts, we need a different psychological approach to the job market, an approach Waterman calls informed opportunism. Workers must be informed about market trends and aware of their own strengths, skills, and priorities.

They need to be constantly scanning for opportunities so that when one comes along that fits them well, they can jump at it. Waterman offers myriad ways for people to get to know themselves, and strategies to help them be ready for the uncertainty ahead. She identifies four steps to career planning based on informed opportunism: (1) understanding career realities, (2) self-assessing, (3) synthesizing data and setting priorities, and (4) acting—and then keeping the process moving. Her case studies help readers quickly apply the principles presented in her chapter.

6 BEYOND BALANCE TO LIFE QUALITY: The Integration of Work and Life

Betsy Collard and H. B. Gelatt, longtime professionals and forward thinkers in the field, have teamed up to help us rethink the issue of trying to balance work and life. They suggest that the balance framework is no longer helpful in our interconnected and boundariless world; seeking equilibrium may be counterproductive. They call for (1) reframing the issue in terms of life quality, (2) identifying the two components of life quality—that is, how time is spent and how people feel and think about that expenditure, (3) identifying the mental barriers to achieving life quality, and (4) questioning the common wisdom of simplification. Collard and Gelatt do a masterful job of making their case and helping the reader understand the concepts through questions for reflection and several exercises. You are likely to view your own life differently after reading this chapter.

7 VALUES: A Key to Meaningful Work

Mark Guterman and Terry Karp share their expertise as developers of a new process for understanding values. Taking this familiar topic in career counseling a step further, they begin with a discussion of the place of values in our lives and offer a variety of methods to help clients find and declare their values. These include both such familiar techniques as journaling and defining moments identification and a unique research-based card sort and mapping technique, ValueSearch, designed to identify the patterns in values. Guterman and Karp identify eight motivational goals or categories in values and four ways to map them: universality and/or benevolence lead to a self-transcendence theme; tradition and/or security lead to a conformity theme; power and/or achievement lead to a self-enhancement theme; and excitement and self-direction lead to an openness to change theme. Using their system, it becomes easier to take what seem to be disparate values and identify a pattern for clients to understand. The system also more clearly articulates values conflict. The authors offer explanations and examples to help readers quickly grasp their work and learn to apply it.

8 MULTICULTURAL CAREER COUNSELING: Awareness, Knowledge, and Skills for the Changing Face of the Workplace

Rosie Phillips Bingham has long been a leader in helping psychologists and career development specialists become more effective in culturally diverse settings. In her chapter, she illustrates the importance of career management professionals recognizing their own worldview—that is, the lens they use to understand the world around them. She offers a model for understanding how racial identity develops and explains how that affects the career counseling process. She presents ways in which career counselors and clients can prepare themselves for the process. Included are several checklists, such as the *Multicultural Career Counseling Checklist,* to help counselors organize and carry out their counseling interventions in ways that are sensitive to their clientele and to themselves. Bingham's frameworks and practical suggestions can help career management professionals increase their level of awareness, knowledge, and skill in multicultural career counseling.

9 DEVELOPMENTAL CAREER COUNSELING: Different Stages, Different Choices

Judith Grutter is a longtime contributor to the field of career counseling—in her career counseling practice, in her conceptual frameworks, and in her training business. In this chapter she focuses on how clients at different developmental stages face different issues and therefore need different interventions. She looks at the stages of identity formation, exploration, commitment, career entry, career progression, career refinement, and career disengagement, helping us understand each stage and what clients "need" to do to successfully navigate each one. Using the frameworks of Holland's RIASEC codes and psychological type, Grutter walks us through ways to help clients learn about the world of work, choose a work path, become initiated into their first job, understand how to promote themselves, assess their life's work and its meaning, expand their horizons, and look at what retirement might mean. Her many examples, practical tips, and useful strategies illustrate her points as well as facilitate our applications of them.

10 USING THE STRONG INTEREST INVENTORY® AND MYERS-BRIGGS TYPE INDICATOR® INSTRUMENTS TOGETHER: The Whole Is Greater than the Sum of Its Parts

Jean Kummerow contributes her experience both as a trainer teaching professionals throughout the world about the *Strong Interest Inventory*® and *Myers-Briggs Type Indicator*® (MBTI®) instruments and as a career counselor utilizing these instruments directly to help her clients. This chapter is the most specific of all the chapters, with its emphasis on direct career counseling interventions through the combined use of these two popular career assessment instruments. Both instruments are well-known throughout the world as tools for helping people understand themselves and their career interests. Kummerow offers an introduction to each instrument, but the focus of the chapter is on using the two together. She shows how to integrate the results of those two instruments at a statistical level, a personality level, a task level, and a job title level. Combining the two gives more power to the assessment than using them separately. Numerous case examples and exercises are presented to help readers and their clients in their own integration process.

International readers will also find this book relevant to their practices and lives. Several worldviews of the career development concepts are mentioned, although those of major focus are of Euro-North American origins. These concepts have spread throughout the world and seem applicable globally. Readers in many countries will notice a number of the same trends in their workplaces even while most of the statistics presented here are based on U.S. data. We're all facing a quickly changing international marketplace and the challenges and joys of technology!

Let me mention just a few facts to indicate why some topics are covered in these chapters. Several authors write of the importance of health care benefits in career decision making. The United States does not have universal health care. Employers generally provide health insurance to full-time workers and some part-time workers in jobs at certain levels; the government provides health care for the elderly, disabled, and very poor. Thus, finding a job with health care benefits is important to many workers, and some are hesitant to take risks in moving to part-time work, self-employment, or a new employer if it jeopardizes their health care benefits.

In at least one chapter, wage figures are mentioned. To help put these in context, a job paying $10 (U.S. dollars) an hour equals an annual salary of approximately $21,000. In the United States in 2000, poverty guidelines were set at $8,350 annually for a single person or $17,050 for a family of four. (Some consider these guidelines too low and even suggest doubling or tripling the numbers for a more accurate picture of a "decent" standard of living.) Nearly 13 percent of the United States population lives below these guidelines.

There are many challenges in career development work everywhere. It is my wish that this book can help *all* of us better meet those challenges.

Another prominent feature of this book is its practical focus with exercises and discussion questions to make career development issues readily applicable to clients. The exercises in this book are examples for use with clients, and permission is granted to reproduce them for individual client use only. Reproduction for any other purpose, including resale, *requires* written permission for use from the publisher.

So there you have it—a walk through the book and the highlights of each chapter along with an invitation for international readers and clients everywhere to apply the material to their own circumstances. I hope you enjoy reading the book as much as I enjoyed editing it, and I trust that you will learn much that can help you in your work and in your life.

Jean Kummerow
St. Paul, Minnesota
May 2000

part ONE

New Directions in the Workplace

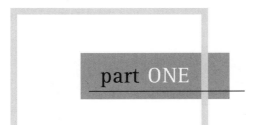

1

The Changing World of Work

PREPARING YOURSELF FOR THE ROAD AHEAD

Wayne F. Cascio

WE ARE LIVING IN THE FUTURE/I'LL TELL YOU HOW I KNOW/
I READ IT IN THE PAPER/FIFTEEN YEARS AGO—John Prine

Many a sage has attempted to forecast new developments in the economy, in technology, in work, and in everyday life. In fact, over the last 30 years or so the pages of many popular publications have been littered with predictions—and many of them have been just plain wrong. As examples, consider two headlines that appeared in the *Wall Street Journal* in 1966 and 1976, respectively: "Airliner That Will Top 4,000 MPH Is Expected Before End of Century" and "Huge Nuclear Facilities Will Help the U.S. Meet Surging Power Demand." I don't claim to have a crystal ball either, but in this chapter I will share with you some ideas about what the future world of work will look like, particularly the trends in organizations and the impact on workers. I'll end with some suggestions for your own career management.

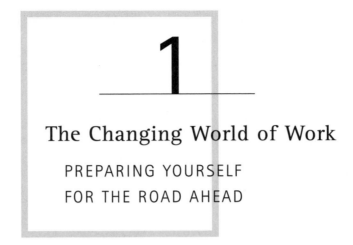

Let's begin by examining how new workplace realities, such as downsizing, reengineering, and restructuring, have produced a revision of the psychological contract that binds workers and organizations to each other. To put the changes into perspective, consider some features of the old contract, and how they have changed to reflect the realities of today's workplaces (for more on this, see Rousseau, 1995, 1996).

Old Psychological Contract	New Psychological Contract
Stability, predictability	Change, uncertainty
Permanence	Temporariness
Standard work patterns	Flexible work
Valuing loyalty	Valuing performance and skills
Paternalism	Self-reliance
Job security	Employment security
Linear career growth	Multiple careers
Onetime learning	Lifelong learning

Do these changes in the psychological contract imply that Americans are not as committed to work as a central activity in their lives? Data from the annual General Social Survey (a multitopic survey administered to roughly 1,500 adult, English-speaking men and women) suggest that the answer is no (National Research Council, 1999). The following item from the survey was asked in 1973 and again in 1996: "If you were to get enough money to live as comfortably as you would like for the rest of your life, would you continue to work, or would you stop working?" In 1973, 69 percent of Americans said they would continue to work. In 1996, 68 percent said they would continue to work—virtually no change. In the same surveys, respondents indicated the job characteristic most important to them continued to be an intrinsic one: work is important and gives a feeling of accomplishment.

Although there appears to be continuity in the centrality of work in the lives of Americans, this is not to imply that dramatic changes are not occurring in the world of work. Business trends that seem immutable and unstoppable are driving much of the change. These include the following (Bulkeley, 1998; SHRM, 1996; Ulrich, 1998):

- **Globalization**—a term that refers to commerce without borders, along with the interdependence of business operations internationally. The growth of the global market is accelerating with the growth of the Internet. And the Internet has changed the rules of business competition forever. Booksellers such as Amazon.com provide 24-hour-a-day supermarkets that ship their products anywhere. Using software from Net

Perceptions, Amazon.com analyzes purchases and suggests other books that customers will probably like. Market research with customers indicates that the suggestions are often right on target. Get ready to take advantage of global competition online, whether you are looking to buy or sell a car, a house, or a bouquet of flowers.

- **Technology**—Historians of technology are debating whether advances in digital technology are ushering in a new era. Digitization is (1) the conversion of physical phenomena (for example, distance, time) and meaningful symbols such as words and numbers into binary (digital) electronic signals, and (2) the use of those signals to control machines and to create or manipulate information (National Research Council, 1999). It is having at least three effects: (1) It is changing the mix of jobs. New jobs, many in the computer science area, have arisen, while jobs in other operations that revolved around manual or mechanical means of processing information, such as printing press operators, telephone operators, and bank tellers, have declined. (2) The skills required to do many jobs are either increasing or decreasing, especially those using information-processing technologies. Evidence suggests that more workers have experienced an increase in skills as a result of digitization (National Research Council, 1999). (3) It is changing the types of skills needed, reducing some of the manual and sensory-based skills and increasing the analytic and information-processing requirements of many production jobs. This means rapid changes in the knowledge and skill content of jobs, along with changes in the analytical and interactive aspects of work, and this has important implications for the design of education and training systems.

- **Change**—Changes in demographics, markets, technologies, the design of jobs, and organizational restructuring drive the need for continuous learning and produce increased stress, the redefinition of careers, and opportunities for new products and services. As Heraclitus said about 2,500 years ago, "Nothing endures except change." Time has not dulled the validity of that statement. (Chapter 2 documents several of these changes.)

- **Intellectual capital**—knowledge, information, intellectual property, and experience that can be put to use to create wealth and to enhance human welfare (Stewart, 1997). Intellectual capital is found in three places in an organization: its people, structures, and customers. Intellectual capital is therefore composed of human capital, structural capital, and customer capital. Human capital includes the knowledge, skill, and capability of individuals to provide solutions to problems that customers think are important. Structural capital includes everything that remains when the employees go home—databases, customer files, software manuals, and so forth. Customer capital is the value of an organization's relationships with the people with whom it does business, including suppliers. Human capital is particularly important, especially in the context of how an organization competes for business in the marketplace (its competitive strategy), because human capital is the source of innovation and renewal. After all, money talks, but it doesn't think. Machines work efficiently, but they don't invent. Thinking and inventing are done by people, the most valuable asset in today's organizations.

- **Speed in market change**—the need to be in constant touch with customers, along with more strategic partnering to penetrate new markets or to gain competitive advantage in old ones. To stay ahead, companies are moving from reengineering to e-engineering, for the Internet permits instant communication with every supplier, partner, and customer—and, in many cases, lets them communicate with each other. Dell Computer, for instance, lets customers configure their own PCs online and then track assembly and shipping status. The result? Happy customers and continued growth.

- **Cost control**—the need to keep the costs of doing business at the lowest possible levels in order to be competitive. Outsourcing, strategic partnerships, variable pay schemes, and flattened organizational hierarchies have served to lower costs and have spawned dramatic changes in the structure of work. Among the most visible changes is the increased use of teams. Teams move discretion to lower organizational levels, and cross-functional teams enhance horizontal communications, coordination, and problem solving across traditional functional boundaries (for example, specialists in human resources working with finance, manufacturing, and sales staff).

TOWARD A GLOBAL MARKETPLACE

The global village is getting smaller every day. Satellite dishes in the world's most remote areas beam live television feeds from CNN and MTV. Cross-cultural exposure, if not actual interaction, has become the norm. In this emerging economic order, foreign investment by the world's leading corporations is a fact of modern organizational life. Firms in the European Union have invested almost $250 billion in the United States, while U.S. firms have invested more than $230 billion in the European Union. More than 800 multinational companies have regional headquarters in Hong Kong alone (Kraar, 1997). Today foreign investment is viewed not just as an opportunity for U.S. companies investing abroad but also as an opportunity for firms in other countries to develop subsidiaries in the United States and elsewhere. A single marketplace has been created by factors such as the following:

- Global telecommunications enhanced by fiber optics, satellites, and computer technology
- Giant multinational corporations such as Gillette, Unilever, and Nestlé, which have begun to lose their national identities as they integrate and coordinate product design, manufacturing, sales, and services on a worldwide basis
- Growing free trade among nations (exemplified by the European Union; the Association of Southeast Asian Nations, ASEAN; Mercosur, a free-trade area that includes Argentina, Paraguay, and Brazil; and the North American Free Trade Agreement among Mexico, the United States, and Canada)
- Financial markets being open 24 hours a day around the world
- International investment among multinational companies of $315 billion in 1996 alone, of which $96 billion came from U.S. companies ("Foreign Money," 1997; Solomon, 1997)
- Foreign control of more than 12 percent of U.S. manufacturing assets and employment of more than 3 million U.S. workers

- Employment of about 75,000 expatriate U.S. employees overseas
- The emergence of global standards and regulations for trade, commerce, finance, products, and services

As a consequence of this onslaught of cross-cultural exposure and interaction, it might appear that the world's cultures are growing more homogeneous. Don't be fooled. A quote from T. Fujisawa, cofounder of Honda Motor Co., suggests otherwise: "Japanese and American management is 95% the same, and differs in all important respects" (Adler, Doktor, & Redding, 1986). In other words, while organizations are becoming more similar in terms of structure and technology, people's behavior within those organizations continues to reveal culturally based differences.

Culture, according to Harry Triandis, a cross-cultural psychologist at the University of Illinois, provides implicit theories of social behavior that act like a "computer program," controlling the actions of individuals. Cultures include unstated assumptions about the way the world is. These assumptions influence thinking, emotions, and actions without people noticing that they do. Attributes such as sense of self and space, dress and appearance, food and eating habits, verbal and nonverbal communication, time and time sense, beliefs and attitudes, and work motivation are some typical dimensions along which cultures differ. Members of cultures often believe that their ways of thinking are obviously correct, and need not be discussed.

It is precisely because aspects of culture are not often discussed that opportunities for cross-cultural misunderstandings abound. Organizations will face ongoing challenges to find ways to help reduce such misunderstandings and to help people deal more effectively in a global environment. It is important to note, however, that the global environment that is characterized by multiple cultures from different racial or ethnic groups is often local as well. That is, many cities, neighborhoods, and workplaces comprise multiple cultures from different racial or ethnic groups. Some important issues to address include

- Helping people achieve a deeper understanding and appreciation of their own culture and that of others and to value the differences that each reflects
- Helping people span the boundaries between their own personal cultural experiences and those of the organizations they work in

- Helping managers and employees understand how the work of the organization (for example, through its work design or management styles) modifies their interactions with host-country nationals, whether those interactions are in an employer-to-employee or employee-to-customer context

THE INFORMATION REVOLUTION

Just as the Industrial Revolution brought about wrenching changes in the nature of work, and in the attitudes and habits of workers, the Information Revolution will transform everything it touches—and it will touch everything. Day by day, the information economy continues to expand. Just look at the growth of the computing, communications, and entertainment industries. As Thomas Stewart notes in his influential book *Intellectual Capital* (1997), every country, company, and individual depends increasingly on knowledge—patents, processes, skills, technologies, information about customers and suppliers, and experience. No force can stop, or even slow, the revolution that is going on all around us.

To illustrate just the broadest outline of this revolution, consider these startling facts:

- Industries that transport information are growing faster than those that transport goods. International voice telephone traffic has been increasing at a rate of about 16 percent per year, data traffic about 30 percent a year, and Internet traffic faster still (Stewart, 1997).

- Nike is a shoemaker that makes no shoes. Rather, its work is research and development, design, marketing, and distribution—all knowledge-intensive services.

- The substitution of information for inventory is reinventing retailing, and has led directly to the creation of the virtual department store ("The Virtual Mall," 1998). CUC International, an electronic shoppers club, has no inventory whatsoever. All it has is a catalog with a list of available items. To place an order, a customer either calls a toll-free number or accesses the company's Internet home page. CUC passes the order on (taking a commission), and it is then shipped directly from the manufacturer. The company stocks nothing but sells everything.

Knowledge has become the fundamental ingredient of what we make, do, buy, and sell. As a result, managing it—finding and growing intellectual capital, storing it, selling it, and sharing it—has become the most important economic task of individuals, businesses, and nations.

Consider the explosive growth of commerce on the Internet. In 1998, businesses spent $43.1 billion on Internet-based purchases from other corporations. In 1999, that figure was expected to rise to almost $110 billion (Anders, 1999). At the level of the individual firm, General Electric will save $500 million in two years by purchasing $5 billion in goods via the Internet. In 1998, Cisco Systems, a firm that makes routers for the Internet, sold over $5 billion (U.S.) in goods over the Internet. In addition, 7 out of every 10 requests to Cisco for technical assistance were fulfilled electronically, at satisfaction rates that surpassed those involving human interaction ("The Corporation of the Future," 1998).

U.S. consumers spent $3 billion on Internet-based purchases in 1998 and almost $12 billion in 1999, and they are expected to spend more than $41 billion by 2002 (Anders, 1999). In Japan, consumers spent about $1.7 billion in 1999, with the volume of purchases expected to swell to about $8.5 billion by 2001 (Spindle, 1999). Finally, e-commerce in Europe has gone from almost zero in 1997 to a projected $5 billion by 2003. To put Europe's relatively slower Internet usage in context, note that legal and telecommunications issues have hampered its quick expansion there. For example, even local telephone calls are billed by the minute, so the longer one stays connected, the larger one's phone bill grows (Gruner, 1999).

Indeed, the volume of online traffic is doubling every 100 days. This is reflected in sales growth among Internet-based firms. As an example, consider that the 1997 sales by the first Internet bookstore, Amazon.com, were $148 million. That was up 825 percent over 1996 sales. The nation's largest automobile retailer, Republic Industries, Inc., sold an estimated $500 million of cars through the Internet in 1999. Instead of relying on independent online services, Republic's close to 400 franchisees receive sales leads and build relationships through its AutoNation USA site. In the near future, consumers logging on to autonationusa.com will have the choice of surfing it by themselves or having an "Internet vehicle consultant" help them search for the right car or truck. When consumers are ready to buy, they are passed on to an Internet sales consultant at a dealership near them (Warner, 1999).

Consider one final fact: the employees of the companies that enable Internet-based commerce, or that transact Internet-based commerce, are all knowledge workers. This raises a fundamental issue—namely, what is knowledge work?

The Nature of Knowledge Work

Knowledge work—the work of planning, supervising, scheduling, and managing—used to be the province of the professional—the lawyer, the engineer, the teacher. Now it is frequently part of the job description of the hourly worker as well. Why? Because for most people today, information is the most important raw material they need to do their jobs. People are hired on the basis of what they know and can do. What they earn depends on the market value of the portfolio of skills and knowledge that they offer the employer. As an illustration of this, consider the change in perspective on mergers and acquisitions of progressive companies.

Rather than acquire firms merely to speed growth or to boost market share, Cisco routinely employs acquisitions to capture intellectual assets and next-generation products. Says John Chambers, Cisco's chief executive officer, "Most people forget that in a high-tech acquisition, you really are acquiring only people. . . . That's why so many of them fail. At what we pay, at $500,000 to $2 million an employee, we are not acquiring current market share. We are acquiring futures" ("The Corporation of the Future," 1998).

Indeed, Cisco's belief in this philosophy is so strong that it measures the success of every acquisition first by employee retention, then by new product development, and finally by return on investment. How has Cisco done in holding onto the intellectual assets it buys? Overall turnover among acquired employees is just 6 percent a year, two percentage points lower than Cisco's overall employee turnover. The company works hard to embrace employees acquired in deals, and often gives the most talented ones key jobs in the new organization. In fact, three of Cisco's main businesses are led by former CEOs of acquired companies.

Leveraging Knowledge

An ongoing challenge for those who rely on knowledge to do their jobs will be to transmit both new knowledge and accumulated wisdom rapidly.

This challenge will be especially difficult in geographically dispersed operating environments, such as many firms face. To facilitate the leveraging of knowledge, new structures are needed. One such structure is the "knowledge database."

So-called "knowledge databases" are cropping up inside large and small corporations as the practice of "knowledge management" begins to take off ("Does Anyone Around Here Know. . . ?," 1997). Its goal is an ambitious one: to allow every person in an organization to be able to access the collected know-how, experience, and wisdom of his or her colleagues. Big consulting firms are leading the way. Thus Andersen Worldwide developed its Knowledge Xchange; Booz, Allen & Hamilton set up Knowledge On-Line; KPMG Peat Marwick, a Knowledge Manager; and Price Waterhouse, something called Knowledge View. Among companies surveyed for Bain & Co.'s annual survey of management techniques, only 27 percent said they used knowledge management, and only a quarter of those said they used it in any substantial way. Still, corporate interest remains high as the portion of corporate assets defined as intellectual capital increases (Lancaster, 1997).

Actually, a day at work 10 years from now in the interconnected world of voice, data, and video will probably feel pretty much the same as it does now. What will change, however, is the amount of information available to the decision maker and the speed with which opinions can be gathered and synthesized. Search engines will change the role of libraries. The Internet and computers will facilitate lifelong learning. All of this implies greater process control, improved quality, and greater accountability than ever before (Bulkeley, 1998).

NURTURING THE HUMAN SIDE OF BUSINESS

In the 21st-century world of work, with its virtual teams, virtual offices, and even virtual organizations, the need to nurture the human side of business will be greater than ever. Issues of workplace fairness, justice, and work-life balance will not go away. Organizations will still face challenges in recruiting and retaining talented employees who will be committed to their jobs; in training new leaders to manage the performance of diverse employees (full-time, part-time, temps, and contract employees); and in managing the "people side" of mergers and acquisitions. There will always be a need for talented people to address those issues.

Consider the challenge of balancing work and home life when operating globally, 24 hours a day. With digital phones, you can be reached any time, anywhere. E-mail is filling up every hour. New items are coming in continually. How do you balance that (McGuire, 1998)?

The answer is with flexibility—both personal and organizational—and effective time management skills. This also implies that the demands of a faster pace of work will require a stable personality, and more and more firms will turn to personality assessment to identify workers and managers who are psychologically suited to perform work in the types of environments the firms operate in—and to screen out those who are not. Candidates who score high on dimensions of flexibility, agreeableness, emotional stability, and conscientiousness are good bets to succeed.

Another hot career area is "coaching." One study that examined which jobs are likely to grow most rapidly in the future identified "personal counselors" (along with personal home organizers, retirement planners, and genetic engineers) as jobs in this category (Minehan, 1999). While the idea of coaching as a managerial role has taken hold in team-based work environments, it will be a major focus of training programs in leadership development. Leaders in the kinds of 21st-century organizations described here will need to be master coaches because their roles will involve engendering loyalty from a diverse group of subordinates, even though the organization cannot guarantee jobs to anyone.

Leaders will also be responsible for managing the performance of members of virtual teams and teleworkers whom they do not physically see on a regular basis. Positions such as "Director of Socialization" will be developed to provide on-site counseling and to direct social activities (Minehan, 1999). There is well-developed literature on the topic of performance management (how to define performance, facilitate performance, and encourage performance), and those same principles can and should be applied in virtual work environments. In a nutshell, expect the demand for continued professional training and development in areas such as team building, executive assessment, feedback, and coaching to grow, not diminish, in the future world of work.

Much is made in the popular press about companies competing for the "best and the brightest." For those who fit that description, jobs will always be available. The fact is, however, that most of us are neither the best nor the brightest. Will there be a place for us in the new economy? The answer is a resounding yes. Services, which now account for 74 percent of the gross domestic product of the United States, and 79 percent of all employment, are expected to account for all of the net growth in jobs in the next decade (Cascio, 1995). It's not the manufacture of fewer goods as much as the effects of improved technology and more efficient manufacturing processes that allow the same or a greater amount of goods to be produced with fewer workers. As the ranks of manufacturing workers shrink, the ranks of workers in services—in fields as diverse as health care, financial services, retail sales, and business services—will expand.

Many service jobs require modest levels of intellectual skills, combined with well-developed interpersonal skills, along with high levels of adaptability, empathy, initiative, and an ability to work under stress. People of modest intellectual ability and well-developed interpersonal skills can capitalize on the increasing emphasis on interpersonal interactions in service jobs—those involving frontline customer contact with people, whether the people are called patients, clients, or customers.

The need for interdependence and more direct interactions with people increases the importance of skill in communications, problem solving, and negotiations. Considering all of the changes described thus far, what do the changes imply for individual careers, for the way that we define career success, and for career management?

WHAT A CHANGING WORLD OF WORK MEANS FOR WORKERS

In thinking about careers in the evolving world of work, it is important to emphasize the increasingly temporary nature of relationships between individuals and organizations. Said a victim of three corporate downsizings in four years, "A job is just an opportunity to learn some new skills that you can then peddle elsewhere in the marketplace" ("Working Scared," 1993). While such a view might appear cynical to some, the fact is that responsibility for career development ultimately belongs to each individual. This is painfully obvious to those who have been victims of downsizing or have struggled through a merger of organizational cultures. Their concept of loyalty has changed forever. The following sections examine this issue in greater detail.

The 1990s: Constant Restructuring, Mergers, and Acquisitions

At least since the mid-1980s, employment downsizing has been regarded as the preferred route to improve corporate efficiency. Indeed, *Newsweek* magazine commented that "Firing people has gotten to be trendy in corporate America, in the same way that building new plants and being considered a good corporate citizen gave you bragging rights 25 years ago" (Sloan, 1996, p. 44). This trend continued unabated throughout the 1990s. For example, in 1998 U.S. corporations announced over 600,000 staff cuts. Conversely, the robust U.S. economy generated 236,000 net new jobs a month in 1998, and workers enjoyed an average 2 percent wage increase after inflation ("A Tale of Two Job Markets," 1998).

Numerous articles have documented the downsizing that has been occurring for white-collar job holders. Many of the articles have focused on the negative consequences to individuals, families, and communities of people losing their jobs. Others, particularly in the business press, have extolled the benefits of companies making themselves "lean and mean." Regardless of one's perspective, virtually all observers agree that the phenomenon of employment downsizing has produced fundamental structural changes in our economy and has had painful impacts on the American labor force.

Downsizing has caught on in many industrialized countries. A study of six of them (Canada, France, Germany, Great Britain, Japan, and the United States) found that more than 90 percent of firms had downsized, and more than two-thirds were planning to do so again (Wyatt, 1993). In March of 1999, Sony Corporation announced a major asset restructuring. It plans to eliminate 20 percent of its factories and 17,000 of its worldwide workforce by 2003 ("Sony's Shake-Up," 1999). In short, downsizing is a global phenomenon, and it is far from over.

The accelerating pace of mergers and acquisitions is another trend that is affecting careers in organizations. Thousands of mergers and acquisitions have taken place over the last decade among both large and small companies. To appreciate the magnitude of this development, consider that in 1988 there were a total of 3,921 deals worth about $300 billion. In 1998, however, there were 11,260 deals worth over $1.5 trillion ("A Decade of M&A Activity," 1999). In general, after a buyout, the merged company eliminates staff duplications and unprofitable divisions. Restructuring, including downsizing, often leads to similar effects—diminished loyalty from employees. In the wave of takeovers, mergers, downsizings, and layoffs that characterized the 1990s, millions of workers have discovered that years of service mean little to a struggling management or to a new corporate parent. This leads to a rise in stress and to a decrease in satisfaction, commitment, intentions to stay, and perceptions of an organization's trustworthiness, honesty, and caring about its employees (Gutknecht & Keys, 1993; Kleinfeld, 1996; Schweiger & DeNisi, 1991).

Companies counter that today's competitive business environment makes it difficult to protect workers. Understandably, organizations are streamlining in order to become more competitive and more flexible in their response to the demands of the marketplace. But the rising disaffection of workers at all levels has profound implications for employers.

U.S. companies now lose half their employees every four years, half their customers in five years, and half their investors in less than 12 months (Reichheld, 1996). Median time on the job for all ages is now about four years ("Job Mobility," 1997; Work Week, 1997). Furthermore, employee turnover is expensive. Companies report that the fully loaded cost of losing a typical worker is $50,000 (Reingold, 1999). Soon managers will hold seven to ten jobs in a lifetime, up from three to four in the 1970s. Some 10 percent of the American workforce actually switch occupations every year (Henkoff, 1996).

Problem or Opportunity?

Is there an opportunity to profit from all of the wrenching changes that are going on? Companies like Monsanto, United Technologies, and Xerox recognize an opportunity to create value in the midst of such turmoil. How? By understanding that they can only retain loyal customers with a base of loyal employees (Reichheld, 1996; White & Lublin, 1996). Sears Roebuck & Company found as a result of a large-scale, two-year study involving more than 800 stores that the most important determinants of how an employee will behave in front of a customer (that is, in terms of his or her service helpfulness) are his or her attitudes toward the job and the company. Service helpfulness, together with the customer's perceptions about the quality and value of the merchandise, affect the likelihood that the customer will recommend Sears to others, and the likelihood that he or she will return to

Sears (customer retention). Customer retention, in turn, affects financial outcomes, such as changes in profitability and sales growth. Statistical analyses showed that this employer-customer-profit chain is causal in nature, and lagged in its effects. That is, employee attitudes at time one drive customer impressions at time two, which drive changes in financial outcomes at time three (Rucci, Kirn, & Quinn, 1998). The lesson? It really matters what employees think about their jobs and the company for which they work. It affects their behavior on the job, their commitment to doing a good job, their willingness to "go the extra mile" to satisfy a customer or to help a fellow employee (organizational citizenship), and their willingness to stay with the current employer. Creating a loyal base of employees is an opportunity for companies to create value in the marketplace. That's a win-win result for all concerned.

The New Meaning of Loyalty

The concept of loyalty that seems to be emerging is not the same as it has been traditionally—blind allegiance to a company. Today, progressive companies are trying to build loyalty to a vision or mission, to individual supervisors, or to members of a work team. Instead of a 20- or 30-year horizon, many firms are thinking in terms of shorter employment relationships, those of three to five years in duration. While they cannot provide guarantees of lifetime employment, they can offer their employees fixed-term employment contracts with options for renegotiation and extension. These are the same mechanisms used by professional sports teams to attract and retain top talent. As we have just seen, to the extent that they can decrease the defection rates of customers, employees, and investors, firms are likely to realize substantial growth, profits, and lasting value.

Career Success Redefined

In the past, organizations took primary responsibility for managing the careers of their employees. Not so anymore. In the evolving world of work one's career is shaped and managed more by the individual than by the organization (Hall & Mirvis, 1995). But what is the meaning of "career success"?

The tradition-oriented "organization man" of the 1950s had a clear definition of success and a stable model for achieving it. However, the constant threat of restructuring or downsizing in the late 1990s has forced employees at all levels to explore alternative models of career success, and they are confronted with a variety of possibilities. As a consequence, organizations are finding today's employees harder to manage. But they are also finding them to be highly motivated and committed to tasks they value (Rousseau & Wade-Benzoni, 1995).

In practical terms, what does this mean for the concept of development and success in the work career? Is it occupational success? Job satisfaction? Growth and development of skills? Successful movement through various life stages? Traditionally, career development and success have been defined in terms of occupational advancement, which is clear and easy to measure. However, throughout the 1990s, in response to tougher global competition and the threat of being taken over, companies have thinned out their ranks to become more efficient and profitable. That means less hierarchy and fewer rungs on the corporate ladder. At the same time, the large number of baby boomers (those born between 1945 and 1964) and baby busters (born 1965 to 1976), including record numbers of business school graduates, have come of age and are competing for the remaining rungs. The result is human resource management problems that organizations have never faced before. The impact on employees will be more stress, more burnout, and more psychological withdrawal. Alternative means of satisfying employees' career aspirations will be needed.

Consider a new model of career progress: In the future more careers will be cyclical—involving periodic cycles of skill apprenticeship, mastery, and reskilling. Lateral, rather than upward, movement will constitute career development, and cross-functional experience will be essential to multiskilling and continued employability. Late careers increasingly will be defined in terms of phased retirement (Hall & Mirvis, 1995). In this new world, the ultimate goal is psychological success, the feeling of pride and personal accomplishment that comes from achieving one's most important goals in life, be they achievement, family happiness, inner peace, or something else (Hall, 1996).

Increasing Concern for Work-Life Balance

Tight labor markets in the late 1990s, largely a function of a vibrant, expanding economy, have led many employers to rethink how to help their valued workers serve clients better while at the same time striking a better balance between their work lives and their personal lives. With the demand for talent in many fields far outstripping the available supply, many organizations have shifted their focus from finding new employees to retaining experienced ones. As a framework for viewing this issue, consider the following facts about the American workforce (Bond, Galinsky, & Swanberg, 1998):

- Fully 85 percent have some day-to-day family responsibility, and virtually identical proportions of men and women report work-family conflicts.
- Among wage and salaried workers, 46 percent are parents with children under 18 who live with them at least half-time.
- Among married employees, 78 percent have spouses or partners who are also employed.

For workers who are parents, consider the following facts about childcare issues (Johnson, 1999):

- Nearly one in five American workers (19 percent) have children under age six living at home.
- More than one-third of employees in the United States must have childcare arrangements in place in order to come to work.
- Among employed parents, 29 percent experienced some kind of childcare breakdown in the last three months, and 33 percent spend time regularly on the job worrying about care.

Childcare breakdowns are associated with absenteeism, tardiness, impaired concentration, and less marital and parental satisfaction.

At a more general level, family and personal concerns are a source of stress in all workplaces (Johnson, 1995, 1999):

- In professional service firms, well over half the employees can be expected to experience some kind of work-family stress in a three-month period.
- Staff members with work-family conflict are three times more likely to consider quitting (43 percent versus 14 percent).

- Staff members who believe that work is causing problems in their personal lives are much more likely to make mistakes at work (30 percent) than are those who have few job-related personal problems (19 percent).

Conversely, employees with supportive workplaces report greater job satisfaction and more commitment to helping their companies succeed. Thus an evaluation of Johnson & Johnson's work-life programs found that while employees appreciated and made use of the company's array of progressive policies, the factors most often associated with people's ability to balance work and nonwork roles were a supportive supervisor and workplace culture (Families and Work Institute, 1993).

Even the most progressive work-life policies are useless, and can even be counterproductive, if the company culture does not support them. When supervisors or coworkers do not support employees taking parental leave or using flextime, the policies themselves will fail to promote the kind of commitment and organizational attachment employers hope for. Leading companies know this, and they are reexamining the ways in which work is performed, managed, and rewarded. Fran S. Rodgers, chief executive officer of the Boston consulting firm WFD, Inc., aptly expressed this new attitude: "Judge people on results, and give them a lot more latitude in how they meet those results. Treat people like adults" (Rodgers, in Lublin, 1997, p. R4).

CAREER MANAGEMENT IN A CHANGING WORLD OF WORK

The previous sections provided the context for and trends in the changing world of work. Now I offer an emerging model of career management, one based on self-reliance, and offer some tips on handling two inevitable events in everyone's career: finding a job and leaving your current job for a new one.

Self-Reliance[1]

Consider this stark fact: In today's corporate environment, employees are ever more likely to crash into the ranks of the unemployed with no safety net, and it could happen over and over again. Moreover, candor about career issues is in short supply at many companies these days. Bottom line: Career survival is up to each individual—not the company. The advice to everyone: Consider yourself to be self-employed, responsible for your own career development, CEO of You, Inc. This new approach is based on an underlying assumption that would have been considered heresy 10 or 20 years ago in the paternalistic, "we'll take care of you" environments of many companies—that self-reliance is the key to career management in the 21st century. Remember, it's a new psychological contract between employers and employees.

In the past, many companies assumed responsibility for the career paths and growth of their employees. The company determined to what position, and at what speed, people would advance. That approach worked reasonably well in the corporate climate of the last three decades. However, the corporate disruptions of the 1990s have rendered this approach to employee career development largely unworkable.

Acquisitions, divestitures, rapid growth, and downsizing have left many companies unable to deliver on the implicit career promises made to their employees. Organizations find themselves in the painful position of having to renege on career mobility opportunities their employees had come to expect. In some cases, employees who expected career growth no longer even have jobs.

Increasingly, corporations have come to realize that they cannot win if they take total responsibility for the career development of their employees. No matter what happens, employees often blame top management or "the company" for their lack of career growth. One company changed its approach to career growth as a result of pressure from its professional workforce. Employees felt suffocated by 20-plus years of management's determining career progress for them. Task teams worked with top management to develop career self-management training for employees and career counseling skills for managers. The resulting increases in employee productivity, enhanced morale, and decreased turnover of key employees have more than justified the new approach to employee career management.

Company Responsibilities

Although the primary and final responsibility for career development rests with each employee, the company has complementary responsibilities. The company is responsible for communicating to employees where it wants to go and how it plans to get there (the corporate strategy), providing employees with as much information about the business as possible, and responding to the career initiatives of employees with candid, complete information. One of the most important contributions a company can make to each employee's development is to provide him or her with honest feedback about current job performance. Employees, in turn, are responsible for knowing what their skills and capabilities are and what assistance they need from their employers, asking for that assistance, and preparing themselves to assume new responsibilities.

This approach to career management can be summed up as follows: Assign employees the responsibility for managing their own careers, then provide the support they need to do it. This support takes different forms in different companies but usually contains several core components. These may include

- **Self-assessment.** The goal of self-assessment is to help employees focus on their interests, values, skills, personality preferences, and preferred work environments. In so doing, they are likely to set realistic career goals that are appropriate for them personally. Companies may provide a variety of ways to self-assess, including, for example, ability tests, interest inventories, and personality measures.

- **Career planning.** The companies teach employees how to plan their career growth once they have determined where they want to go. Employees learn what they need as well as how to read the corporate environment and to become savvy about how to get ahead in their own companies.

- **Supervisory training.** Employees frequently turn first to their immediate supervisors for help with career management. At Sikorsky Aircraft, for example, supervisors are taught how to provide relevant information and to question the logic of each employee's career plans, but not to give specific career advice. Giving advice would relieve the employee of responsibility for managing his or her own career.

- **Succession planning.** Simply designating replacements for key managers and executives is no guarantee that those replacements will be ready when needed. Enlightened companies are adopting an approach to succession planning that is consistent with the concept of career self-management. They develop their employees broadly to prepare them for any of several positions that may become available. As business needs change, broadly developed people can be moved into positions that are critical to the success of the business.

The practice of making career self-management part of the corporate culture has spread rapidly over the last several years. Companies are using this approach to build a significant competitive advantage. Given today's turbulent, sometimes convulsive, corporate environments, plus workers who seek greater control over their own destinies, it may be the only approach that can succeed over the long term.

Individual Actions

While companies may provide help with career management, it is up to individuals to act, and a number of suggestions are offered below to focus those actions. At some time or another, whether voluntarily or otherwise, almost everyone faces the difficult task of finding a job. Much has been written about recruitment from the organization's perspective. In actual practice, however, organizations search for qualified candidates just as candidates search for organizations. Thus recruitment is a two-way street. How do people find jobs? Research shows that 70 percent land a job through personal contacts, 15 percent through placement agencies, 10 percent through direct mailings of their résumés, and only 5 percent through published job openings (Cohn, 1985; Falvey, 1991). The individual search seems to pay off.

Coping with a Job Loss. Losing a job has become a frequent occurrence over the last decade (as a result of mergers, restructurings, and downsizings), one that is expected to continue as economic conditions change (Uchitelle & Kleinfeld, 1996). Consider this scenario: You are a midlevel executive, well regarded, well paid, and seemingly well established in your chosen field. Then—whammo!—there's a change in business strategy or in economic conditions, resulting in your layoff from the firm where you had hoped to retire. What do you do? How do you go about finding another job? According to management consultants and executive recruiters, the following are some of the key things *not* to do (Rigdon, 1992; "When a Recruiter Comes Knocking," 1996).

- **Don't panic.** A search takes time, even for well-qualified middle- and upper-level managers. Seven months to a year is not unusual. Be prepared to wait it out.

- **Don't be bitter.** Bitterness makes it harder to begin to search; it also turns off potential employers.

- **Don't kid yourself.** Do a thorough self-appraisal of your strengths and weaknesses, your likes and dislikes about jobs and organizations. Face up to what has happened, decide if you want to switch fields, figure out where you and your family want to live, and don't delay the search itself for long.

- **Don't drift.** Develop a plan, target companies, and go after them relentlessly. Realize that your job is to find a new job. Cast a wide net; consider industries other than your own.

- **Don't be lazy.** The heart of a good job hunt is research. Use reference books, public filings, and annual reports when drawing up a list of target companies. If negotiations get serious, talk to a range of insiders and knowledgeable outsiders to learn about politics and practices. You don't want to wind up in a worse fix than the one you left. Unfortunately, studies indicates that only about 5 percent of job applicants do any research on a company before an interview (Work Week, 1995).

- **Don't be shy or overeager.** Since personal contacts are the most effective means to land a job, pull out all the stops to get the word out that you are available. At the same time, resist the temptation to accept the first job that comes along. Unless it's absolutely right for you, the chances of making a mistake are quite high.

- **Don't ignore your family.** Some executives are embarrassed and don't tell their families what's going on. A better approach, experts say, is to bring the family into the process and deal with issues honestly.

- **Don't lie.** Experts are unanimous on this point. Don't lie, and don't stretch a point—either on résumés or in interviews. Be willing to address failures as well as strengths. Discuss openly and fully what went wrong at the old job.

- **Don't jump the gun on salary.** Always let the potential employer bring this subject up first. But once it surfaces, thoroughly explore all aspects of your future compensation and benefits package.

Those who have been through the trauma of job loss and the challenge of finding a job often describe the entire process as a wrenching, stressful one. Avoiding the mistakes shown above can ensure that finding a new job will not take any longer than necessary.

Switching Jobs. If organizations cannot match the career expectations of their employees, one option for employees will be to switch organizations. Guidelines for doing this fall into the following major categories (Bolles, 1996; Farnham, 1996; Henkoff, 1996).

Selecting a Field of Employment and an Employer

- You cannot manage your career unless you have a macro, long-range objective. The first step, therefore, is to think in terms of where you ultimately want to be, recognizing, of course, that your career goals will change over time.

- View every potential employer and position in terms of your long-range career goal. That is, how well does this job serve to position you in terms of your ultimate objective? For example, if you aspire to reach senior management by 2005, consider the extent to which your current job helps you develop a global orientation, develop public speaking skills, practice a "bring out the best in people" leadership style, and learn to manage cultural diversity. These are now and will continue to be key requirements for such senior positions (Aburdene, 1990).

- Accept short-term trade-offs for long-term benefits. Certain lateral moves or low-paying jobs can provide extremely valuable training opportunities or career contacts.

- Consider carefully whether to accept highly specialized jobs or isolated job assignments that might restrict or impede your visibility and career development.

Knowing Where You Are

- Always be aware of opportunities available to you in your current position, such as training programs that might further your career development.
- Carefully and honestly assess your current performance. How do you see yourself, and how do you think higher management sees your performance?
- Try to recognize when you and your organization have outlived your utility for each other. This is not an admission of failure but rather an honest reflection of the fact that there is little more the organization can do for you and that, in turn, your contribution to the organization has reached a point of diminishing returns. Here are five important symptoms for when you might consider moving on (Petras & Petras, 1989).

    1. You're not excited by what you are doing.
    2. Advancement is blocked.
    3. Your organization is poorly managed and is losing market share.
    4. You feel you are not adequately rewarded for your work.
    5. You are not fulfilling your dreams.

Planning Your Exit

- Try to leave at your convenience, not the organization's. To do this, you must do two things well: (1) Know when it's time to leave (before it's time), and (2) since downsizing can come at any time, establish networking relationships while you still have a job.
- Leave your current organization on good terms and not under questionable circumstances.
- Don't leave your current job until you've landed another one, for it's easier to find a new job when you're currently employed. Like bank loans, jobs often go to people who don't seem to need them (Petras & Petras, 1989).

MAKING THE MOST OF YOUR CAREER

A variety of forces is helping to shape the future world of work, from global product and service markets, to new technology and Internet-based commerce, to mergers, acquisitions, and corporate restructuring. However, we can impart this to our clients: Organizations have lots of jobs, but you have only one career. It is important to make the most of that career, whether you're thinking of changing jobs or starting to find one. Exercise 1.1 raises questions about workplace changes that are likely to affect you. These are important milestones, and they need to be managed carefully. You are in charge of that. Fortunately, tools are available to help you succeed. It's up to you to make use of them.

EXERCISE 1.1

EVOLVING WORKPLACE ISSUES

Reflect on the following questions. You may then wish to discuss your responses with others.

1. As an employee, what changes in the psychological contract that binds workers and organizations to each other have you observed or experienced?

2. As an employee, how are the following business trends shaping your work?
   - Globalization
   - Technology
   - Change
   - Intellectual capital
   - Speed in market change
   - Cost control

3. As an employer, how has the Information Revolution affected your business? What implications does it have for your employees and their careers?

4. What does the concept of loyalty mean to you in the current work environment we face?

5. What does the concept of career success mean to you in the current work environment we face?

6. As a job seeker, in what ways are you increasing your self-reliance?

____

____

7. As an employer, what opportunities do you provide to your employees for

   Self-assessment ____________________

   Career planning ____________________

   Supervisory training ____________________

   Succession planning ____________________

REFERENCES

Aburdene, P. (1990, September). How to think like a CEO for the 1990s. *Working Woman,* pp. 134–137.

Adler, N. J., Doktor, R., & Redding, S. G. (1986). From the Atlantic to the Pacific century: Cross-cultural management reviewed. *Journal of Management, 12,* 295–318.

Anders, G. (1999, July 12). Buying frenzy. *The Wall Street Journal Reports: E-Commerce,* pp. R6, R10.

Bolles, R. N. (1996). *The 1996 what color is your parachute?* Berkeley, CA: Ten Speed Press.

Bond, J. T., Galinsky, E., & Swanberg, J. E. (1998). *The 1997 national study of the changing workforce.* New York: Families and Work Institute.

Bulkeley, W. (1998, November 16). Corporate seers. *The Wall Street Journal,* pp. R37, R39.

Cascio, W. F. (1995). Whither industrial and organizational psychology in a changing world of work? *American Psychologist, 50,* 928–939.

Cohn, G. (1985, November 19). Advice on what not to do as the search continues. *The Wall Street Journal,* p. 37.

The corporation of the future. (1998, August 31). *Business Week,* pp. 102–106.

A decade of M&A activity. (1999, March 9). *Business Week,* p. 96.

Does anyone around here know . . . ? (1997, September 29). *Fortune,* pp. 279–280.

Falvey, J. (1991, Fall). A new set of rules for the "real world." *Managing Your Career.* Chicopee, MA: pp. 39, 41.

Families and Work Institute. (1993). *An evaluation of Johnson & Johnson's work-life programs.* New York: Author.

Farnham, A. (1996, January 15). Casting off: Three who did it right. *Fortune,* pp. 60–64.

Foreign money keeps flooding into the U.S. (1997, May 19). *The Wall Street Journal,* p. A1.

Gruner, S. (1999, July 12). Late to the party: The European Internet market is heating up, at last. *The Wall Street Journal Reports: E-Commerce,* p. R25.

Gutknecht, J. E., & Keys, J. B. (1993). Mergers, acquisitions, and takeovers: Maintaining morale of survivors and protecting employees. *Academy of Management Executive, 7*(3), 26–36.

Hall, D. T. (1996). Protean careers of the 21st century. *Academy of Management Executive, 10*(4), 8–16.

Hall, D. T., & Mirvis, P. H. (1995). Careers as lifelong learning. In A. Howard (Ed.), *The changing nature of work* (pp. 323–361). San Francisco: Jossey-Bass.

Henkoff, R. (1996, January 15). So, you want to change your job. *Fortune,* pp. 52-56.

Job mobility, American-style. (1997, January 27). *Business Week,* p. 20.

Johnson, A. A. (1995, August). The business case for work-family programs. *Journal of Accountancy,* pp. 53–57.

Johnson, A. A. (1999, February 25). *Strategic meal planning: Work/life initiatives for building strong organizations.* Paper presented at the conference on Integrated Health, Disability, and Work/Life Initiatives, New York.

Kleinfeld, N. R. (1996, March 4). The company as family no more. *The New York Times,* pp. A1, A8–A11.

Kraar, L. (1997, May 26). The real threat to China's Hong Kong. *Fortune,* pp. 85–94.

Lancaster, H. (1995, August 29). Professionals try new way to assess and develop skills. *The Wall Street Journal,* p. B1.

Lancaster, H. (1997, December 9). Contributors to pools of company know-how are valued employees. *The Wall Street Journal,* p. B1.

McGuire, P. (1998, July). Wanted: Workers with flexibility for 21st century jobs. *APA Monitor,* pp. 10, 12.

Minehan, M. (1999, February). Forecasting future trends for the workplace. *HR Magazine,* p. 176.

National Research Council (1999). *The changing nature of work: Implications for occupational analysis.* Washington, DC: National Academy Press.

Petras, K., & Petras, R. (1989). *The only job book you'll ever need.* New York: Simon & Schuster.

Reichheld, F. F. (1996). *The loyalty effect.* Boston: Harvard Business School Press.

Reingold, J. (1999, March 1). Why your workers might jump ship. *Business Week,* p. 8.

Rigdon, J. E. (1992, June 17). Deceptive résumés can be door openers but can become an employee's undoing. *The Wall Street Journal,* pp. B1, B7.

Rodgers, F. S., quoted in Lublin, J. S. (1997, September 19). Coopers & Lybrand tackles turnover by letting its workers have a life. *The Wall Street Journal,* p. R4.

Rousseau, D. M. (1995). *Psychological contracts in organizations: Written and unwritten agreements.* Thousand Oaks, CA: Sage.

Rousseau, D. M. (1996). Changing the deal while keeping the people. *Academy of Management Executive, 10*(1), 50–59.

Rousseau, D. M., & Wade-Benzoni, K. A. (1995). Changing individual-organizational attachments. In A. Howard (Ed.), *The changing nature of work* (pp. 290–322). San Francisco: Jossey-Bass.

Rucci, A. J., Kirn, S. P., & Quinn, R. T. (1998, January/February). The employee-customer-profit chain at Sears. *Harvard Business Review,* pp. 82–97.

Schweiger, D. M., & DeNisi, A. S. (1991). Communication with employees following a merger: A longitudinal field experiment. *Academy of Management Journal, 34,* 110–135.

SHRM/CCH Futures Study. (1996, June 19). *HR's survival depends on developing competencies to manage future issues.* Washington, DC: Author.

Sloan, A. (1996, February 26). The hit men. *Newsweek,* pp. 44–54.

Solomon, C. M. (1997, January). Global business under siege. *Global Workforce,* pp. 18–23.

Sony's shake-up. (1999, March 22). *Business Week,* pp. 52, 53.

Spindle, B. (1999, July 12). The route to Asia. *The Wall Street Journal Reports: E-Commerce,* p. R22.

Stewart, T. A. (1997). *Intellectual capital.* New York: Doubleday.

A tale of two job markets. (1998, December 21). *Business Week,* pp. 38, 39.

Uchitelle, L., & Kleinfeld, N. R. (1996, March 3). On the battlefields of business, millions of casualties. *The New York Times,* pp. 1, 14–17.

Ulrich, D. (1998, January/February). A new mandate for human resources. *Harvard Business Review,* pp. 124–134.

The virtual mall gets real. (1998, January 26). *Business Week,* pp. 90, 91.

Warner, F. (1999, February 18). Car race in cyberspace. *The Wall Street Journal,* p. B1.

When a recruiter comes knocking, be ready to respond. (1996, August 6). *The Wall Street Journal,* p. B1.

White, J. B., & Lublin, J. S. (1996, September 27). Some companies try to rebuild loyalty. *The Wall Street Journal,* pp. B1, B2.

Working scared. (1993, April 17). *NBC News.*

Work Week. (1997, February 11). *The Wall Street Journal,* p. A1.

Work Week. (1995, October 31). *The Wall Street Journal,* p. A1.

Wyatt Company. (1993). *Best practices in corporate restructuring.* Washington, DC: Wyatt.

NOTES

[1]Material in the following sections has been adapted from W. F. Cascio. (1998). *Managing human resources* (5th ed., pp. 193–194, 337–338, 342–343, and 363–364). Burr Ridge, IL: Irwin/McGraw-Hill. For more information on the new approach to career self-management, see Morin, W. J. (1996, December 9). You are absolutely, positively on your own. *Fortune,* p. 222. See also Hall, D. T. (1996). Protean careers of the 21st century. *Academy of Management Executive, 10*(4), 8–16. See also Schein, E. H. (1996). Career anchors revisited: Implications for career development in the 21st century. *Academy of Management Executive, 10*(4), 80–88.

2

Planning for the 21st-Century Workforce

KEY TRENDS THAT WILL SHAPE THE EMPLOYMENT AND CAREER LANDSCAPE

Andrea Saveri and Rod Falcon

Career management and professional development specialists will have their hands full in the 21st century. Both the composition of the workforce and the nature of work and jobs are undergoing profound transformation. Although the labor force is growing very slowly, there are significant changes in its makeup—formative work experiences, expectations, and needs—as well as significant changes in the nature of work and careers. Work is becoming a very distinct individual experience and the workforce is extremely heterogeneous and multifaceted. There are no simple blueprints for careers or skills that will apply across the range of work situations. Career planners and professional development specialists will have to learn to detect the distinct context of workers and work to deliver effective services in a broad range of work situations. This chapter begins with some of the most significant changes in the composition of the workforce in the first decade of the 21st century followed by some of the key changes in jobs and the nature of work.

THE 21ST-CENTURY WORKFORCE— SLOW GROWTH, BIG CHANGES

The first striking feature about the workforce in the first decade of the 21st century is that it will grow much more slowly than in any other decade since the 1960s. Growth in the labor force will continue to slow down to less than 1 percent by 2010. Not until well into the second decade of the 21st century will the impact of the *echo boomers* (those born between 1977 and 1994) begin to affect the rate of labor force expansion. Figure 2.1 shows workforce growth in the last four decades of the 20th century.

During the 1970s the labor force grew at an average annual rate of 2.6 percent. Roughly 2.4 million workers entered the workforce each year, and employers had a large number of workers from which to choose. Throughout the 1980s and 1990s, labor force growth slowed about .5 percent each decade. Employers found themselves with a shrinking labor pool in which they could not skim from the top as they had done in past decades. Between 2000 and 2010, the labor pool will continue to shrink. Despite its decline, the labor force will undergo significant changes in composition and structure.

The workforce in 2010 will have distinct characteristics compared to the labor pool of the early 1990s. We've identified six key trends that will create some of the most profound change in the workforce:

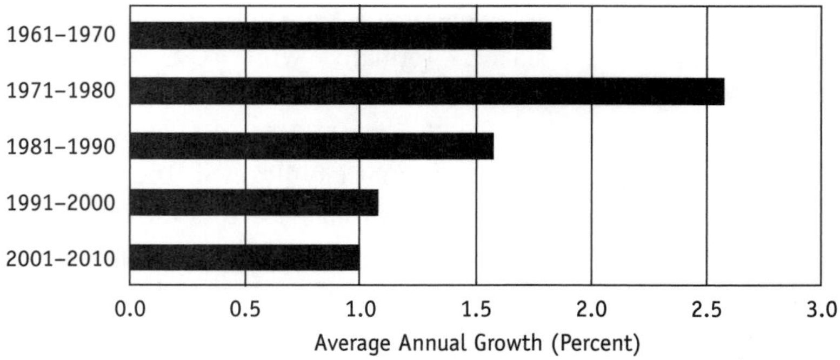

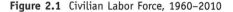

Source: Institute for the Future, "The Future Workforce," 1998c; U.S. Bureau of the Census, *Statistical Abstract of the United States: 1998,* 1998 (Table 164, p. 403); Fullerton, H. N., Jr., "Labor Force 2006," 1997, p. 25.

Figure 2.1 Civilian Labor Force, 1960–2010

- An intergenerational workforce creates challenges and opportunities.
- Demographic diversity changes the homogeneous workforce majority.
- Women pioneer cutting-edge work alternatives.
- Youth culture transforms the nature of organizational work.
- Labor mobility contributes to nonlinear career paths.
- Global work becomes a local experience.

An Intergenerational Workforce Creates Challenges and Opportunities

Table 2.1 shows that there will be over 154 million workers by 2010. This amounts to a net increase of 13 million workers in the first decade of the 21st century—the smallest increase since the 1960s.

Table 2.1 Workers in the Civilian Labor Force Age 16 and Over, 1960–2010

Year	Workers (Millions)
1960	69.6
1970	82.8
1980	106.9
1990	126.1
2000	141.1
2010	154.1

Source: Institute for the Future databases; U.S. Bureau of the Census, *Statistical Abstract of the United States: 1998,* 1998 (Table 164, p. 403).

One key demographic shift illustrates the dynamic change within the labor force age structure. The labor force, like the population in general, is aging. Figure 2.2 on the following page shows the changing composition of age cohorts. By 2010, the average age of workers will be well over 40.6 years—a number driven by the aging baby boomers.

The baby boom life cycle continues to have huge impacts on all aspects of American life. In the first decade of the 21st century, its impact on the workforce will be no less. The youngest baby boomer will turn 46 years old

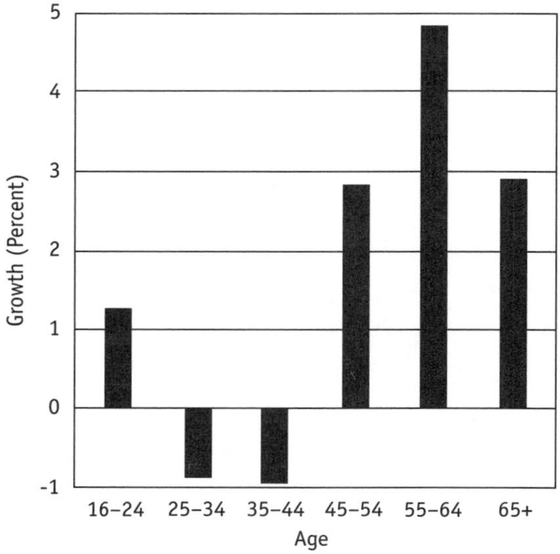

Source: Institute for the Future databases; Fullerton, H. N., Jr., "Labor Force 2006," 1997, p. 25.

Figure 2.2 Projected Growth in the Labor Force by Age Cohort, 2001–2010

in 2010 and the oldest will turn 64, increasing the number of workers in those age categories. They will be at the peak of their work life and their decision to transition to retirement or continue working will have a profound impact on the workforce and on larger social issues in general.

The much smaller baby bust cohort (Generation X—those born between 1965 and 1976) currently ranges in age from 25 to 36 years. This group is developing its career trajectory and expectations of work and organizational relationships at a time of great technological innovation and organizational change. This generation will account for 16 percent of the total population by 2010 and will become the middled-aged workers with growing families and older parents. This age cohort will make up a smaller share of the workforce in the future than in the past; its share will drop by about 1 percent. This means that traditional issues related to families with young children and older parents may not dominate organizations the way they have in the past. Their concerns and issues will compete with those of many older, mature workers (some ex-retirees reentering the workforce) and younger workers entering the workforce for the first time.

The next generation of young workers, the so-called echo boomers, represent the next cohort of workers to watch. It will take until 2020 for their full impact to be felt in the labor force. By 2010 this generation will range in age from 16 to 33, and for the first time in decades, the number of young workers will increase. These workers will have been educated during the online era and will have had their first work experiences in organizations where e-mail, intranets,[1] and portable communications devices were the norm. Their formative media and work experiences will have a profound impact on their expectations of employers and of work itself. This effect is discussed later in this chapter.

As baby boomers move through middle age and into preretirement and retirement, the number of workers will be spread across the age cohorts in a slightly more balanced pattern. Figure 2.3 shows that by 2010 the number of workers aged 16 to 24 will just about equal the number of workers 55 years and older. These cohorts are similarly represented by women and men. The result will be workers that span life cycle and work cycle stages; have diverse technology experiences at home, school, and work; come from different work or educational backgrounds; and have a wide range of formative experiences with employers and employment arrangements.

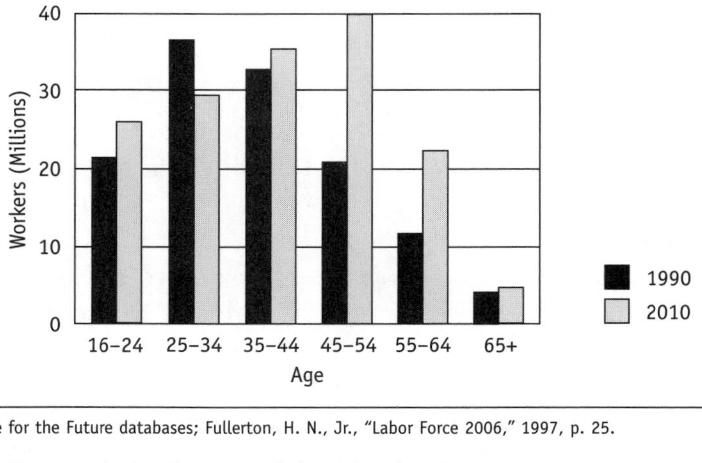

Source: Institute for the Future databases; Fullerton, H. N., Jr., "Labor Force 2006," 1997, p. 25.

Figure 2.3 Age Structure of the U.S. Labor Force, 1990, 2010

Young workers entering the workforce will have undertaken collaborative work projects at school, had part-time or temporary work during the summers, and used Internet-based networking and community building, which are all activities in which work and play are highly integrated. Older workers (particularly baby boomers) will have had experiences during the downsizing of the 1980s and 1990s in traditional organizations that shifted to more flexible horizontal structures, where teamwork and independent contract work loosened traditional notions of hierarchy and employment. Women who entered the professional workforce in large numbers in the 1970s and 1980s will have learned to balance careers and household responsibilities, and will have pioneered strategies to leave and reenter the workforce on their own terms.

What these different groups of workers will have in common is an expectation and desire for flexibility about how they fit work into their lives. A single model and set of assumptions about the duration of careers, the pathway for building a career, the meaning of work and a job, and the relationship with employers will not apply to all workers. Companies will need to identify various motivations and work values and create conditions under which workers can construct a work life that is both meaningful for themselves (however the worker defines that) and productive for the employer. Counselors will have an important role as mediator and liaison between workers and employers, helping them both develop new work patterns.

Demographic Diversity Changes the Homogeneous Workforce Majority

Ethnic and racial identity is another critical factor shaping diversity within the workforce. The number of Americans of ethnic and racial identity is growing rapidly, contributing to a society in which a homogeneous majority is becoming less dominant. Although the population today remains largely white and non-Hispanic, the number of Hispanics, Asians, African Americans, and Native Americans is growing faster than the population as a whole. Figure 2.4 shows this growth. Increasing immigration and higher birth rates among these groups drive this trend.

The national picture, however, does not tell the whole story of diversity: Hispanic, Asian, African American, and Native American populations are not evenly distributed across the United States, making diversity more pronounced in certain regions than in others. As seen in Figure 2.5,

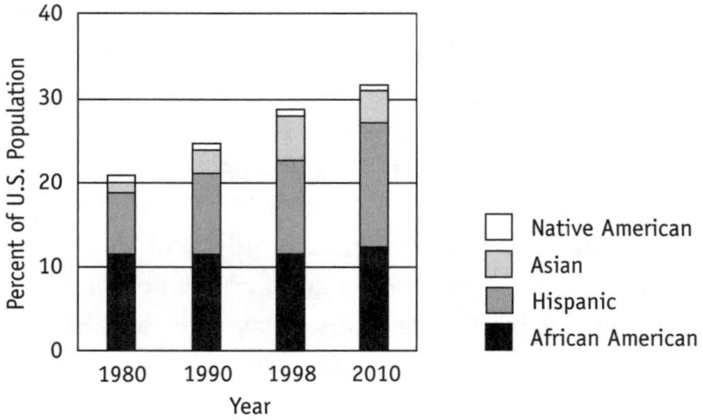

Source: U.S. Bureau of the Census, *Statistical Abstract of the United States: 1998,* 1998 (Tables 37, 38; pp. 37–38).

Figure 2.4 Diversity in the U.S. Population, 1980–2010

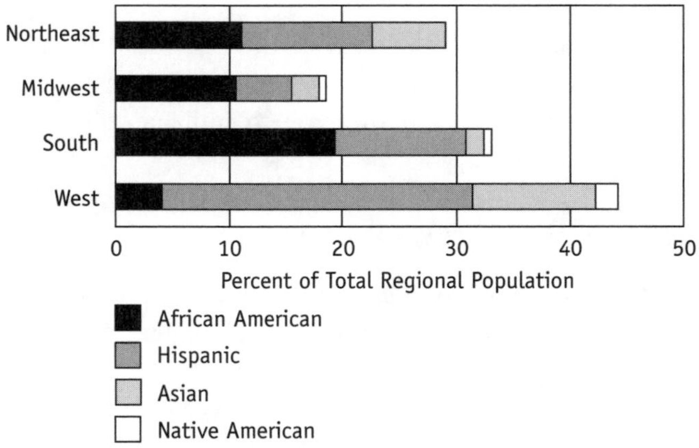

Source: U.S. Bureau of the Census, *Statistical Abstract of the United States: 1998,* 1998 (Tables 37, 38; pp. 37–38).

Figure 2.5 Projected Ethnic Diversity by Region in 2010

the highest concentration of ethnic and racial diversity is found in the West and South, a pattern that will continue into the 21st century.

Diverse populations will bring distinct experiences and outlooks to the workplace. Their cultural and historical legacies will be important factors, along with circumstances such as age and technology experience. These factors shape notions of family, community, communication, work, and the future. Combined with the increasing age diversity among the population, ethnic and racial diversity will continue to challenge homogeneous patterns of household and work life.

The meaning of work will be redefined as different groups of workers reach key stages in their lives and draw from their past experiences to make sense of future options. Workers with diverse age, ethnic and racial, technological, and work experience profiles will look for new options at the workplace to fit with their idiosyncratic household needs. The 14-hour corporate job in the same office day after day (for some of us) and the five-day, 9-to-5 job (for others of us) will no longer be the only options.

Strategies such as job sharing, telecommuting, part-time work, temporary work, self-employment, contract employment, and employment with dynamic start-ups rather than established companies are among the options for workers to develop a work life that meets their particular needs at various times in their life cycle. All workers, however, will value the ability to develop a work style that is in sync with their personal lives and family goals. Companies will have to learn to accommodate these work patterns, philosophies, and expectations if they are to build a resilient, adaptable organization.

Women Pioneer Cutting-Edge Work Alternatives

The changing pattern of women's participation in the workforce will be a major source of its growth and compositional change. Women are one of the fastest-growing groups of new entrants into the labor force. They will account for over 62.8 percent of all new workers between 2001 and 2010 and will make up almost half (49 percent) of the total labor force—up from 38 percent in 1970. Women's participation in the labor force (that is, the percentage of women who are in the workforce) for every age group has increased continuously since 1970, as seen in Table 2.2.

Less than half of women, 43.3 percent, were in the workforce in 1970, compared with 79.7 percent of men. Since the 1970s, the gap between men's and women's participation in the workforce has been closing. By 2006, 61.4 percent of women will be in the workforce, only 12.2 percent less than men. Their contribution to the world of work is clearly more than just their large numbers. Women have had a long history of developing alternative strate-

Table 2.2 Labor Force Participation Rates, 1970–2006

	1970	1980	1990	1996	2006	Percent Change 1996-2006
Total Civilian Labor Force	60.4	63.8	66.5	66.8	67.6	.8
Men *(all ages)*	79.7	77.4	76.4	74.9	73.6	-1.3
Women *(all ages)*	43.3	51.5	57.5	59.3	61.4	2.2
20–24	57.7	68.9	71.3	71.3	71.8	.5
25–34	45.0	65.5	73.5	75.2	77.6	2.3
35–44	51.1	65.5	76.4	77.5	80.2	2.7
45–54	54.4	59.9	71.2	75.4	79.9	4.5
55–64	43.0	41.3	45.2	49.6	55.8	6.2
65+	9.7	8.1	8.6	8.6	8.7	.1

Source: U.S. Bureau of the Census, *Statistical Abstract of the United States: 1998,* 1998.

Note: Rates are based on the civilian noninstitutional population of each specified group and represent the proportion of each specified group in the civilian labor force. For example, the civilian labor force participation rate is the proportion of persons aged 16 and over in the civilian noninstitutional population who work.

gies in order to fit work into their lives and accommodate the demands of a male-dominated workplace.

Since the 1970s, women who wanted careers have had to pioneer strategies for integrating work and home life, balancing the responsibilities of both worlds. Professional women who wished to pursue careers followed career survival strategies that remained essentially unchanged for most of the 20th century. Although the actual occupations and the number of women working have changed dramatically, the strategies have not (as identified by Slater & Glazer, 1987). This legacy has created a history of adaptation and flexibility that will suit women and men well in the future workforce. The strategies include

- **Superperforming.** Sometimes called "supermoms," superperforming women are amazons who juggle family responsibilities and work life by essentially working overtime at both, sometimes with the assistance of a "shadow mom" at home (a babysitter or housekeeper).

- **Voluntary subordination.** Women have also used the strategy of taking supportive rather than leadership roles in the organization and professions, or followed the "family track" instead of the "rat race" model for career success. Even women educated in professional schools may choose to take more supportive roles in organizations in order to spend more time with their families or avoid the pain of gender discrimination in certain "fast track" professions. This strategy explains why women dominate supportive roles in the medical field, for example, where the majority of nurses, therapists, dieticians, and physician assistants are women, while only 24 percent of physicians are women. In recent years, however, the ratio of women in leading rather than supportive positions has begun to shift–increasing numbers of women are receiving professional training and pursuing traditionally male-dominated fields such as medicine, law, engineering, and the sciences. For example, according to the Association of American Medical Colleges, women accounted for 43 percent of new enrollments in 1998.

- **Career innovation.** One of the most exciting strategies for professional women has been to forge new career areas where they can make their own rules and carve out new niche markets or entire occupations. New occupations, in particular, may be less hierarchical and/or more flexible to issues of particular interest to women, such as day care or other family needs.

- **Institutional separatism.** Entrepreneurship presents an answer for many professional women leaving the corporate world seeking to build their own work environments and cultures. Between 1977 and 1992, the number of women-owned businesses expanded rapidly by 15 percent each year. Women business owners now account for more than one-third of all businesses in the United States. Women-owned businesses will continue to grow at a rapid pace.

These adaptive career management styles will be increasingly important in the next decade, as organizations change internal structures and relationships with other enterprises; technology continues to shape work environments, team processes, and management possibilities; and distributed, remote work becomes more popular. Although actual career strategies for women may begin to change, women's experiences and skills in adapting to workplace conditions will be increasingly valuable in an ever-changing world of work. In fact, new models of work may be adapted from women to

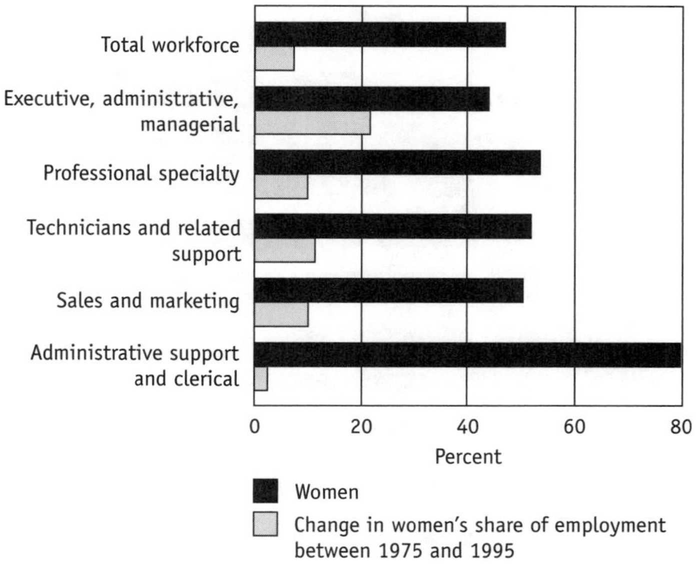

Source: Wooton, B. L., "Gender Differences in Occupational Employment," 1997.

Figure 2.6 Women's Occupational Employment, 1975–1995

benefit the entire organization. Women will be good sources of employment and career innovation for other workers. Men, who traditionally have not had to use such creative strategies in order to succeed in the workplace, may conversely find it more difficult to adapt to new work styles and practices or respond creatively to changing organizational structures.

Although important issues still persist, such as the gap in wages for men and women, women have made impressive gains in executive, administrative, and managerial occupations. They fill 43 percent of these positions—high-level jobs that require fundamental competencies in decision making, long-term thinking, team leadership, and visioning. Figure 2.6 shows the change in women's participation in various types of occupations between 1975 and 1995, with the largest gains in executive, administrative, and managerial positions.

Some of the biggest gains in the past decades have been in medical and health management, technical writing, purchasing, economics, financial management, and personnel and labor management. Women's movement

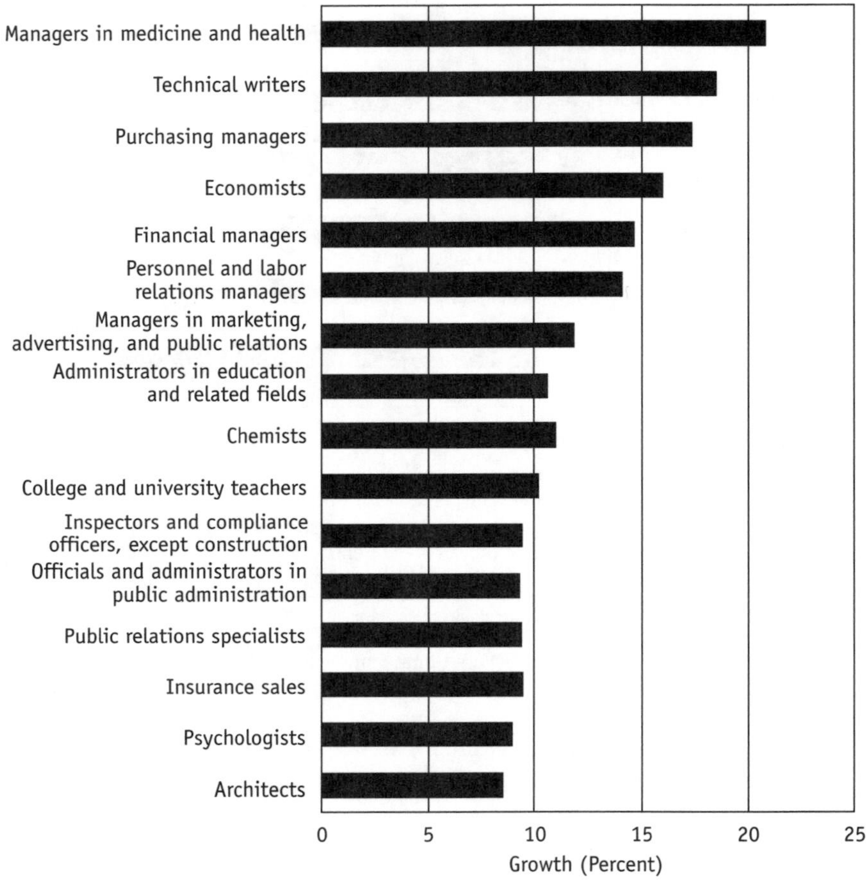

Source: Wooton, B. L., "Gender Differences in Occupational Employment," 1997.

Figure 2.7 Employment Gains for Women, 1985–1995

into these fields reflects their ability to pioneer in new fields rather than simply adapting to traditionally male-dominated occupations. However, despite these impressive gains, the statistics reflected in Figure 2.7 indicate that women have had trouble reaching the top levels of management in anything but token numbers.

Despite the barriers, women will continue to enter management at middle and executive levels and bring with them the tradition of pioneering alternative career paths in complicated organizations, where opportunities are not always stated in straightforward ways. They will bring with them vast experience in developing work strategies that accommodate their larger lives and home responsibilities. Career counselors should look to pioneering women in the workplace for alternative work styles, practices, and career paths. The experience of women and their career management strategies over the last 20 years have lessons and examples for all workers in the changing landscape of work.

Youth Culture Transforms the Nature of Organizational Work

A distinct youth culture, developed in a hyperconnected communications and information age, will shape the future of work and workplaces in the early 21st century. The echo boomer generation will have a significant impact on the workplace; their notions of meaningful work and careers, and their assumptions about the role of technology will be distinctly different from those of the generations before them.

In particular, expectations of how technological devices fit into daily life will be significantly different for the echo boomers based on their formative experiences with new media technology. Past interactions with technologies—especially during younger, more formative years—create a person's current expectations and attitudes toward them. As people mature, their early formative experiences with various technologies create a tacit knowledge base that shapes their outlook on the way technologies integrate into daily life. The way an average 15-year-old and an average 50-year-old envision a personal computer in their lives is rooted in a foundation of distinct technology and media experiences over time.

As Figure 2.8 on page 46 shows, people born in the late 1970s and 1980s are the first generation to grow up with interactive household media and technology—interactive in the sense that the user controls and affects what happens on the screen, or in the game, or in the outcome of the particular experience. They grew up with VCRs, video games (TV, arcade, and PC based), complex remote controls for channel surfing through expanded cable programming, and early handheld devices such as the Walkman®. As they started to come into adolescence, pagers, electronic pets (for example, Tamagotchi), cellular phones, the Internet and the World Wide Web began to fill their lives. Their younger siblings born in the 1990s probably played with (or teethed on) old remote control units and broken cordless phones,

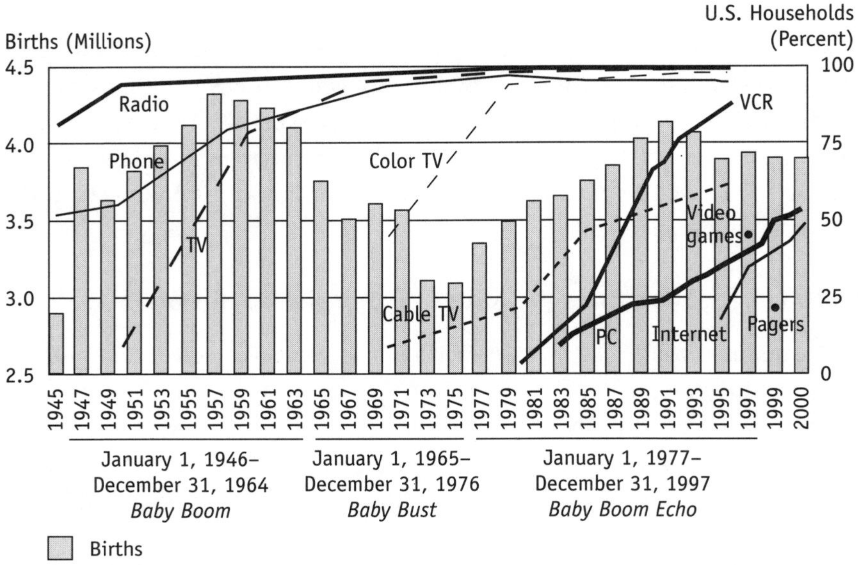

Source: Institute for the Future, Outlook Project working documents, 1999; U.S. Bureau of the Census, *Statistical Abstract of the United States: 1998,* 1998 (Table 915, p. 573).

Note: • indicates the percentage of households with video games (43% in 1997) and pagers (24% in 1998); sources are IFTF-commissioned national surveys).

Figure 2.8 Diverse Formative Technology Experience—Boom, Bust, and Echo

and saw themselves on TV in home videos in addition to viewing the popular cable TV figures and celebrities.

This group is the first to wear their technology as fashion and to bring it or find it in many places in their lives, such as friends' houses, schools, pizza shops, arcades in malls, and other public places. They are experiencing adolescence with personal messaging devices in their backpacks, their own phone lines or voice mail boxes, and their own web pages. The ability to communicate with friends, parents, or relatives at any place and at any time is a given in their environment. They will carry these experiences with them into the workplace. This group will drive the rate of growth of the workforce in the next two decades as shown by the increase in the number of births between 1977 and 1994. By 2020, the number of workers aged 26 to 43 (echo boomers) will explode—a pattern not seen since the baby boomer generation.

Table 2.3 Computer Use by 11- to 18-Year-Olds (Percent)

	Daily	1–3 Times /Week	2–3 Times /Month	Never
At home	22.1	27.0	11.6	39.2
At school	28.4	40.0	20.0	11.6
At public library	1.0	6.7	46.4	46.2
At friend's/relative's house	2.2	11.5	46.7	39.7
At girls'/boys' club	—	0.6	12.6	96.9

Source: Institute for the Future, Anticipating Consumer Desire, Outlook Project, SR-626, June 1997a.

Young people today live in a media-rich world and expect technology to be part of their environment. They use computers, for example, at home, at school, at friends' houses, and even in public spaces like libraries, community centers, and stores. Almost half use a computer at least several times a week at home; almost 70 percent do so at school. Table 2.3 shows the results of a survey of 11- to 18-year-olds regarding frequency of computer use.

A wide range of new media devices and services surround young people in their homes and in their bedrooms, as shown in Figure 2.9 on page 48. And more than half of young people report that communication devices and services are good ways for them to keep in touch with their friends when they're not in school. Girls indicated a slightly higher use of technology for social communication.

The allure of new media technologies, however, is not simply devices and gadgets. Rather, new media represent opportunities for interaction with friends in customized environments, such as online MUDs (multi-user domains),[2] conference calls, and unique pager code languages specific to groups of kids. This generation's experiences with communication and information technologies represent intensive learning processes. In short, kids are experiencing their adolescence through the new tools of connection and creation, and in turn are shaping the continued evolution of these tools in household and work life.

Why is this important? Today's children will carry these early technology experiences with them as they shape their careers. They will be the first

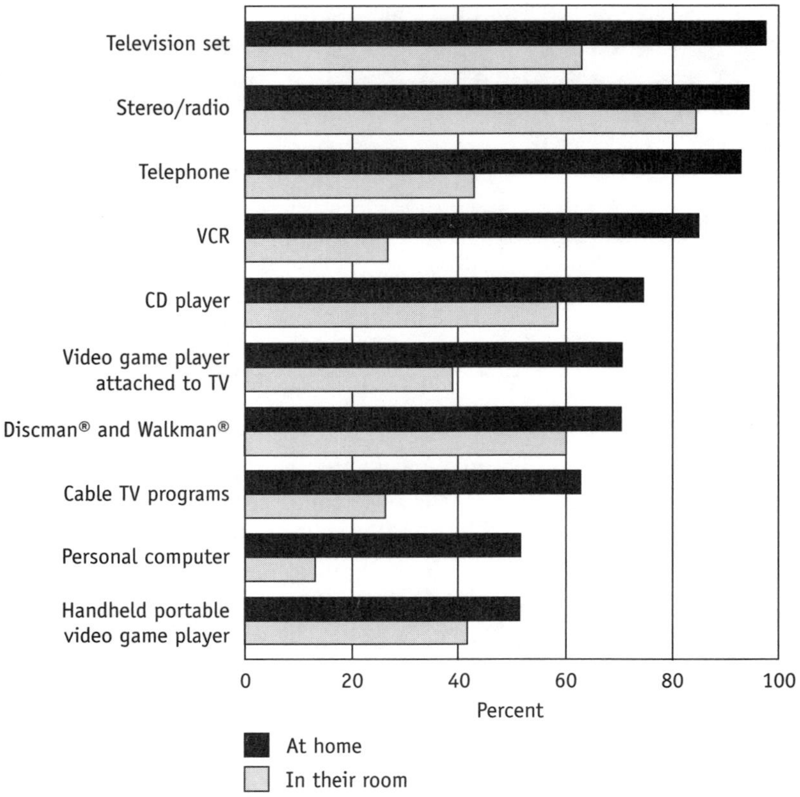

Source: Institute for the Future, Anticipating Consumer Desire, Outlook Project, SR-626, June 1997a.

Figure 2.9 Media Use by 11- to 18-Year-Olds
(Percentage of 11- to 18-year-olds who have media items at home and in their room)

workforce of the new knowledge economy who also grew up in it. They will bring new expectations of and familiarity with technology to their careers, changing the way technology is used in the workplace and creating new workplace cultures. Their sense of physical distance, social proximity, relationship building, and individual and group identity will be shaped directly from their early play and experimentation with media and technology. Expect to see this group pioneer new learning and communications environments, collaboration processes, and career paths. The oldest segments of this generation (age 23 in 2000) are already entering the workforce.

Labor Mobility Contributes to Nonlinear Career Paths

In the new work world, knowledge work will involve ongoing, interdependent project work among specialists and professionals. The work will be organized and performed in teams and informal groups across organizational and geographic boundaries. Managing information that is developed with distributed colleagues (geographically dispersed across domestic and international locations) or delivered to remote customers will be an important work practice. Workers will need to continually develop skills to become valuable contributors in these webs of interdependence and collaboration.

Career development will become less determined by the hierarchy of specific job titles and more by the nature of specific work projects accomplished with other professionals across companies. Interdependent, cross-boundary work creates the need for workers to develop diverse work experiences and build a rich portfolio of skills and a broader knowledge base. Career mobility becomes a strategic part of the career development process. By working in different parts of the company or with other companies (partners or suppliers), workers can create opportunities to add to their career portfolio. In effect, workers becomes self-reliant, managing the evolution of their own careers. Below are two examples of workers who describe the importance of actively assessing the experience gained on the job.

> I joined as an engineer. But I made it clear when I joined that I wanted to have the option of a [career] change at some time in the future. A year after I joined, I had the opportunity to move over into marketing. The product that I had been hired to work on was launched [into the market] so I moved over to marketing with it and I performed the launch.—*Young female engineer, 1998*

> I began to think about how I could enter the industry. Many of my coworkers had difficulty making the move [from high-tech research to industry] because people felt that if you were at [the research company] more than five years you were going to be branded for the rest of your career with a résumé showing [only] research. So they felt [that] less than five years [was] the optimal time to get into industry and [get] hands-on experience with commercial products and pressures of shipping schedules, and then try to find a way to move into other areas where you wanted your career path to go.—*Female high-tech manager, 1998*

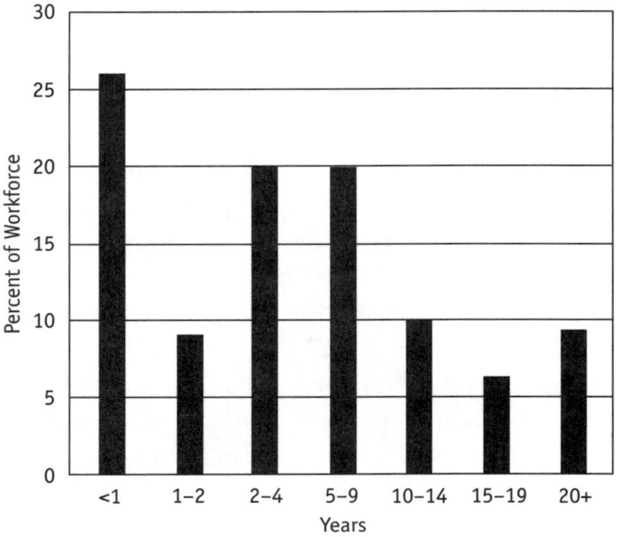

Source: U.S. Bureau of Labor Statistics, "Employee Tenure in the Mid-1990s," 1997.

Figure 2.10 Tenure with Current Employer (U.S. Workforce)

Figure 2.10 shows that in 1996 more than half of U.S. workers had been with their current employer for four years or less.

While almost half of workers have longer-term relationships, five years or more, with one employer, their mobility within a company will increase as they work in different departments and on different teams. They will become intrapreneurs—workers who continually seek and develop new career options and skill-building opportunities within a company, often contributing new ideas and innovations. The challenge for an individual worker is to see each job as a piece of a broader ongoing career path. This requires the active assessment of individual work experiences, skills, and goals. It also requires future workers to be able to transcend the boundaries of their intellectual and knowledge domains and understand the links between their expertise and that of their colleagues. Cross-disciplinary learning will become important for these workers. They will learn new ways of applying their knowledge in diverse work contexts.

Shorter tenure with an employer is not simply a function of young workers learning new skills and moving into new positions with new

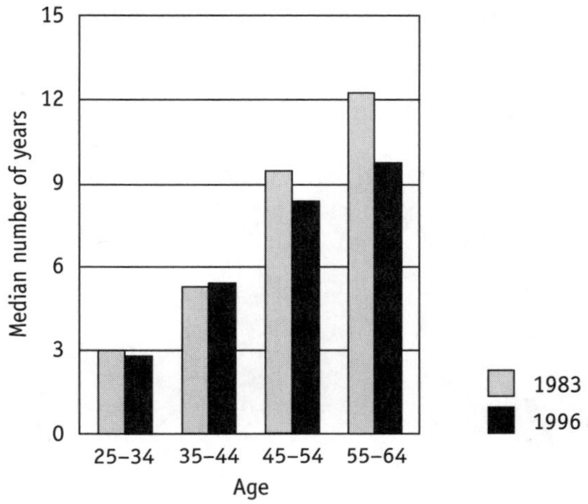

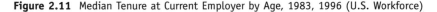

Source: U.S. Bureau of Labor Statistics, "Employee Tenure in the Mid-1990s," 1997.

Figure 2.11 Median Tenure at Current Employer by Age, 1983, 1996 (U.S. Workforce)

employers. Figure 2.11 shows that older workers are already beginning to reduce their length of tenure with employers.

Workers between the ages of 25 and 44 had about the same length of tenure with their employers in 1983 and 1996. However, workers in their late 40s and 50s spent fewer years with the same employer in 1996 than in 1983. As a result of these changes, career paths—both within an organization and across many organizations—no longer will reflect the traditional ascending ladder, where career growth implies steady advancement and the steps to achieve it are explicitly articulated. Careers now take a more cyclical, spiral path that may change directions, bosses, or employers. Figure 2.12 on page 52 shows that for self-reliant workers, there may be more than one way to get from one stage of a career to another.

In the new world of work, employers will continue to support workers, but individuals will take more control over their career paths and seek what is necessary to achieve continuous professional satisfaction, growth, and effectiveness. Developing methods to support career self-reliance will become a strategic goal for companies. As employees shift from the old parental model, under which companies took care of them, to the new model, whereby they take responsibility for their own careers, they will

Old Career Model: The Step Ladder	New Career Model: The Spiral
Career growth is driven by tenure and performance	Career growth is driven by diverse experience and performance
Linear, one-direction path	Cyclical or circuitous path
Hierarchical path moves up	Horizontal path moves around
Long-term, single employer	Multiple relationships with employers
Career dependent	Career self-reliant
Focus on discrete competencies	Develop competencies in multiple contexts, portfolio keeps evolving

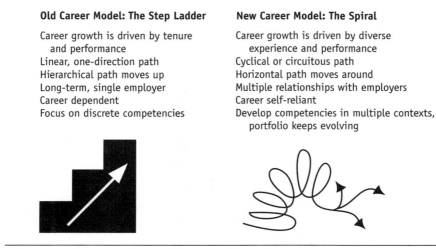

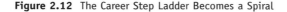

Source: Institute for the Future, Career Revisited, Outlook Project, SR-644, 1997b.

Figure 2.12 The Career Step Ladder Becomes a Spiral

challenge both the human resources and information technology departments to accommodate the new approach. The old HR model that pushes information to employees by means of leaflets, manuals, and benefit books is rapidly giving way to a new model that provides employees access to information on demand and interactive electronic environments. The human resources and information technology departments have an opportunity to work closely to help workers identify ways to create value for the firm while continuing their own professional development.

Global Work Becomes a Local Experience

The global workforce now numbers 2.5 billion people. Only about 15 percent live in high-income, developed countries—Australia, New Zealand, Canada, Japan, Western Europe, and the United States—as defined by the Organization for Economic Cooperation and Development (OECD). In 2025, the OECD countries' share of the global workforce will drop to 10 percent, or 384 million. See Figure 2.13 for a projection of the 2025 world labor force.

In the 21st century, the most dynamic labor growth will come not from these countries but from the other regions of the globe, including East Asia and the Pacific, South Asia, Latin America and the Caribbean, Central Asia,

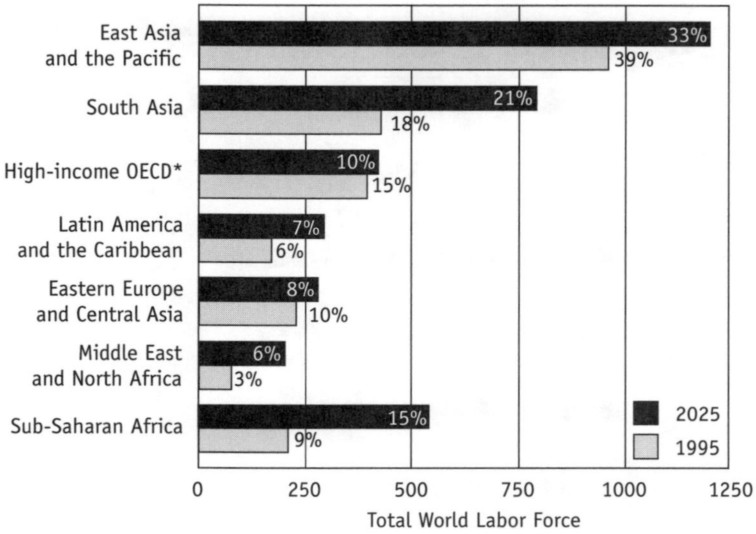

Source: Institute for the Future, demographic databases, 1999; World Bank, *World Development Report,* 1995; International Labour Organization, *World Labour Report,* 1995.

Note: Percentages represent proportion of total world labor force.

*The Organization for Economic Cooperation and Development (OECD) includes Australia, Austria, Belgium, Canada, Czech Republic, Denmark, Finland, France, Germany, Greece, Hungary, Iceland, Ireland, Italy, Japan, Korea, Luxembourg, Mexico, Netherlands, New Zealand, Norway, Poland, Portugal, Spain, Sweden, Switzerland, Turkey, United Kingdom, and United States.

Figure 2.13 Projected World Labor Force by Region (Millions of Workers), 1995, 2025

the Middle East, and Africa. South Asia, for example, will gain 3 percent of the global workforce, adding 339 million workers, and Sub-Saharan Africa will jump 6 percent, adding 323 million workers. In the 21st century, global work will truly be global, encompassing countries and cultures that vary considerably.

In addition to lower labor costs, these emerging economies will have increasing numbers of skilled workers, as indicated in Figure 2.14 on page 54 by the number of people projected to be enrolled in secondary education over the next 15 years.

These emerging skilled workers will be critical for both local enterprises and multinational companies partnering with local enterprises. They represent not only a productive workforce but also workers who will

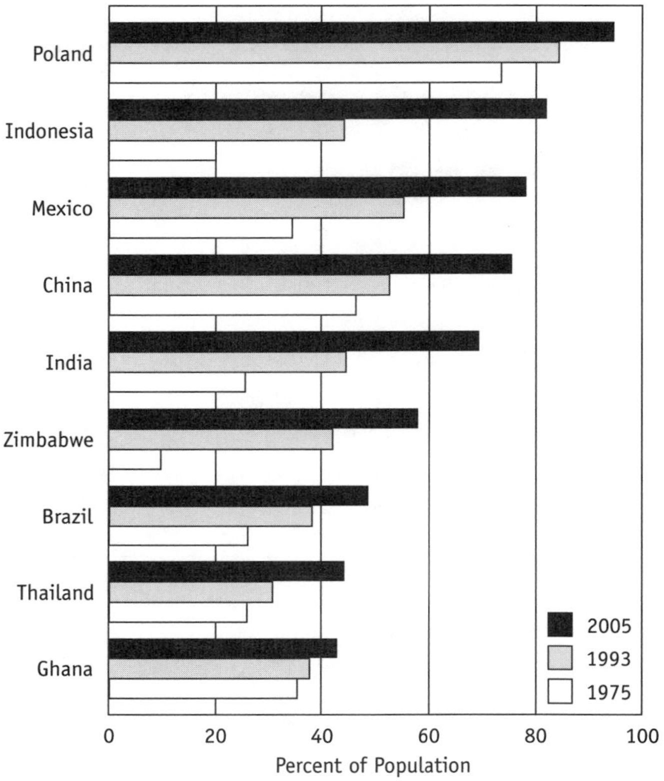

Source: World Bank, *World Development Report,* 1995.

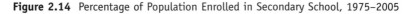

Figure 2.14 Percentage of Population Enrolled in Secondary School, 1975–2005

contribute to their country's middle class. By the year 2000, over half of the employees working for foreign affiliates of multinational corporations were projected to be in developing countries, as shown in Figure 2.15.

The distribution of global information and knowledge work creates opportunities for local workers to gain new work experiences, skills, and training, and for global companies to tap into local and cultural knowledge. Harnessing creative local talent and cultural know-how will be critical for multinational organizations as they begin to develop, market, and sell more services and value-added products requiring higher levels of collaboration and joint development.

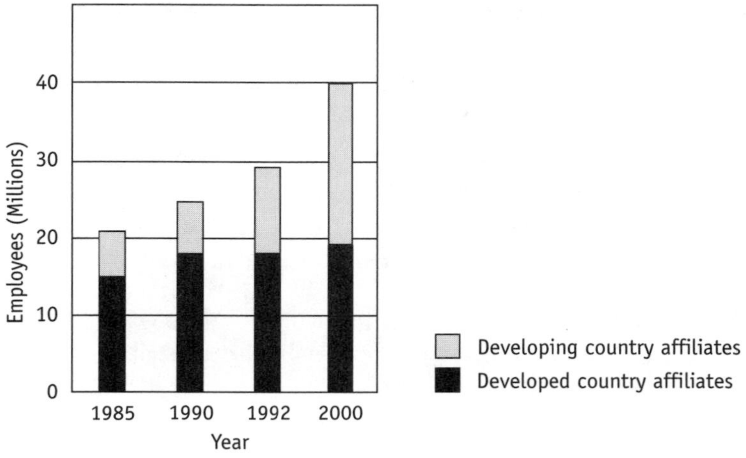

Source: Institute for the Future, demographic databases, 1999; *World Investment Report*, 1995; International Labour Organization, *World Employment Report*, 1995.

Figure 2.15 Employment in Foreign Affiliates of Transnational Corporations (Millions of Employees), 1985–2000

For U.S. workers, this means that more work will involve teaming with foreign counterparts on a regular basis. Globally distributed teams will share electronic workspaces, traveling only at team start-up for trust building and other critical stages of collaboration. Workers in the United States as well as in other countries will have to become familiar with telecommunications tools, information-sharing software, and other groupware (technology tools and systems that support group work and collaboration). Distributed work, in which team members and other work colleagues are located in various geographic locations, will become a global norm for most workers in the 21st century.

IMPLICATIONS

The following are some of the most important human resource and management-related issues that counselors, career coaches, and trainers will have to consider as a result of the changing gender and age structures, mobility, and globalization of the labor force.

- **Lifelong learning and skill development.** Workers will need to constantly assess and build their portfolio of skills and expertise. The returns for investment in education and skill development will remain high as occupations experiencing growth continue to require higher levels of education and sophisticated skill sets. The responsibility, however, for skill development and training will fall on the individual employee. Counselors will need to integrate a skill development plan into their career development discussions with their clients.

- **Multiple careers and new meaning in work.** Many older workers, particularly the boomer generation, are enjoying better health and longer lives and will not be ready to retire. They will enjoy many different careers and work options for longer, productive, lifelong engagement than generations in the past. Older workers will begin to reexamine the meaning of work and careers, move into flexible work arrangements, or even start second or third careers. Counselors will need to be aware of these changing preferences across all of the age cohorts as they work with clients.

- **Women as older workers.** Labor force participation rates among women have been increasing since the 1970s, when they entered the workforce in record numbers. As these women mature, they will drive the changing age structure of the workforce. These women, well into their careers, will be looking for different career and work options. Career counselors will need to work with these clients where work and life cycle patterns intersect, creating a distinct set of issues for this group.

- **Intergenerational issues in the workplace.** The workforce will be generationally diverse. Managing and working across the age cohorts will be challenging. Differences in work styles, sense of timing and pace, meaning in work, and needs will be difficult to generalize across the workforce. With increases in longevity, for example, retirement patterns will be less predictable. Older workers may need new kinds of assistance and information to help them plan their transitions out of and back into the workforce. At the same time, organizations will need to create learning and advancement opportunities for their young workers. A workforce with a range of age cohorts provides organizations with many creative perspectives and diverse knowledge bases. Age cohorts can help bridge cultural gaps created by social, cultural, and technological backgrounds.

Creating opportunities for intergenerational learning and mentoring will be an important strategy for leveraging the distinct and equally valuable skills and experiences of older and younger workers.

- **Self-reliant workers.** Companies should not fear their self-reliant, mobile, career-oriented employees. Self-reliant workers will drive the creativity and innovation in companies. Opportunities for them to develop their own careers and leadership within the boundaries of the company will be critical. Companies that retain the best workers will allow for varied spiral career paths within the company.
- **Women's innovations in career development and employment models.** With experience in developing alternatives for circumventing the limitations of traditional work structures, women will be key sources of innovation for new work styles, organizational structure, and team processes. As the workforce becomes more diverse, developing creative alternatives for how to work will be essential to the 21st-century organization.
- **Young employees and the electronic workspace.** New young workers will bring distinct expectations and experiences with them as they enter the labor force. They will take the electronic workspace to new horizons in the 21st-century organization. Their exploratory and integrative approach with media tools will open new opportunities for leveraging cyberspace as a corporate work environment.
- **Global literacy.** The globalization of work will be common for every worker, even for those who never travel or leave the home office. The key to leveraging a global workforce is developing team processes that challenge traditional assumptions and don't favor a single center. Electronic tools–voice mail, electronic mail, intranets, videoconferencing, and fax–will be critical for creating a supportive and shared work context that allows trust to build across borders.

21ST-CENTURY JOBS—AN EXPANDING SERVICE ECONOMY

The continued expansion of service industries and greater penetration of information and communications technologies will shape the nature of work and jobs in the 21st century. Three important trends are

- An expanding service-producing economy will drive job growth.
- Customer-oriented jobs will shape the nature of work.
- Selecting and managing communications media will be a key work activity.

As jobs grow in the service sector, there will be more polarization between jobs requiring high and low levels of education, specialized training (in specific fields and technical knowledge), and firsthand work experience. Opportunities for high-paying jobs in information-intensive and knowledge-oriented fields (such as health services, retail services, professional services, and government industries) will be limited to those with high levels of education and demonstrated skill, through either past job experience or specialized training. Low-skill jobs will also grow in these industries, but they will be comparatively low paying, offering little chance for advancement or job mobility. Occupations in fields with the largest growth will focus on information management, customer support and management, and service development and delivery. Developing strategies for new knowledge acquisition and opportunities for skill improvement will be extremely important to workers in the 21st-century job market.

An Expanding Service-Producing Economy Will Drive Job Growth

Employment growth will be driven largely by the continued shift to a service-producing economy. Data from the U.S. Bureau of Labor Statistics forecast that 95 percent of all new jobs created between 1996 and 2006 will be in the service-producing sector. Employment in the goods-producing sector is expected to grow by less than 1 percent between 1996 and 2006. While this sector retains high value for the economy, its employment base has been stable for the last two decades—remaining at about 24.5 million jobs. This will account for 16.5 percent of total employment—a decrease from 18.2 percent in 1996. Table 2.4 shows the percentage of growth in these sectors.

The service sector includes a wide range of service industries including transportation, wholesale trade, retail trade (which directly serves the customer), financial services—including real estate and insurance services—government services, and professional and personal services (encompassing education and business, health, legal, social, entertainment, personal, and

Table 2.4 Number of Jobs in Major Industry Sectors (Millions), 1986–2006

Year	Service Producing	Percent of Total	Goods Producing	Percent of Total
1986	74.2	63.0	24.5	20.8
1996	93.3	69.7	24.4	18.2
2006	111.9	75.2	24.5	16.5

Source: U.S. Bureau of the Census, *Statistical Abstract of the United States: 1998,* 1998.

Note: Percentages are for nonfarm employment and therefore do not add to 100 percent. Agriculture, private household, and unpaid family work account for the remaining percent.

Table 2.5 Number of Jobs in Major Industry Categories (Millions), 1986–2006

	1986	1996	2006
Goods Producing	24.5	24.4	24.5
Mining	0.78	0.57	0.44
Construction	4.8	5.4	5.9
Manufacturing	18.9	18.5	18.1
Service Producing	74.2	94.3	111.9
Transportation and utilities	5.2	6.3	7.1
Wholesale trade	5.8	6.5	7.2
Retail trade	17.9	21.6	23.9
Finance, insurance, and real estate	6.3	6.9	7.7
Services	22.3	33.6	44.9
Government	16.7	19.4	21.1
Agriculture	3.3	3.6	3.6
Private Households	1.2	0.93	0.76
Nonfarm Self-Employed and Unpaid Family	8.1	9.1	10.2

Source: Institute for the Future databases; Franklin, J. C., "Industry Output and Employment Projection to 2006," 1997.

miscellaneous services). All of these categories increased from the mid-1980s to the mid-1990s and will continue to grow in the next decade, as shown in Table 2.5. They accounted for 94.3 million jobs in the mid-1990s and will grow to over 111 million in 2006.

Jobs in retail, government, professional, and personal services will contribute the biggest increases in the next decade. Professional and personal

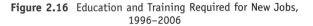

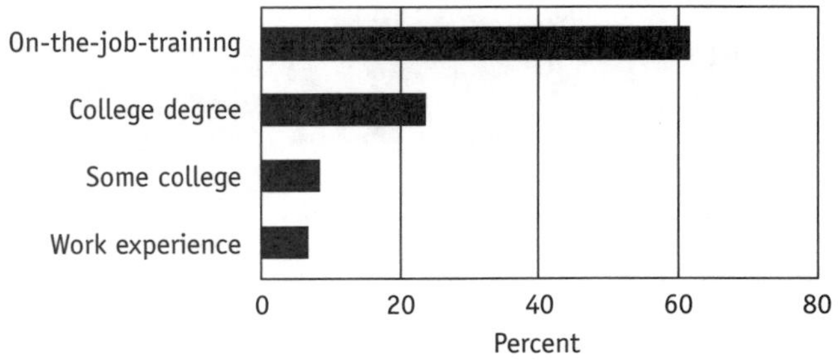

Source: Silvestri, G. T., "Occupational Employment Projections to 2006," 1997.

Figure 2.16 Education and Training Required for New Jobs, 1996–2006

services and retail trade categories will add 11.3 million and 2.3 million jobs, respectively, to the economy—for a total of 68.8 million jobs by 2006. Together they will make up 73 percent of new jobs and 46 percent of total employment by 2006. Government will grow by 1.7 million jobs.

Another characteristic of this pattern of job growth is the range of levels of education and training required for these jobs. Most new job openings—created from actual job growth and job replacement—are in the highest- and lowest-level skill areas. Over one-fourth of all new jobs require at least a bachelor's degree. Many require a bachelor's degree with work experience and some require postgraduate degrees. Currently, 16 percent of the U.S. adult population holds at least a bachelor's degree. See Figure 2.16 for a breakdown of education and training needed for new jobs.

According to the Bureau of Labor Statistics, occupations that require a bachelor's degree or more pay about 42 percent more than the average job, while those requiring work experience plus a bachelor's or higher degree pay 63 percent more than average. It clearly is worthwhile to increase educational attainment to at least a bachelor's degree to reap the benefit of a growing service economy.

Many new jobs requiring a high school diploma or less rely on on-the-job training (from a few months to a year) to prepare workers. These jobs pay considerably less and are characterized by high turnover and little job mobility. Many are found in the retail and personal services categories.

Customer-Oriented Jobs Will Shape the Nature of Work[3]

What does growth in the service sector mean for workers? A shift to a service-oriented economy means that work processes are being designed to get closer to the customer—to learn more about the customer, to provide more customized goods and services, and to anticipate new customer needs. Employment growth reflects these new organizational concerns and strategic needs.

An expanding service-producing economy creates two major challenges for the next decade:

- Employers need to reorganize to support the shift from a focus on producing products to a focus on servicing global customers with products and services.
- Employees need to develop information management and communication skills to support service delivery and learn how to address the desires, preferences, and conditions of customers.

Workers increasingly will find themselves in positions that focus on learning about customer needs, customer perceptions, and how to differentiate their products with value-added services. Fewer workers will be producing goods and more will be managing and coordinating production processes. Workers will need to be able to troubleshoot problems as they arise, often making decisions based on their own knowledge and experience and with input from their coworkers. They will frequently be comparing the status of their individual and group's performance to company and industry benchmarks. This will require good information management, collaborative work skills, and sophisticated use of information and communications media.

Three employment areas in the service sector are growing faster than overall labor force growth. These jobs help companies

- Move goods to the customer (such as wholesale trade, retail trade, and freight carriers)
- Provide services directly to the customer (such as hotels, recreation, travel services, auto repair, and health services)
- Provide business support services (such as software, advertising, finance, or consulting services)

Table 2.6 Employment Growth in Customer-Oriented Jobs, 1996–2006

Average Annual Rate of Change of Selected Industries			
Goods Producing	**Percent**	**Consumer Services** *(cont'd)*	**Percent**
Mining	-2.5	Auto repair services	3.3
Construction	0.9	Other repair services	1.3
Manufacturing	-0.2	Health practitioners	3.9
		Misc. health services	5.3
Goods Disbursing		Social services	3.7
Freight	1.7		
Wholesale trade	1.1	**Business Services**	
Retail trade	1.0	Computer & data	
		Processing	7.6
Consumer Services		Financial services	1.0
Hotel & lodging	1.4	Media/advertising	1.1
Personal services	0.9	Personnel supply	4.3
Amusement & recreation	3.1	Personnel services	2.5

Source: Franklin, J. C., "Industry Output and Employment Projections to 2006," 1997 (Table 4, p. 44).

In the next decade, jobs that move products to customers, support the customers' needs, or deal directly with customers will continue to grow. Table 2.6 shows that jobs involved in freight services, hotel and lodging, recreation, auto repair, health practitioner offices and other health services, computer-related services, and personnel (staffing) services will have above average job growth in the next decade.

Industry growth alone doesn't tell the whole story of the job market changes. Another critical characteristic of the shift to a service-based economy is the extent to which those jobs require intensive information and knowledge management skills, such as managing and analyzing data and making decisions about sales, customer preferences, inventories, consumer market patterns, and other strategic business issues. Increasingly, workers will have to bring some special skill or knowledge to the workplace, and work interactively with information and customers. This will include employees at retail counters and customer service desks as well as managers and other executives.

Table 2.7 shows the growth in various occupational categories. The fastest-growing occupations are those that require the most specialized training and education—professional specialties and technicians and technical support occupations. And, according to Bureau of Labor Statistics studies, 70 percent of workers who have direct contact with customers—

Table 2.7 Employment Growth by Major Occupational Categories, 1996–2006 (Average Annual Growth Rate)

Occupational Category	Percentage of Growth
Executive, administrative, and managerial	1.6
Professional specialty	2.4
Technicians and related support	1.9
Marketing and sales	1.4
Administrative support, including clerical	0.7

Source: Silvestri, G. T., "Occupational Employment Projections to 2006," 1997.

technicians, administrative support, and sales representatives—have been to college. The lesson is that workers will have to develop specialized job experiences and complete higher levels of education (at least college) to gain the most job mobility and opportunities.

Selecting and Managing Communications Media Will Be a Key Work Activity

Service sector jobs that get closer to the customer—involving either direct interaction with customers or indirect support of customer service delivery and maintenance—require sophisticated information management and intense communication with colleagues. In such an environment, messaging (or remote communications) becomes a critical work practice.

Work processes are often distributed geographically and involve high levels of interdependence with coworkers in various parts of the country or world. Customer service centers may be located in a different part of the country than product distribution facilities. Retail service workers may need to consult remote databases to make a decision or communicate with other retail service providers to solve a problem quickly. Choosing the information and communication tools to conduct this type of work is no longer straightforward. Furthermore, communication methods selection has direct consequences for the nature and quality of the interaction.

Rather than just reaching for the telephone to contact a colleague or dropping a document in the mail, workers select from an expanding array of tools that provide communications in various formats. Workers can communicate from any place at any time. They can immediately contact a coworker remotely via a pager or cellular phone. They can send large

Table 2.8 Office Workers' Use of Communication Tools

Tool	Percentage Who Use Daily or Several Times a Week
Desktop PC	96
E-mail	96
Voice mail	95
Fax	89
Internet	71
Intranet	69
Laptop	29
Cellular phone	27
Pager	19

Source: Institute for the Future, *Managing Communications in the 21st-Century Workplace,* IFTF/Pitney Bowes Corporate Communications Study, 1998–1999.

documents and files instantly through electronic mail. Or they can slow down the pace of communication and use regular postal mail. Rather than select any mediated form of communication they can meet face-to-face, if schedules and geography permit. Choices for how and when to communicate and exchange information abound. Knowing how to make the best media choices for particular work tasks and conditions will be a critical skill for knowledge workers in the next decade.

The average office worker today is reported to use six tools regularly at work. Table 2.8 shows a range of widely used communication tools.

E-mail is the most frequently used tool in the office worker's electronic communication toolkit. Other electronic communication methods are also making significant inroads into the workplace, including Internet and intranet access, as seen in Table 2.9. Over the next few years, more office workers will depend on the use of the Internet and intranet as these tools become more widely available.

An Asynchronous Messaging Work Culture. The widespread diffusion of information and communications technologies in the workplace is creating a new genre of work communications—asynchronous messaging (or time-delayed messaging)—and new areas of competency in managing those communications. Early examples of asynchronous messaging are postal mail

Table 2.9 E-Mail, Internet, Intranet Use in 1998–1999

	Percentage
E-mail	31
Internet	23
Intranet	7

Source: Institute for the Future, *Managing Communications in the 21st-Century Workplace,* IFTF/Pitney Bowes Corporate Communications Study, 1998–1999.

and telephone answering machines; the most recent examples of messaging methods include electronic mail, voice mail, pagers, and fax. They are methods in which the sender and receiver do not need to interact at the same time (synchronously) to exchange a communication. Workers interacting with coworkers, partners, suppliers, or clients in different time zones can avoid some of the difficulties of finding an appropriate shared hour during the day using asynchronous methods. Workers no longer need to be at their desk to send or receive messages and can begin to create their own patterns for where and when they access their messages using the growing number of messaging devices and services. Indeed, messaging is a mainstay of office communications.

Workers today must actively manage a continuous flow of office communications generated by new anytime, anyplace communications methods. Indeed, a whole new world of responsibilities and roles is emerging to address communications functions and related issues of communications overload, knowledge filtering and transfer, and information exchange. Table 2.10 on page 66 shows the results of a recent national survey that indicates the average office worker interacts with 190 messages per day, including messages sent and received in various electronic and paper methods.

The challenge for office workers is to learn to use new tools as they are adopted by their organizations, departments, and work groups and to integrate them into their workflow. This involves learning which tools are most effective for specific kinds of work and communications—often determined by work groups themselves. This means learning to identify and communicate individual tool preferences for certain kinds of communications and specific people, such as supervisors or customers. To communicate effectively, workers will need to learn the communication styles of their

Table 2.10 Number of Messages Sent and Received by One Office Worker in an Average Day

Communication Method	Total	Sent	Received
Telephone	52	23	30
Interoffice mail	18	8	10
E-mail	30	13	17
Voice mail	22	9	13
Post-it notes	11	7	5
U.S. Postal Service	18	6	12
Telephone message slips	10	6	4
Fax	15	6	9
Pager	3.5	2	2
Cellular phone	3.3	2	1
Overnight courier/messenger	3.4	2	2
U.S. Postal Service Express Mail	3.2	1	2
Total Communications Per Day	**190**	**84**	**106**

Source: Institute for the Future, *Managing Communications in the 21st-Century Workplace,* IFTF/Pitney Bowes Corporate Communications Study, 1998–1999.

coworkers, bosses, and others who may have different technology abilities. Some may prefer voice mail to electronic mail, and others may prefer certain methods of communication when they travel compared to when they are at the office. These specific preferences need to be communicated among workers to avoid frustration and to ensure that communications are effectively delivered, received, and read.

As workers gain more access to new tools, they will need to develop strategies for managing the volume of messages that they receive each day. Techniques for filtering and screening messages will be important for sorting through communications and getting to the important messages. Sometimes, special features of specific tools (such as e-mail or voice mail features) can help organize and prioritize communications. But other times, individuals and groups need to develop their own social guidelines and etiquette for handling intense communications.

Young Workers and Adoption of New Tools at the Office. Young workers moving into the workforce will directly influence tool diffusion and adoption in the workplace as they will have already learned to use and experiment with

Table 2.11 Percentage of Workers Who Use E-mail on a Regular Basis

Age Group	Percent
18–34	36
35–44	28
45–54	21
55+	12

Source: Institute for the Future, *Managing Communications in the 21st-Century Workplace,* IFTF/Pitney Bowes Corporate Communications Study, 1998–1999.

new electronic media at school and at home. Current video game technology and interactive toys are providing youngsters with ample opportunity to develop formative experiences with interactive technology that they will carry into the workplace. These experiences will shape their expectations for how they will interact with their coworkers and with information.

Currently, workers between ages 18 and 34 are more likely to use electronic tools such as e-mail, the Internet, and intranet than their older coworkers, as seen above in Table 2.11. As even younger cohorts enter the workplace, this trend will continue. We expect technology-savvy young workers to contribute heavily to the development of new social protocols for communications and asynchronous messaging and to define new forms of electronically mediated work.

Learning how to effectively use communications tools will become an increasingly important area of development for workers as more work is distributed geographically. Learning how to use asynchronous tools and effectively manage messages will become an important basic work skill as more work is conducted across time zones in various locations. Counselors and career professionals should not neglect the importance of such skills and knowledge in working with their clients.

PRACTICAL EXERCISES FOR COUNSELORS

Several key exercises will help counselors better assist their clients in developing strategies to begin or change careers to meet the conditions of the 21st-century world of work. Some are exercises with clients themselves, while others are tasks for counselors to manage, synthesize, and communicate key career information they gather.

Practical Exercises with Clients

To succeed in the 21st-century world of work, individuals will need to make continuous assessments of their career needs, desires, and options throughout the various stages of their work-life cycle. Exercises 2.1 and 2.2 will help clients proactively meet challenges and make course corrections. The exercises will assist clients as they search for and develop career mobility opportunities within their own organization as well as in other organizations.

EXERCISE 2.1

DEVELOP ONGOING CAREER PORTFOLIO ASSESSMENT TOOLS

Counselors should assist clients in developing a portfolio of their career in addition to their traditional résumé, and encourage a regular updating of that portfolio.

- The portfolio should reflect the client's career history with examples of work or documents and other artifacts that represent the experiences and learning of the client at various jobs.
- Make the exercise fun. Everyone is familiar with documenting important family events, vacations, travel, and life histories with pictures, writing, and other artifacts. Apply this technique to the career portfolio and use it to encourage reflection about the career evolution.
- Meet periodically with clients and ask them to explain why certain images or documents were included in the portfolio.
- Ask clients what the images or documents reflect and what their importance is in the evolution of the client's career.
- Ask clients to imagine documenting the pathway of a career as a learning journey—what key individuals were met along the way, what were the key lessons, what were specific bottlenecks at different points along the career, what pieces of work or work events represent key learning and experiences?

Portfolios are good for reflecting on the past. Another important step is to apply that reflection to future work and career options and choices. Workers will need help to identify, communicate, and apply the value of their experiences to new work contexts. As companies develop more cross-industry alliances, cross-functional teams, and global connections, workers will need to apply their skills to new work situations, employers, and problems. Workers should learn how to communicate the value of their past work experiences and skills to prospective employers in a wide range of industries and fields.

EXERCISE 2.2

HELP TRANSLATE SKILLS AND EXPERIENCE TO NEW WORK CONTEXTS

Using their career portfolios, clients can identify specific skills and experiences they acquired in the past and make links to potential jobs and career choices in the future. By building on the career history, counselors can assist clients in anticipating what the portfolio might look like in the future.

- How can past experiences and skills extend both to the future and to new work situations?
- What will be the value of their acquired skills in these new contexts?
- Some of the answers to these questions may require some investigation and research by the client to determine the criteria for value in new jobs, companies, or work environments.
- Counselors can make these exercises individual one-on-one interactions or small-group exercises to leverage the knowledge and expertise of other workers.

Counselors must stress the importance of continuing learning and skill development for workers of all ages. In addition to encouraging reflection and assessment of career experiences and skills, counselors need to help clients build continuous learning into their careers (see Exercise 2.3).

EXERCISE 2.3

DEVELOP A LIFELONG LEARNING STRATEGY FOR CLIENTS

Learning and skill acquisition strategies will need to be sensitive to age groups, gender, ethnicity, and life stage. Some may prefer peer mentoring opportunities (for example, senior executive women, workers in start-up companies, or temporary and contract/freelance workers) so that they can share a common context, whereas others prefer independent coursework and study.

- Counselors can help clients identify the learning strategies that work best for them now and understand how those strategies may need to change in the future.
- Clients may need encouragement to explore learning resources available on the World Wide Web. These resources range from interactive discussions and exercises to traditional web page documents for downloading and reading. Web-based learning may be particularly helpful to certain groups of workers (working moms, multiple job holders, temporary or contract workers) since they may need to access material from home or from work at whatever time suits them.

Specifically, counselors should help clients think through the implications of the service economy on the future of their careers and the kind of learning and skills that will be most useful (see Exercise 2.4).

Messaging and information exchange is a key work practice in the knowledge economy. Successful workers in any type of job in the 21st century will need to be skilled at using communication tools to retrieve, evaluate, share, and create information and knowledge. This includes technical skills (operating specific devices) as well as social skills related to tools use (knowing what tool to use, when, and how to shape particular communications for effectiveness; see Exercise 2.5).

EXERCISE 2.4

HELP CLIENTS DEVELOP SKILL LINKS TO THE SERVICE ECONOMY

Outline clients' current and desired career or work situations and identify how this work relates to the customer.

- Where in the distribution chain of products or services to the customer does their job fit?
- Do they interact directly with the customer?
- Are they primarily dealing with information that supports the customer?
- Does their job require them to learn from the customer in order to develop new products and services?
- In describing how clients' career portfolios might look in the future, identify how their work will relate to the customer and what kinds of skills will be important.
- What are ways of acquiring those skills or that expertise? Use this to develop a strategy for skill and experience acquisition for the client. Some skill development may be possible to accomplish in the context of the client's current employment; however, some may require special coursework, reading, and practice outside of their job.

Tasks for Counselors

Counselors will need to prepare themselves to help clients in the 21st century. This will include enhancing their own background knowledge of the changing context of work, building networks with other professionals, identifying employment niches to better help selected workers, and utilizing a variety of communication methods themselves as they leverage technology. Exercises 2.6 through 2.9 are designed to focus counselors on those important tasks.

EXERCISE 2.5

EVALUATE COMMUNICATION STRATEGIES TO INCREASE EFFECTIVENESS

Social protocols are the agreed-upon rules or guidelines that emerge from groups of tool users to help them manage communications. Some workers, for example, scan e-mail by subject and name to answer important ones first, or they use the return receipt preference to make sure a message has been received. Some groups develop their own codes or rules, such as agreeing to leave brief voice mails and use e-mail or fax for longer messages. As specific devices exist within an organization or team, workers learn to develop and model social protocols to facilitate their use of various tools.

When users don't know the social protocols, they can experience frustration, which can lead to some workers rejecting certain tools and creating potential communication bottlenecks within teams, work groups, and departments. As more workers adopt and use technologies for their work, they will need to develop and share their preferences for how to use them. Learning to use new technologies and to develop shared protocols for use will be an ongoing activity for workers.

- Counselors should encourage group discussions on effective communication and messaging skills.
- Sessions in which clients share their most effective and least effective messaging and communications techniques will broaden the group's knowledge of what works, why, and for whom. These can include individual stories of why certain communication methods (for example, e-mail, voice mail, or face-to-face) worked better or worse in certain work situations.
- Have the group dissect why a particular method failed to deliver a desired outcome or why it was effective. Individuals can apply these tips to their own work context.
- Encourage clients to be more reflective about the tools they use and to think ahead about the consequences of using a particular tool. For example, will e-mail or voice mail be easier to access for the colleague on the road or in another country?
- In small groups, have each client describe his or her own communication method preferences and those of coworkers. Do they match up? Are there conflicts?
- Discuss ways that they can choose the right tools for effective communication in the correct context and avoid those that don't work well.

EXERCISE 2.6

DEVELOP KNOWLEDGE BASE OF THE CHANGING CONTEXT OF WORK

Workers seeking career guidance will require high levels of interaction and engagement with information about companies, industries, and professional development. Counselors will be expected to have cutting-edge information about trends in employment and work life. In particular, counselors should understand the implications for their clients of the shift from goods-producing to service-producing jobs. Their clients are having this experience firsthand. Counselors cannot afford to become out of date with the big picture of change.

- Counselors should develop their own databases of resources specific to particular industries and occupations.
- Counselors should be able to communicate key trends and implications for various types of clients.
- Counselors should be able to help clients see their own careers in a broader context of change and evolution.

EXERCISE 2.7

LEVERAGE TECHNOLOGY TO CREATE ANYTIME, ANYPLACE SERVICES

Work is becoming more mobile and reliant on communication technologies—so that coordinating time for counseling and coaching may be difficult.

- Making a number of communication options available to clients will be important and expected.
- Making resources available online—such as tools for career self-assessment, career development process guides, and job listings—will help counselors better serve their clients. Clients will appreciate and benefit from the convenience of accessing information and choosing the media that best suits their specific needs.
- Using e-mail newsletters, web sites with opportunities for clients to contribute comments and suggestions, reviews, and scheduled online discussion forums may bring in some clients who cannot physically come to career management offices or participate during traditional hours. It will also help build a sense of community around specific topics of interest to the client base, which is an important way to start customizing services.

EXERCISE 2.8

BUILD A STRATEGIC NETWORK THAT MATCHES THE DIVERSITY AND NEEDS OF CLIENTS

Counselors should continually update their own networks of counselors, professionals, and providers they use to deliver services to clients to make sure that they span the age range, cultural background, and needs of clients.

- Counselors may have a list of referrals for more specific or in-depth training, but this list may not represent the diversity of clients. Are there traditional assumptions guiding the selection of these referral professionals and services?
- It will be important for counselors to reassess and identify new ways to leverage their networks in the most effective way for themselves and their clients—as information sources, potential employers, and partners.

EXERCISE 2.9

MAKE SURE TO TARGET EMPLOYMENT NICHES

Counselors ought to review their services and assess their relevance to the special needs of particular groups of workers, such as temporary and contract workers, employees in start-up companies, self-employed and small proprietors, those who work primarily at home, and other kinds of nontraditional workers.

- How can counselors' services (context and delivery) apply to these distinct groups of workers? How are these groups of workers underserved in the career guidance field?
- Are there special skills or knowledge that are particularly relevant to these different groups?
- Customizing programs and services for workers in new forms of employment and in newly forming industries will fill a gap in this part of the market for career services.

REFERENCES

Franklin, J. C. (1997, November). Industry output and employment projections to 2006. *Monthly Labor Review,* pp. 39–57.

Fullerton, H. N., Jr. (1997, November). Labor force 2006: Slowing down and changing composition. *Monthly Labor Review,* pp. 23–38.

Institute for the Future. (1997a, June). Anticipating consumer desire for new media at home: Lessons from connected households. Outlook Project, SR-626.

Institute for the Future. (1997b, October). Career revisited: A shift to self-reliance. Outlook Project, SR-644.

Institute for the Future. (1997c). *The new consumer changes the face of the workforce.* Corporate Associates Program, *8*(2).

Institute for the Future. (June 1998a). Digital kids: Key trends to track. Outlook Project, SR-657.

Institute for the Future. (1998b). From information to knowledge: Harnessing the talent of the 21st-century workforce. *Ten Year Forecast.*

Institute for the Future. (1998c). The future workforce: Slower growth, big change. *Ten Year Forecast.*

Institute for the Future. (1998d). Older workers: Coming to a century near you. *Ten Year Forecast.*

Institute for the Future. (1998-1999). Managing communications in the 21st-century workplace. IFTF/Pitney Bowes Corporate Communications Study.

Institute for the Future. (1999). Working documents. Outlook Project.

International Labour Organization. (1995). *World Labour Report.* Geneva, Switzerland: International Labour Office.

Silvestri, G. T. (1997, November). Occupational employment projections to 2006. *Monthly Labor Review,* pp. 58–83.

Slater, M., & Glazer, P. M. (1987). "Prescriptions for professional survival." In J. K. Conway, S. C. Bourque, & J. W. Scott (Eds.), *Learning about women: Gender, politics, and power* (pp. 119-135). Ann Arbor: University of Michigan Press.

U.S. Bureau of the Census. (1998). *Statistical abstract of the United States: 1998.* (118th ed.). Washington, DC: U.S. Government Printing Office.

U.S. Bureau of Labor Statistics. (1997). *Employee Tenure in the mid-1990s.* Washington, DC: U.S. Government Printing Office.

Wooton, B. L. (1997, April). Gender differences in occupational employment. *Monthly Labor Review.*

World Bank. (1995). *World development report: Workers in an integrating world.* Washington, DC: International Bank for Reconstruction and Development.

World investment report: Transnational corporations and competitiveness. (1995). United Nations Conference on Trade and Development, Geneva, Switzerland.

NOTES

[1]Intranets are proprietary companywide computer webs for internal corporate communications that use the protocols and standards of the public Internet.

[2]Multi-user domains, known as MUDs, are text-based worlds that allow online, real-time interaction between players or participants. For example, MOOSE Crossing, created by Amy Bruckman as part of her doctoral work at the MIT Media Lab, is an interactive, text-based online environment in which children create characters, objects, artifacts, and stories as a form of enjoyment and learning.

[3]For a more detailed discussion, see The Institute for the Future Report "The New Consumer Changes the Face of the Workforce."

3

A New Deal for a Learning Economy*

JOBS AND CAREERS IN POSTINDUSTRIAL SOCIETY

Stephen A. Herzenberg, John A. Alic, and Howard Wial

For decades, the U.S. economy has been shifting from a structure centered on manufacturing to one dominated by services. Our society has become postindustrial—we have a new economy that needs new practices and policies to improve job opportunities and productivity performance. This chapter seeks to spell out those practices and policies.

Doing so requires an analytical framework that can make sense of the new economy in all its diversity. Our framework is grounded in the dynamics of service industries and the labor market. At the core are four *work systems*. Each represents a different basic approach to production and to controlling how hard or how well people work. Together, they capture the full range of ways in which production can be organized. Understanding the four work systems is a first step toward understanding jobs and careers as

*This chapter draws heavily from *New Rules for a New Economy: Employment and Opportunity in Postindustrial America* by Stephen A. Herzenberg, John A. Alic, and Howard Wial, 1998, especially chapters 3, 5, and 7. For a fuller treatment, additional examples, and more extensive references, readers are encouraged to consult that source.

they are today and envisioning them as they could be—in a future with organizations and institutions changed to expand career opportunities for all workers.

The analysis of work systems points to three problems that limit opportunities in today's economy, contributing to wage inequality and limiting mobility to better jobs. The first problem is the nature of many jobs. The new economy doesn't consist only of high-paying jobs as computer programmers, web page designers, physicians, and airline pilots. About a quarter of U.S. employment falls into low-paid, labor-intensive categories: nurse's aides and hospital orderlies, truck drivers and janitors. Many of these jobs are in small work sites—independent nursing homes and childcare centers, fast food outlets and building sites—detached from social networks that could lead to advancement.

A second problem is the uncertainty and insecurity now part of many "good" jobs. Mergers, restructuring, and downsizing destroy jobs of managers and professionals as well as secretaries and clerical workers. Career trajectories are less predictable. Those who, in the old economy (through the 1970s), could look forward to stable employment in a big company with opportunities to advance now face the kinds of uncertainties with which less skilled workers have always lived.

Third, many of the service industries that now dominate the economy exhibit poor productivity performance, as measured by government statistics. (We generally prefer the term "performance" because it suggests the qualitative dimensions of service output as well as the quantitative.) Lagging performance limits the rate at which wages and living standards can grow. Work systems based on low-wage, "unskilled" jobs restrict performance unnecessarily, while undercutting worker motivation and career incentives. Why is performance poor when businesses could reorganize production to raise performance? In part because many businesses have been content to compete based on low wages and in part because we've lacked a production model suited to services that can lead to widespread improvement (as standardization and scale economies did for mass manufacturing in the old economy). We present such a model and consider its implications for improving economic performance and for creating better jobs for workers.

We present solutions to the three problems and show (1) how to reorganize work to reduce the number of low-wage, dead-end jobs; (2) how to create new pathways out of low-wage jobs, within and across industries; and (3) how to strengthen the career development infrastructure for those outside the high-skilled occupations that already benefit from such supports. These strategies hinge in part on policy reforms, which would promote new forms of worker associations that could pick up some functions performed by organization-level job ladders in the old economy. The chapter closes with suggestions for career consultants, workers, and others on how to navigate today's turbulent economy.

Our analysis offers insights into how individuals can prosper by building careers that take them into successively better jobs, with different employers (*staircase careers*) or within a single organization (more common in the old economy). But our primary aim is to suggest a collective reconstruction of the economy, so that all Americans can look ahead with optimism rather than unease. We hope too that international readers will learn from our ideas. The issues we discuss are not unique to the United States, nor are the practices and policies that we advocate.

Of all key actors, career counselors are perhaps best placed to grasp the changes we describe and to act on that understanding. Every day, counselors see different facets of the new economy. We hope our analysis will help in putting those facets together, revealing a larger context in which the new economy could work to the benefit of all working Americans, not just the elites who prospered in the 1990s.

THE FOUR WORK SYSTEMS

Each of the work systems—tightly constrained, unrationalized labor-intensive, semiautonomous, and high-skill autonomous—relies on different mechanisms to regulate how work is done and to induce workers to act in ways consistent with the employer's goals. Table 3.1 on page 80 outlines these work systems, which differ in knowledge and skill requirements and in the extent to which skill transfers across organizations. Table 3.2 on page 82 gives estimates of the share of employment in each system for both services and manufacturing.

Tightly Constrained Work System

The jobs in the tightly constrained work system consist of closely prescribed tasks controlled by a combination of technology and

Table 3.1 Work Systems Summary

	Tightly Constrained	Unrationalized Labor-Intensive	Semi-autonomous	High-Skill Autonomous
Examples	Telephone operators, fast-food workers, check proofers	Some nurse's aides, hotel maids, long-distance truck drivers, child-care workers, clerical home workers	Clerical and administrative jobs with relatively broad responsibilities, low-level managers, some sales workers, UPS truck drivers	Physicians, high-level managers, laboratory technicians, electricians, engineers
Business strategy/ markets served	High volume, low cost; standardized quality	Low cost, low volume; often low or uneven quality	Volume and quality vary	Low volume (each job may differ); quality often in the eye of the beholder
Extent of organizational rationalization	High (jobs designed by management)	Low	Moderate	Low to moderate
Task supervision	Tight	Loose	Moderate	Little
Output monitoring/ quantitative performance measurement	Machine or technological pacing common	Quantitative measurement in some cases	Quantitative measurement in some cases	Quantitative measurement rare
Formal education/ credentials	Low to moderate	Low to moderate (skill often unrecognized)	Moderate	High
Formal, organization-specific training	Minimal	Minimal	Significant for those who climb internal job ladders	Varies

Table 3.1 Work Systems Summary (cont'd)

	Tightly Constrained	Unrationalized Labor-Intensive	Semi-autonomous	High-Skill Autonomous
On-the-job training	Limited	Some informal, unrecognized OJT from other workers	Limited to moderate	Substantial
Pay	Often flat hourly; some bonuses linked to output or profits	Sometimes piece rate; sometimes flat hourly	Often flat hourly; some bonuses linked to output or profits	Usually salary; salary or profit share may be linked to billing, attracting clients
Screening of job applicants	Limited	Little	Careful	Usually very careful
Internal job ladders	Limited except in some union organizations	No	Important	Important for some workers
Mobility across organizations	Lateral mobility in some cases	Lateral, no upward mobility	Most experience not portable	Lateral mobility; upward mobility in some professions

Source: Reprinted from Stephen A. Herzenberg, John A. Alic, and Howard Wial, *New Rules for a New Economy: Employment and Opportunity in Postindustrial America,* Table 6, pp. 42–43. Copyright © 1998 The Twentieth Century Fund. Used by permission of the publisher, Cornell University Press.

organizational practice, much like an assembly line. This category includes the jobs most influenced by the tradition of scientific management, which today often means computer monitoring as well as supervisory oversight. Only about 4 percent of U.S. service sector employment falls into the tightly constrained category, including telephone operators, data entry clerks, and fast-food workers such as the hamburger flippers so closely identified in the public mind with dead-end service jobs. Service workers with tightly constrained jobs earned a median wage of $5.75 in 1996, nearly 30 percent

Table 3.2 U.S. Employment by Work System, 1996 (Percent)

	All Industries	Service	Manufacturing
Tightly constrained	5	4	10
Unrationalized labor-intensive	25	26	15
Semiautonomous	30	29	34
High-skill autonomous	41	40	40

Source: Reprinted from Stephen A. Herzenberg, John A. Alic, and Howard Wial, *New Rules for a New Economy: Employment and Opportunity in Postindustrial America,* Table 7, p. 45. Copyright © 1998 The Twentieth Century Fund. Used by permission of the publisher, Cornell University Press..

Note: Totals may not add to 100 because of rounding.

Occupational categories in the Current Population Survey can only be matched to work systems on the basis of somewhat arbitrary choices. Therefore, figures are rough approximations. See Herzenberg, Alic, and Wial, 1998, for the basis for these estimates.

below the median in this work system in manufacturing (where many better-paid, longer-tenured workers are still represented by unions).

Tightly constrained jobs rarely require much in the way of skills, and those skills rarely transfer across employers (for example, knowing the location of menu items on the McDonald's cash register). Training usually takes a few days or weeks, rarely more than a few months. The fast pace and high stress common in the tightly constrained work system contribute to high levels of turnover—often 100 percent or more annually. With opportunities for promotion limited, some workers move from one employer to another in search of a few cents more per hour or a more congenial working environment.

Here's an example of a tightly constrained work system:[1] In a cavernous office that looks like an auditorium during exam period, desks face the front and windows have been blacked out (Horowitz, 1994). In the "cage" (an old banking term for the money-handling area), workers slit envelopes, remove checks, and sort the remaining contents at the rate of three envelopes a minute. At the rows of desks, clerks enter the amount on each check into computer terminals; their quota is 8,500 keystrokes an hour. Everyone's performance is monitored. A manager watches from an elevated platform that workers call the "pedestal" or the "birdhouse." Other supervisors monitor workers from the back of the room. A black globe containing television cameras hangs from the ceiling.

The office is Electronic Banking Systems, Inc. (EBS), in Hagerstown, Maryland. EBS specializes in processing donations to charities and advocacy groups. It typifies the "lockbox" processing that is increasingly the province of organizations specializing in "back-office" operations. Inexperienced workers start at the minimum wage.

"This is a controlled environment," says Ron Eden, the owner of EBS. From his upstairs office, Eden can monitor video images from eight cameras around the processing center. Using remote control, he can zoom in on a worker's desk. Tracking productivity, not only keystrokes but also the number of errors each worker makes, helps him weed out those who fail to keep up.

"It's got to add stress when everyone knows their production is being monitored. I don't apologize for that," Eden says. He is also unapologetic about a rule forbidding talk unrelated to the task. "I'm not paying people to chat. I'm paying them to open envelopes," he says. The windows are blackened, he adds, because "I don't want them looking out—it's distracting. They'll make mistakes."

Some people circumvent the silence rule. "If you don't turn your head and sort of mumble out of the side of your mouth, supervisors won't hear you most of the time," one worker explained. She said her fiancé avoids her for a couple of hours after work "because I don't shut up—I need to talk, talk, talk." Others find it hard to leave the routine behind at the end of the day. One said her husband complained that she awakened him at night "shuffling my hands in my sleep" as if still opening envelopes.

Unrationalized Labor-Intensive Work System

Many more Americans—26 percent of service workers, 15 percent of those in manufacturing—hold unrationalized labor-intensive jobs than find themselves in the tightly constrained work system. The 1996 median wage in the unrationalized labor-intensive work system was $6 per hour in services and $6.40 in manufacturing.

The fundamental characteristic of this work system is that tasks vary irregularly, so they cannot be easily systematized or "rationalized." Workers are expected to figure out for themselves how to do what needs to be done—care for residents in a nursing home, load or drive a truck, or clean an office building. Employers—with low capital costs and the ability to hire unskilled workers at low wages—have few incentives to systematically analyze work in order to enhance productivity or to train their employees. Moreover, their customers may not recognize quality (for example, in childcare) or reward it (in low-end retailing).

Those who have never worked in an unrationalized labor-intensive job may perceive the skills required as low and generic (cleaning, lifting, driving, caregiving). Admittedly, training and opportunities for career advancement are limited. Even so, furniture movers, uncredentialed short-order cooks, and many others in this work system often develop skills and know-how that make them much more productive than novices. Though employees typically pick up skills from coworkers, rarely do they receive substantive or problem-solving training that would help them build on their informal know-how or devise innovative approaches to their tasks. Nor do employers spend much time and effort asking how technology might improve performance. Because skills transfer easily across organizations, occupational tenure may be lengthy even though job tenure tends to be low.

Within the unrationalized labor-intensive work system, we define three subcategories—quantitative control, socialized/customer control, and simple control.

- **Quantitative Control.** When employers can easily measure output and reject low quality, as with hotel housekeepers or janitors, they usually pay a fixed amount per unit of output (that is., a piece rate) or require workers to complete a fixed set of tasks in the workday. Hotel housekeepers we interviewed, for example, clean about 17 rooms a day. At $6 an hour with an eight-hour day, this comes to a little less than $3 a room. Supervisors or quality inspectors check each room. After a little on-the-job training from a coworker, hotel housekeepers are largely left to accomplish their tasks as they see fit.

- **Socialized/Customer Control.** In nursing homes, childcare centers, and other unrationalized social service work, managers have no way to measure output. Workers themselves are responsible for how well the job is accomplished. Quantity and quality depend on informally acquired know-how and on workers' sense of obligation to those in their care. Because quality is difficult to evaluate, the market may not reward it. Roughly half of nursing home residents, for instance, cannot communicate their wants and needs. For facilities that draw Medicaid and Medicare funds, state regulations ordinarily set minimum staffing levels. Nursing homes outside the high-end private-pay parts of the industry pay the lowest wage that will attract the number of staff required by law (or close to that number).

Childcare centers now look after nearly 30 percent of American children for at least part of the day. As in nursing homes, low pay, few benefits, and difficult working conditions result in a high rate of turnover. Many who have the disposition for this work and find it rewarding leave in frustration for better pay in other occupations. Labor accounts for 70 percent of costs in childcare centers, even though the median wage was only $6 per hour in 1996 (identical to the figure for the unrationalized labor-intensive work system as a whole). Although childcare employees have higher average levels of education and training than nurse's aides, the quality of care, as in nursing homes, tends to reflect worker attitudes plus whatever knowledge (and good or bad habits) they bring to the job. Parents cannot observe what goes on; young children may not be able to convey the reasons for happiness or unhappiness; language barriers sometimes exist between providers and parents. Even if they could identify higher-quality care, many working parents could not afford it.

When internalized commitment to the job contributes to high effort levels among unrationalized social service workers, a strong work ethic creates a further disincentive for employers to consider other means of improving performance.

- **Simple Control.** Employers commonly resort to simple control where wages are low, task variety impedes quantitative control, and worker commitment is weaker than in the socialized/customer control category. Examples include much of independent retailing, low-skill office work (including temporary work), and casual labor and nonprofessional self-employment. In these settings, where employers believe, often incorrectly, that there is little potential to improve performance through technology or job redesign, performance varies widely. Performance often depends on the personal relationship of supervisor to worker and on whether supervisors have carrots (a small raise, flexible hours) or sticks (inflexible, bad, or few hours; the worst assignments) that can be used to motivate or coerce workers.

As one example of an unrationalized work system, imagine a nursing home—small, somewhat run-down, but clean (Eaton, 1997).[2] Arianne, a nurse's aide, arrives at 6:20 A.M. and begins by setting aside a supply of clean towels and sheets. Because several of her coworkers have called in sick, Arianne must care for an additional six residents this day, 16 altogether. She begins waking residents, changing their diapers, and washing them. Half are lying in wet or dirty sheets. Shortly after 7:30, Arianne wheels the eight residents she has dressed to breakfast and returns for the rest. She skips her 10-minute scheduled break at 8:30 to answer two patient call lights. Later that morning one of Arianne's patients suffers a cardiac arrest and goes by ambulance to the hospital. Arianne is momentarily relieved that she has one fewer person to care for, then immediately feels guilty.

After her own half-hour lunch break, Arianne takes the 15 residents to the dining room and later changes diapers again. She also has to finish paperwork from the previous day. "If it's not documented, it didn't happen," says the director of nursing. Arianne asks, "Isn't it better to take care of someone than to write down that you did?" Now she is trying to remember who had a bowel movement, what they ate, who had a bath. From 1:30 P.M. to 2:30 P.M., she takes residents to activities and gives two baths, interrupted by call lights. She asks the charge nurse for help, but no one is available. She is too busy to chat with residents, who like to hear about her children and talk about their own grandchildren. Leaving a little after 3:00 P.M., Arianne catches the bus for her second job, the dinner shift at another nursing home.

In contrast to the check processors at EBS, Arianne has autonomy over her daily tasks. But she earns only $6.50 an hour. She would like to get her high school equivalency certificate, but cannot manage school on top of two jobs. Her family has no health insurance because she cannot afford the co-payment. Arianne has been looking for a promotion to rehabilitation aide, which pays $6.75 an hour and requires less lifting and running. But there are 40 nurse's aides in the 90-bed home and only one rehabilitation aide.

Semiautonomous Work System

Semiautonomous workers, like those in the unrationalized labor-intensive system, perform tasks that cannot be technically controlled or monitored because of variety and/or complexity, or because workers' movement over wide areas makes close supervision difficult. The semiautonomous work system differs from the unrationalized labor-intensive system in that jobs, though nonprofessional, require substantial specialized learning. Much of this knowledge and skill is organization-specific. Examples include: clerical, administrative, or secretarial work that depends on mastery of proprietary computer systems (more than 80 in one insurance company we visited) or a bureaucracy's "standard operating procedures"; low-level management; sales positions requiring significant training in selling techniques, product attributes, or both (for example, selling tailored clothing or new cars); customer service representatives whose jobs are not subject to machine pacing; airline flight attendants; and drivers for service-oriented companies such as Federal Express or United Parcel Service. About 29 percent of service workers hold semiautonomous jobs. Many have considerable seniority, contributing to comparatively high wages—a 1996 median of $10 an hour. Employers rely on financial incentives, along with organizational culture and peer pressure, to align worker behavior with organizational goals and limit turnover to retain organization-specific skills.

In contrast to the unrationalized labor-intensive work system, organizations recognize the skills required in semiautonomous jobs and systematize the transmission of working knowledge to inexperienced employees. In contrast to the tightly constrained work system, task variety limits the scope for rationalization. For instance, package express drivers now carry handheld terminals that automate pick-up and delivery "paperwork"—but they still must drive the truck and find the address. Peer pressure and commitment to high-quality work motivate many semiautonomous workers, but are less powerful forces than in the high-skill autonomous work system, which depends more heavily on occupational pride, expertise, and self-management.

Because semiautonomous workers acquire substantial repertoires of skills relevant only to their current employer, and because companies lose productivity while training replacements, worker and employer share an interest in a long-term relationship. As a result, the semiautonomous work system has offered good opportunities for several generations of Americans who entered the labor market without a college degree or specialized skills. They could expect to advance along internal job ladders, aided by company-provided training and on-the-job learning. Some employers provided profit sharing or commissions to cement their relationships with semiautonomous employees. But in recent years, economic restructuring—mergers, downsizing, reengineering—has dissolved many of these long-standing relationships.

Some semiautonomous workers, including sales representatives, secretaries, and many managers, acquire a combination of organization-specific and occupational skills that permits them to move from one employer to another, rising as they negotiate a staircase career. However, workers who lose a long-held job may face a good deal of new learning—and a pay cut—at a new place of employment.

Now let's enter the ornate, 19th-century headquarters complex of Mount Rushmore Mutual, a large insurance company, which houses a full-fledged semiautonomous work system.[3] Gloria, a senior service representative, works in a fifth-floor cubicle. She can reach almost anyone in the company by means of elevated walkways in a set of buildings that spans three city blocks. The company pays well for the area and, so far, provides jobs for life.

Gloria came to Mount Rushmore Mutual out of high school 21 years ago when a friend of her mother's told her about an opening. She started as a messenger in underwriting, then moved to filing. Soon she became a secretary in the investment department. Now, as one of a team of 17 workers who service policies marketed by field agencies in six states, Gloria has reached the top of the company's nonmanagerial job ladder. She calls herself a cheerleader, and she looks and acts the part.

Most of the time, Gloria and her colleagues deal with routine matters—address changes, tax questions, billings, reinstatement of lapsed policies. But she also handles complaints that customers have taken to their state insurance commission. On her team, members rotate between four-month stints on the phones answering questions and three months off the phones. Six of Gloria's team members have more than six years of seniority. As Chris, their manager, says, "Since it takes two years to get up to speed, we don't want people leaving; it's only in the second year that the lightbulb goes on." The company has begun to require a college degree even for entry-level clerical positions. Still, when Chris asked other managers to imagine doing without two of their team members, then two more, they usually wanted to keep the most experienced workers over the college educated—in some cases, to their own surprise.

The company tracks the number of cases handled by each worker, but Chris doesn't show these figures to employees until their third year. Chris knows that some people deal with problems briskly while others, though slower, may be better at ferreting out a customer's underlying concerns. A labor organization represents Mount Rushmore Mutual's "nonexempt" employees. But with an open shop agreement, workers do not have to belong to the union, and only two members of Gloria's team have joined. In teams with older workers and less admired managers, a majority belong to the union. Some employees and union officials have been complaining of work intensification. But even if that were the case, it's not clear what choice workers would have but to accept the pressures. What they know isn't worth much to another company, even in insurance. The only jobs older, less educated workers in this Midwestern city could hope to find would pay perhaps half as much.

High-Skill Autonomous Work System

High-skill autonomous workers basically manage themselves—even if, like electricians, nurses, and teachers, they are formally subordinate to another professional or a manager. With expertise often recognized by professional, technical, or craft credentials, their skills are useful to many employers. Personal commitment to the standards of the occupation plays a critical role in maintaining performance. In traditional professions, such as law and the clergy, intraoccupational and intraorganizational advancement hinges on a combination of formal but subjective review (before making partner or bishop) and personal social networks ("who you know"). Two-fifths of service workers fall into this work system, making it the largest of the four. It is also the most rapidly growing. Earnings are well above those in the other work systems, with a 1996 median wage of $15 per hour in services, $16 in manufacturing.

In contrast to the tightly constrained and unrationalized labor-intensive work systems, employers of high-skill autonomous workers usually screen carefully and provide substantial formal and informal support for on-the-job learning and supplementary education and training. As for the unrationalized labor-intensive system, employers may have little understanding of what determines performance and how it could be measured or improved. Although employers may track output and quality—the number of lines of code generated by computer programmers, for example, or the mortality rate of surgeons—performance evaluation has a large subjective element usually dependent on peer judgment. (Some blocks of computer code are "better" than others; some surgeons take harder cases.) Indeed, the complex, nonroutine, and intangible nature of much craft and professional work makes defining performance, never mind evaluating it, a sometimes insurmountable task. Workers themselves may develop a rough internal consensus about what constitutes good performance, but this may or may not coincide with the interests of employers or customers.

To illustrate high-skill autonomous work, imagine a 38-year-old urban planner. Nathan began to learn his trade in graduate school. His mentor, a former city manager, helped him understand the realities of urban politics and bureaucracy and introduced him to the skills of interviewing informants in the field—getting people to tell their own stories in their own ways. From the teaching and writing of his theoretically oriented dissertation advisor, Nathan gained a worldview that still guides how he thinks about urban problems. He came to appreciate the discipline it took his advisor to avoid imposing his own interpretations on Nathan's evidence from the field.

Since leaving graduate school a decade ago, Nathan has changed employers four times. "I'm still learning," he says, "even though I still do pretty much the same things as at the beginning. Watching professionals try to manage has been an eye-opener. Then I try to do it myself and screw up about as badly." Before his last transition, caused by budget cuts following the population decline in Detroit, Nathan feared he might have to take a job that would be "a paycheck, not a calling." But after two months, he stopped fretting. Now he says, "I know people all over the country who're in the same boat. We care about cities, worry about their future, and look out for one another."

Throughout his career, Nathan benefited from both formal training and informal guidance from more experienced workers. This is characteristic of the high-skill autonomous work system. So is the self-motivation that makes him pull the occasional all-nighter 10 years out of graduate school. A prototypical knowledge worker, he understands that his reputation and network of colleagues matters more than whether his current job lasts. As he puts it, "So long as I don't land on my head, I'll land on my feet."

Although work is organized in an infinite variety of ways, the four work systems capture the essentials. Each could be subdivided, but none of the four could be folded into one of the others. The four work systems should help the reader make sense of the range and variety of service work—from hamburger flipper to master chef, piece-rate poodle washer to veterinarian—and its consequences for careers. Some jobs fit squarely in one of the four categories. Others fit less neatly. In addition, the defining mechanisms of each work system may be supplemented with mechanisms identified with one of the others. Some jobs not categorized as high-skill autonomous, for example, rely to some extent on self-motivation. Furthermore, some traditional occupational categories span work systems. Sales jobs, for instance, include clerks in low-wage, low-skill, high-turnover positions best categorized as unrationalized labor-intensive (in some department stores, for instance). They also include tightly constrained telemarketers who must follow a script when the householder picks up on a computer-generated call. Others fall into the semiautonomous work system. Sales personnel at the Wolf Organization's lumberyards, profiled on pages 102 and 103, get substantial training, average more than $40,000 per year in salary and bonuses, and can advance to become yard managers or higher. Some of those who sell financial services likewise benefit from considerable training and may develop a commitment to the job like that of high-skill autonomous professionals. Stockbrokers and insurance agents are representative of the high-skill autonomous work system.

Many jobs also include tasks that are incidental to the distinctive core of the work. Professionals, for example, spend much of their time on mundane tasks that don't draw on their specialized training and experience. They may do their own filing and sneak away after jamming the copy machine. It is the core of the job that determines the work system with which it should be identified.

Employers select the work system(s) they rely on. Their decisions depend largely on business strategy, choice of technology, and organizational history. Often smaller organizations do whatever the rest of their industry does. But businesses have much more latitude than managers may think to design work in ways that improve both job quality and performance. We return to this point later and show that service work can be reorganized to shrink the less desirable categories, particularly the unrationalized labor-intensive system, and to create better jobs regardless of work system.

Table 3.3 Work Systems, Business Organization, and Career Paths, Mid-1960s

Work System	Business Organization	Career Paths
Tightly constrained	Stable, often unionized organizations	Many within one organization
Unrationalized labor-intensive	Predominantly small organizations (including manufacturing)	No advancement within or across organizations; mobility across organizations
Semiautonomous (middle managerial, many administrative, clerical, sales employees)	Predominantly growing or stable organizations, many hierarchical	Most within one organization; some across employers
High-skill autonomous (professional, upper managerial)	Growing organizations, some hierarchical, vertically integrated; some nonprofit organizations; some professional partnerships	Some within one organization

Source: Reprinted from Stephen A. Herzenberg, John A. Alic, and Howard Wial, *New Rules for a New Economy: Employment and Opportunity in Postindustrial America,* Table 12, p. 145. Copyright © 1998 The Twentieth Century Fund. Used by permission of the publisher, Cornell University Press.

HOW WORK SYSTEMS AND CAREER PATHS ARE CHANGING

We now turn to the meshing of the four work systems with corporate organization and career paths in the old economy and the new. Table 3.3 shows that in the old economy, middle-class wages and security were rooted in individual organizations. The middle class encompassed blue-collar workers in high-wage manufacturing jobs. Many of these jobs were in the tightly constrained work system—for example, assembly lines in unionized organizations. Millions of white-collar nonprofessionals with semiautonomous jobs also earned middle-class wages. This group ranged from secretaries to supermarket managers to loan officers in banks. Men or women without a college degree, if they were white, could often get such jobs through informal social networks of family and friends (as did Gloria, the insurance worker), perhaps after a few years in a "bad" entry-level job. For example, a bank teller could become a loan officer and a branch manager. Since the 1970s, many of these opportunities have been closed off.

Table 3.4, on page 94, summarizes the economy and labor market of the 1990s. There are more low-wage, dead-end jobs and fear of layoff from good jobs. Newly created jobs in the tightly constrained work system, such as those in telephone call centers, rarely pay a decent wage. Downsizing and reengineering have cut into the career ladders that once led to better jobs for semiautonomous workers. All workers, including those in the high-skill autonomous system, face greater economic insecurity. Even physicians confront falling wage levels. Not only have deregulation and more intense competition forced restructuring in industries ranging from telecommunications to retailing, but with many more Americans attending college, employers can now screen by requiring a diploma even if formal education has little relevance for the particular job. (Credentials often signal trainability as much as concrete skills.) Wage gaps between bad jobs and good have widened. This is the darker side of a dynamic, innovative economy: Curtailment of mobility paths makes it more difficult to move from bad jobs to good and even the good jobs are less secure.

Table 3.5, on page 95, based on case studies and crude quantitative analysis (all that is possible with existing data sources), summarizes the dynamics of change in the four work systems. The employment share of the tightly constrained work system—small to begin with—is slowly diminishing. Most service jobs that can be easily rationalized and automated, such as telephone operator and fast-food worker, have already been moved into the tightly constrained system. Despite nervousness about electronic sweatshops, comprehensive tightening of the constraints on large numbers of existing jobs is difficult to envision. Even though many of the tasks in, say, health care or trucking or retail trade are routine, they vary unpredictably, making standardization—much less automation—difficult or impossible. Case studies suggest that employment in the unrationalized labor-intensive work system, today accounting for more than a quarter of service jobs and 15 percent of manufacturing jobs, may be growing. With widespread cost-based competition, employers seeking to push down wages turn to the

Table 3.4 Work Systems, Business Organization, and Career Paths, Mid-1990s

Work System	Business Organization	Career Paths
Tightly constrained	Many in small establishments (which may be part of a large organization); some outsourcing to new subsidiaries or independent organizations (check processing, telephone call centers)	Few within one organization
Unrationalized labor-intensive	Small establishments and organizations	No advancement within or across organizations; some horizontal mobility within occupation across employers (nursing homes, childcare)
Semiautonomous	Less stable organizations, some growing rapidly, some slowly, sometimes linked in business networks; fewer vertical hierarchies	Some one-organization careers; more attachments for a few years (with organization-specific skills of little help to mobility)
High-skill autonomous	Some professional partnerships; less stable, less hierarchical organizations, sometimes linked in business networks	Some across employers; some within one organization

Source: Reprinted from Stephen A. Herzenberg, John A. Alic, and Howard Wial, *New Rules for a New Economy: Employment and Opportunity in Postindustrial America,* Table 13, p. 146. Copyright © 1998 The Twentieth Century Fund. Used by permission of the publisher, Cornell University Press.

Table 3.5 Work System Dynamics

Work System	Major Forces of Change	Likely Impacts (within the work system)	Advancement Prospects	Job Security
Tightly constrained	Continuing rationalization, computer-based automation	• Declining number of jobs • Wages, benefits already low in most cases—little change • Generally positive implications for productivity and service quality	Poorer: more dead-end jobs with no prospect of internal advancement	Poorer: more outsourcing, permanent layoffs
Unrationalized labor-intensive	Spread of low-cost business strategies, wage-based competition	• Growing number of jobs • Downward pressure on wages and benefits • Neutral or negative implications for productivity and service quality	Still poor: low-wage jobs unconnected to better ones	Little change: some dead-end jobs are secure
Semiautonomous	Reengineering, continued spread and growing sophistication of information technologies	• Declining share of jobs • Greater dispersion in wages and benefits as compensation rises for those with skills in high demand relative to those with more generic skills • Employment instability tends to erode productivity and service quality	Worse: skills of value only to current employer but organization-specific job ladders breaking down	Worse: more reengineering, permanent layoffs
High-skill autonomous	Technological change permitting lower-skilled employees to replace a few high-skill autonomous workers; continued growth in demand for new technical skills (e.g., for electronic commerce)	• Continued growth in number of jobs likely, but some high-skill autonomous jobs may come to resemble unrationalized labor-intensive • Wages likely to rise for new and scarce skills, decline for some traditional professions (e.g., physicians, lawyers)	Still good in most cases	Little change: skills widely recognized and valued by many employers

Source: Reprinted from Stephen A. Herzenberg, John A. Alic, and Howard Wial, *New Rules for a New Economy: Employment and Opportunity in Postindustrial America,* Table 2, p. 13, and Table 9, p. 76. Copyright © 1998 The Twentieth Century Fund. Used by permission of the publisher, Cornell University Press.

unrationalized labor-intensive work system. In long-distance trucking, for example, government regulation and union influence checked low-wage competition before 1980. Deregulation turned the game in the truckload portion of the business into low labor costs, especially for shipments of low-value goods (Belzer, 2000). From 1978 to 1990, inflation-adjusted wages declined almost 50 percent for these drivers. It's no surprise that truckload carriers faced a severe driver shortage in the second half of the 1990s.

As long as many workers have less paid employment than they want, the unrationalized labor-intensive work system will likely flourish, in part within the underground economy and self-employment (off-the-books cleaning, lawn, and repair services; street retail sales). The Information Age has brought forth a new way of absorbing "surplus" labor: telephone commission sales by minimally trained telemarketers—virtual begging. Because of the numbers involved and the potential for policy reforms to improve unrationalized labor-intensive jobs, we spend considerable time later in the chapter on this work system.

If the unrationalized labor-intensive work system is expanding, the semiautonomous system appears to be declining—an undesirable trend since these are substantially better jobs, on average. In industries such as retailing, employers have shifted many semiautonomous jobs into the unrationalized labor-intensive system. For instance, department stores, facing stiff competition from both discounters and specialty outlets, have transformed nonprofessional positions that once offered decent wages and benefits along with advancement opportunities—classic semiautonomous jobs—into low-paying, high-turnover positions that require little more than ringing up sales—classic dead-end jobs. In 1960, the median wage in retailing was 76 percent of that in insurance and 81 percent of that in banking. By 1996, retailing wages had fallen to 50 percent of those in insurance and 62 percent of those in banking. Many banks, somewhat similarly, have turned the teller job, which once served as the first step on a ladder that could lead to management, into a part-time position, filling higher-level openings from the outside labor market and typically requiring a college degree. Even where semiautonomous work systems remain, organizational restructuring has upset many of the bureaucratic incentives that induced loyalty. Among middle managers—the archetypal company men (and, in recent years, women)—downsizing has left even many who have kept their jobs wary and resentful.

Employment in the high-skill autonomous work system shows rapid growth. Some of these workers, however, now find their wages behaving like those in the other three systems—that is, dropping. One source of vulnerability, as lower-status technical and blue-collar craft workers have long understood, is precisely the professional pride that enables self-direction. Freelance writers and musicians know that if you love what you do, employers have less need to pay you decently for it. Newly minted scientists stuck in a series of postdoctoral positions are learning the same lesson. Taking for granted worker knowledge and commitment brings the risk of depletion of those resources over time. When this happens, performance suffers, as it does when midcareer professionals (physicians, engineers) do not keep up with advances in occupational practice. The line between high-skill and unrationalized work can begin to blur. The more pervasive this form of de-skilling, the more likely that income gains in the future will be restricted to a narrow band of elite managers and professionals at the top.

THREE PROBLEMS IN THE NEW ECONOMY

The shifts within and between the work systems outlined above lead to wage declines for many workers; curtail upward mobility, especially for those stuck in unrationalized labor-intensive jobs; and contribute to a third problem, stagnant productivity growth. Poor productivity performance limits the rate at which wages and living standards can rise.

Lagging performance has many causes, but again the unrationalized labor-intensive work system is a primary culprit. Employers who choose this work system, relying on cheap workers, make no systematic efforts to raise performance. Employees do not have the training, knowledge, or power to improve performance on their own. Moreover, in some tightly constrained, semiautonomous, and now also high-skill jobs, low or stagnant wages and the high turnover they generate discourage employers from investing in workers or more energetically seeking performance improvements. Even if employers wish to improve quality or efficiency, they may not know how. Most of the prescriptions and methods available to managers reflect approaches developed in the mass manufacturing era, when "scientific management" and industrial engineering contributed to low-cost production of standardized goods. Few service products fit this pattern; in fact, with some exceptions, nearly every service product differs (home mortgages, haircuts, physician visits). One of the insurance companies we visited offers customized packages to each of the 70,000 organizations that purchase its disability policies.

In the rest of this chapter, we present solutions to the three problems of stagnant or declining wages, limited upward mobility, and poor performance. Since the tightly constrained work system has relatively few jobs, we concentrate on the other three. Our starting point is a new model for improving performance, one that fits the new economy of services. We show that better performance requires not only work reorganization but a stronger infrastructure for employee mobility, one that incorporates pathways out of low-wage, entry-level jobs and career paths between organizations for those in good jobs now fearful of the next round of layoffs. In brief, performance improvements depend on learning (and coordination among workers), while workers who learn new skills enhance their prospects for moving to a better job, and such mobility, in turn, fosters further diffusion of knowledge and skills. The solutions we propose would thus feed on one another, helping to generate a postindustrial virtuous circle of rising performance and expanding economic opportunity.

A SOLUTION: THE INTERPRETIVE MODEL OF PERFORMANCE IMPROVEMENT

There is little room for standardizing service production, not only in the unrationalized labor-intensive work system but in the semiautonomous and high-skill autonomous systems. To visualize methods for improving quality and efficiency, we need an alternative model for services that cannot be produced in cookie-cutter fashion. That alternative can be explained by contrasting it with the traditional "engineering model," which evolved with mass manufacturing and underlies much economic theory.

In the engineering model, the first step is the product design, an activity that may begin with R&D and in all cases concludes with a set of precisely specified attributes, that is, "blueprints" (today often held in a computer). Process design follows, leading to a well-defined input-output relationship for production at the lowest cost. Production itself is simply a matter of following a predetermined set of instructions, that is, "process sheets." Quality can be monitored statistically, with costs tracked by traditional accounting methods. Some variant of this engineering model applies throughout manufacturing (although shop-floor workers have more freedom to tinker with the production process when fabricating custom products in small lots). It also applies in some services, including routine banking transactions and self-service supermarkets.

The alternative we propose applies to nonstandard products, for which the process must be tailored to circumstances. It encompasses most of the tasks in most of the jobs in the three work systems that account for 95 percent of today's employment. We call this the "interpretive model." Service production is a matter of interpreting and responding to customer needs until there is a match between what the customer seeks and what workers provide. The product has no predetermined design; its attributes vary with the situation. "Design" and "production" are intertwined and performed by the same workers. Iteration and feedback, adaptation and learning—often in real time—are inherent in the model.

Medical diagnosis and treatment offer an especially clear illustration of the interpretive model. Through dialogue with the patient, examination, and sometimes specialized tests, the physician explores symptoms, elicits a medical history, develops a tentative diagnosis, and prescribes treatment. The patient's response may lead to further detective work, perhaps a change in diagnosis and an altered treatment regimen. The goal, not always achieved, is to bring diagnosis and treatment into congruence through mutual adjustment. The work of nurse's aides, teachers, and sales personnel likewise involves interpretive processes, as, indeed, do the tasks of most workers who produce other than standardized services.

In the engineering model, efficiency gains come through improving the design of the product (by, for instance, reducing the number of parts to be assembled) and process (for example, automation, ergonomic tools), scale economies, and shop-floor learning. Although workers contribute, engineers and managers generally have the initiative and the authority to impose changes. In the interpretive model, performance gains come through improving the capacities of workers to understand and respond to the needs of the situation. In contrast to the engineering model, this kind of improvement cannot be imposed by management, but requires workers to learn through experience and from one another. Such learning takes place within and across work sites and within and across occupations.

Drawing from field examples, we divide the attainable economies into two categories. Employees achieve *economies of depth* through greater understanding of work processes (and the phenomena underlying them) and skill in executing these processes. *Economies of coordination* result when people who work together learn to collaborate more effectively. Partly because learning is cumulative and efforts to tap the potential of the interpretive model so far have been modest, we believe that economies of depth and coordination could contribute to sustained performance improvement over lengthy time periods (as opposed to one-time improvements).

IMPROVING PERFORMANCE THROUGH ECONOMIES OF DEPTH AND COORDINATION

The case studies below illustrate the potential for raising performance in the unrationalized labor-intensive, semiautonomous, and high-skill autonomous work systems. In most of the cases we have examined, both economies of depth and coordination are present, although their relative significance varies.

Home Health Care. In unrationalized labor-intensive jobs, as in most of the home health care industry, managers generally take it for granted that work cannot be organized differently than it is today. Case studies refute such preconceptions and demonstrate that unrationalized labor-intensive jobs can be transformed into paraprofessional positions in which the interpretive capacities of employees are self-consciously developed, resulting in economies of depth and higher-quality care.

Home health agencies typically train their aides only to the legal minimum, provide wages and benefits at the bottom end of the local labor market, offer only irregular part-time work, and accept the high rates of turnover that result (typically 40 percent to 100 percent annually). Worker-owned Cooperative Home Care Associations (CHCA), however, seeks to raise standards of care through greater job quality. It pays $2 to $3 above the minimum wage, offers free health insurance, and distributes hours so that senior aides can work full-time. Annual turnover is less than 20 percent.

CHCA begins with a six-week training program that hones the interpretive capacities of workers, most of them former welfare recipients who average an eighth-grade education.[4] The program is delivered through role playing, games, and demonstrations, avoiding classroom lecture settings in which participants may have a history of failure. One of the principles of the program is to get aides to take the survival and problem-solving skills that they have learned in the "school of hard knocks" and apply them in the work situation.

Aides are told that there is no one right way to solve a problem, that each should be viewed from multiple perspectives, and that choices among the alternatives should be openly discussed with clients (for example, whether to help the client with a bath today or tomorrow). CHCA seeks to build reflection and knowledge transmission into organizational culture through means such as the four *P*s mnemonic: *pull back, paraphrase, present choices,* and *pass it on. Pull back* suggests that aides remove themselves emotionally from the situation as part of being a professional. *Paraphrase* prompts aides to summarize and repeat back what a client has said, to confirm or clarify their interpretation. *Present choices* encourages aides to discuss alternatives, making it more likely that a full range of options will be considered and that the client gets what she or he wants. *Pass it on* reminds aides to include necessary information in their written reports and to discuss their client visits with others who may need to know (contributing to economies of coordination). Call up a CHCA office and try to leave a convoluted message with the receptionist, and you will hear paraphrasing in action.

After initial training, aides get three months of intensive on-the-job coaching. "Coordinators" talk through work situations, teaching aides to reflect on their experience as a means of broadening and deepening their skills. Coordinators act as a mirror and a second set of eyes for trainees seeing situations for the first time. Coordinator and trainee put together a "learning contract" that lists skills and knowledge in which aides need to improve (for example, communicating with supervisors) and spells out how that will be accomplished.

Southwest Airlines. Largely because of their success in achieving economies of coordination, Southwest's semiautonomous workers turn around 737s in an average of 17 minutes, compared with an industry figure of 43 minutes (Hoffer Gittell, 1996). As a consequence, Southwest keeps its planes in the air 11 hours a day rather than the more typical 9 hours. The company remains at or near the top of the industry in on-time arrivals, complaints per customer, and baggage handling performance. Southwest's economies of coordination can be traced to the airline's work organization and human resource practices.

A dozen different functional groups must cooperate to unload passengers, luggage, and cargo from a plane, and then prepare it for another flight.

An operations agent serves as case manager for each flight, tracking it from an hour before arrival at the terminal to 30 minutes after departure and planning and coordinating the "attack" on the plane. Southwest hires and trains with an eye to developing workers who can communicate and cooperate across functional boundaries, and who will enjoy that part of the process. The company's pilots have even been known to help clean a plane if needed. Optional short-term job trading helps ramp, reservation, and operations agents understand one another's responsibilities. When delays occur, Southwest analyzes them less to penalize those responsible than to understand the problem and avoid repeating it. The most common code, "team delay," means that the station takes collective responsibility. At American Airlines (Hoffer Gittell, 1996), by contrast, when a delay meant missed connections, CEO Robert Crandall wanted "to see the corpse" (the individual responsible). The consequences included cover-ups that reduce opportunities for organizational learning and improvement.

Lumberyards. The Wolf Organization, a family-owned business, operates 34 lumberyards in 12 states. With the company taking advantage of economies of coordination and depth to provide better service to its major customers, the small contractors who are mostly homebuilders, sales have increased at a rapid pace.

The work system at Wolf has long been semiautonomous. The company pays full family healthcare coverage and generous pension benefits. It also distributes one-third of annual profits back to employees, many of whom come to the company with no more than a high school education, according to a formula that includes the profitability of the individual lumberyard. CEO Tom Wolf used to think that profit sharing and worker experience alone would guarantee high performance. But he has come to believe that the organization also needs to "give workers the means to improve profitability" by supporting the development of their problem-solving capacities.

An internal school, the Wolf Academy, delivers formal training—about 12 days a year for yard managers and three days a year for other employees. Even so, two-thirds of training is still delivered on the job. The company has identified several dozen experienced employees who are good mentors. They work side-by-side with trainees, making customer calls together, for example. Wolf has also put in place systematic procedures for responding to complaints. In the past, late deliveries or damaged goods were a morality play—you'd blame the supplier or say it 'looks like an installation problem to me.'" Now complaints are an opportunity for learning how to prevent their recurrence as well as to demonstrate Wolf's willingness to accommodate customers. In 1998, Wolf became the first company in its industry to acquire global ISO 9000 certification, an internationally recognized certification of organizational competence. The company viewed ISO 9000 not as a test to be studied for, passed, and then forgotten, but as another means of encouraging critical reexamination of "old practices."

Since the mid-1980s, Wolf's sales have quadrupled. Reflecting improvements in coordination between wholesale distribution centers and lumberyards, and between Wolf and its suppliers, inventory turns have risen from four or five a year (typical for the industry) to the high teens. In the mid-1990s, an industry trade publication refused to print Wolf's sales per employee—the figures were so far above industry norms that the editors didn't believe them. Looking ahead, Wolf managers foresee yards staffed by four people instead of eight or 10, thanks in part to lean inventory management and electronic commerce. Contractors will increasingly order over the Internet with direct delivery from central warehouses to the construction site. Most of the active selling will take place through site visits by Wolf employees. By combining information technology with economies of depth and coordination, the company expects to achieve another doubling of its productivity levels.

Insurance. New clerical employees at Mount Rushmore Mutual, the insurance company whose semiautonomous work system we visited earlier, take 18 months or more to reach "proficiency," attesting to the importance of economies of depth. Mastery of the company's computer systems—which incorporate some 85 software packages—is a key skill in solving customer problems quickly and correctly.

Employees in policy services work in teams, helping to capture economies of coordination as well as depth. Teams of 15 to 20 customer service agents meet, sometimes several times a week, to discuss difficult or unusual cases. By sharing lessons learned in responding to customer inquiries, they deepen and diffuse interpretive capacities. Some teams maintain binders of sample cases and letters to customers. In interviews, even senior workers noted that they benefit from this kind of pooled experience.

Technical Occupations. Untapped potential to achieve economies of depth exists in the high-skill autonomous work system, including among technicians. While the voluminous manuals that burden Xerox copier repair technicians might suggest that these workers follow standard procedures adequate for all contingencies, such an image is far from accurate (Orr, 1996). Their repair manuals include elaborate flowcharts intended to lead them through a series of diagnostic tests, concluding with a prescribed remedy. Nonetheless, Xerox technicians find the manuals and flowcharts to be incomplete, inaccurate, or simply too confusing (unless they already understand the problem, in which case the manual is superfluous). Diagnosing and repairing copiers thus remains an interpretive problem. Formal learning plays a part. When Xerox introduces a new copier model, technicians get classroom training in how the machine works and how it breaks. Nonetheless, field studies find that technicians downplay the importance of training compared to experience.

Xerox repair technicians, like other craft and technical workers—and professionals—learn from the "war stories" they tell one another. Such stories relate specific events but may also serve as warnings or reminders—for example, of unanticipated cause-effect relationships. These cautions carry more weight when presented in the context of a concrete situation rather than an abstract exhortation such as managers might issue. Sometimes technicians will relate a case they have solved, minus the outcome, to challenge or test their peers.

Other groups—physicians, engineers—likewise trade information and the lessons of experience formally (at professional meetings) and informally (over the telephone or during social encounters). Some of these networks link employees of organizations that compete fiercely with one another, as in Silicon Valley. But while occupational communities and work-site based groups are critical repositories of know-how, employers may not recognize and support them. In only a few cases, such as radiological technicians, are they well developed in nonprofessional occupations. Those who repair Xerox copiers do not write down the lessons embodied in their stories. Nor do emergency medical technicians, air traffic controllers, or nuclear power plant operators. Communication remains largely oral and local, so that experience does not diffuse outside personal networks. In contrast to better established professions such as nursing, there is little effort to systematically improve practice. This is true even in high-skilled but relatively new occupations such as computer programming. Because programming remains in substantial part the preserve of gifted individuals, each with his or her own style, idiosyncratic practices drive up the life-cycle costs of debugging, documentation, and maintenance. Employers (and policymakers) would be well served to spend more energy fostering occupational communities as vehicles for diffusing best practices in software (and less energy on seeking access to low-wage immigrant programmers).

CREATING MULTI-EMPLOYER LEARNING AND CAREER INFRASTRUCTURES

As the examples above suggest, support for the advancement and dissemination of knowledge within occupational communities translates directly into higher performance. Workers can do their jobs better and can more easily demonstrate capabilities that help them advance in their careers. How do we get to a world in which the interpretive model can spread beyond a few leading companies, such as the Wolf Organization? And how can we reduce the economic anxiety resulting from low-wage, dead-end jobs and insecurity in good jobs? We argue here that a central part of the solution is to strengthen institutions and membership associations that encourage learning and support careers across organizational boundaries. These institutions would take up responsibilities managed in the past by job ladders (or career paths) in large, hierarchical organizations.

Strengthening a learning and career advancement infrastructure linked to occupations, within industries and across industries, has great potential because, even in our turbulent new economy, workers remain strongly tied to occupations. In the 1980s, 68 percent of workers remained in the same occupation for eight years or more—the same percentage as in the 1970s. Moreover, the number of workers who remained in the same industry for eight years or more dropped only slightly, from 63 percent to 59 percent. By contrast, the number who stayed for eight or more years with a single organization fell from 67 percent in the 1970s to 52 percent in the 1980s (Rose, 1995).

Careers and career paths spanning multiple employers are nothing new. They have been common both in the professions and in unionized occupations (construction workers, musicians, actors). Likewise, chefs and waitpersons move from one elite restaurant to another. In all these examples, credentials and experience are transferable across employers. Often, health and pension benefits are portable as well. For instance, construction unions have negotiated joint union-employer benefit funds that cover all members in a geographical area. Institutions including annual professional meetings, union-run hiring halls, and auditions organized by the Association of Theatrical and Stage Employees facilitate the matching of workers who need jobs with employers who need those workers' skills and knowledge. Although organizations may be unwilling to pay for training, precisely because of worker mobility across organizational boundaries, alternative mechanisms pick up the slack. In unionized construction trades, contributions of as much as $1 per hour to joint labor-management funds support apprenticeship programs. (The unionized construction industry invests over 10 times as much in training as the nonunion sector, relative to share of employment.) High-wage professionals such as physicians and lawyers typically pay for their own education and training (which limits access based on family income). But novices also subsidize training when they "pay their dues" as an apprentice or medical intern—a sacrifice premised on higher wages later as a journeyperson or licensed physician.

The trick is to adapt the kinds of institutions that have supported multi-employer careers and work-related communication in higher-skill occupations to workers in unrationalized labor-intensive and semiautonomous jobs. This would lay foundations for transforming work to raise performance. The examples below show that the necessary adaptation has begun, with innovative entrepreneurs and organizations promoting professional development and building multi-employer careers in non-elite, new-economy occupations. These cases point the way to improved economic performance and better jobs for more people.

Transforming Entry-Level Jobs

If too many Americans are stuck in dead-end jobs, pathways must be created out of those jobs or the work itself must be raised in status, compensation, and skill level. The examples below address both solutions.

Multi-Employer Careers in Health Care. In 1995, leaders from business, labor, government, and nonprofit groups in Madison, Wisconsin, and surrounding Dane County sponsored a study of "community career ladders" aimed at providing employers with better-qualified workers and workers with pathways out of entry-level jobs (Dresser, 2000). The study led to formation of employer-led training partnerships in health care, insurance, and manufacturing.

The Health Care Partnership brings together organizations that employ or represent 10,000 workers—three of Dane County's four hospitals, two clinics, three nursing care facilities, three home health organizations, and five unions. One of the partnership's first projects has been to address a shortage of Certified Nurses' Assistants (CNAs) in nursing homes, a shortage that is a direct consequence of the prevalence of the unrationalized labor-intensive work system. The partnership commissioned a study of turnover among nurse's aides, searching for the best local practices in reducing turnover. Not surprisingly, they found good wages and benefits correlated with lower turnover. So did respect for CNAs, teamwork on the job, and two-way communication with supervisors. The partnership is now encouraging the reorganization of unrationalized into semiautonomous work systems to raise job quality for CNAs and other frontline caregivers, both in nursing homes and among home health agencies. The goal, in essence, is to upgrade jobs to paraprofessional status.

By creating pathways that lead to more skilled work, the Health Care Partnership is trying to attract more CNAs and to increase the local supply of nurses and other high-level positions. These jobs require specialized training and credentials, a substantial hurdle for many CNAs. The partnership found a starting point in a shortage of phlebotomists, technicians who draw blood, carving a condensed training course out of an existing year-long curriculum at Madison Area Technical College. Three classes of 15 phlebotomists have been trained; graduates' wages and skill levels are up and the area's hospitals and clinics are able to fill positions that used to go empty for months. Now the partnership is developing programs for restorative aides and health unit clerks.

In Philadelphia, 85 unionized employers and the local hospital workers' union run a Training and Upgrading Fund. With financing from cents-per-hour contributions set through collective bargaining, about 300 workers have made the transition from entry-level jobs to Licensed Practical Nurse or higher over the last two decades.

The Philadelphia and Madison partnerships supplement work-site–specific job security arrangements with new advancement opportunities, ordinarily although not always at the same employer. As upheavals in health care chip away at job security within particular employers, these mechanisms could become the foundation for security within a multi-employer system. In such a system, benefits and seniority-based job rights would attach to the regional industry, not to the employer. Job definitions and certifications would have to be harmonized across the region, a relatively straightforward task in regulated industries like health care, where many credentials are widely recognized already.

The United Child Care Union. In Philadelphia, a new union of childcare workers is seeking to move the industry's low-wage, high-turnover jobs toward the high-skill autonomous work system. The union, which originated in a collaboration between the founder-directors of two worker-owned childcare centers and the National Union of Hospital and Health Care Employees, hopes to make childcare work less custodial and more like the jobs of teachers.

For roughly a decade, the two worker-owned centers—which go by the name Childspace—have operated on the basis of "quality jobs—quality care." Childspace serves primarily low-income families, relying on outside support to pay a living wage (or close to it) and provide individual health coverage to worker-owners (with only a 10 percent co-pay). Some years ago, Childspace established a separate not-for-profit arm to replicate and diffuse this model. Then, in the mid-1990s, several managers, impatient with the pace at which their approach was spreading, began discussing a partnership with the health care employees' union. The strategy that emerged called for organizing two new unions, one for center-based workers and the other for family providers (who deliver childcare in the home). It also calls for organizing area employers of childcare workers into an association that will collaborate with the unions in systematizing training, credentials, and career paths. The union has now initiated a dialogue with leading employers and childcare advocates about establishing industry-wide labor-management benefit funds and an employment center to recruit new workers and operate as a hiring hall for participating employers.

The United Child Care Union recognizes that the central dilemma in childcare is finding a way to pay workers adequately without depriving lower-income families, who simply cannot pay more, of high-quality care for their children. The union's organizing strategy is aimed at overcoming this dilemma by bringing unionized workers and organized employers together with parents, childcare advocates, and educators to argue politically that society must invest in early education for all children. Taxpayer-supported schools have been a pillar of U.S. society. With more women working and fewer extended families to provide care, it makes sense to extend the schooling system to younger ages. Every year, more research shows that early childhood experiences are critical for later learning. Even today, a fifth of Americans do not graduate from high school. The solution to this problem, which stunts individual lives and carries high social costs, is more likely to be found at the beginning of schooling, not in its later years.

Baltimoreans United in Leadership Development (BUILD). The primary goal in the examples above is to raise the quality of entry-level jobs and link them with higher-skilled positions in related occupations. Baltimore's BUILD case (Fine, forthcoming) illustrates a complementary but distinct strategy: raising wages throughout the high-turnover, entry-level labor market and then institutionalizing advancement out of that labor market.

By the early 1990s, many in Baltimore were disappointed that the city's highly touted and publicly subsidized inner harbor revitalization project had not translated into decent jobs for residents. Their frustration fueled BUILD's 1994 "living-wage" campaign, supported by the coalition of religious and minority groups linked with BUILD, and by the largest city (and national) public-sector union, the American Federation of State, County, and Municipal Employees (AFSCME). This successful campaign established an ordinance requiring private contractors to the city to set pay levels several dollars an hour above the minimum wage. (By 1999, the Baltimore ordinance has served as a model for living-wage campaigns in three dozen cities and counties across the country.)

After winning the ordinance, BUILD established a multi-employer association, affiliated with AFSCME, for workers employed by contractors to the city. Many of these contractors are small and transient. The association has helped stabilize the labor market and overcome workers' sense of isolation. (With the living-wage ordinance already lifting wages, the multi-employer association has not sought recognition as a collective bargaining agent with most of these contractors.)

BUILD has now launched a worker-owned temporary agency to serve local employers in the sectors in which its members work. Because temporary employment is a critical entry point to more stable jobs, operating an agency is one way for the association to enhance opportunities for its members. Through the agency and its links with AFSCME, members may gain preferential access to higher-paying, public-sector jobs.

Multisector worker associations are essential vehicles for enhancing mobility where entry-level positions do not link with higher-level jobs within a particular sector. This problem is acute in low-wage jobs such as janitor, security guard, and contract food service workers. "Central labor councils," which bring together representatives of local unions in a geographical area, are one vehicle for organizing such associations (Gapasin & Wial, 1998).

Multi-Employer Institutions and Membership Associations Above the Entry Level

Occupational communities promote interpretive-model performance improvement and smooth transitions across employers in craft and professional settings. Membership associations can take on similar functions among less skilled workers, even though occupational identities may be weaker than in high-skill fields, especially at the outset. Because industrial unions had largely defensive roles in the old economy, the notion of worker associations as central players in performance improvement and career security is foreign to most observers. The reality in much of the new economy, however, is that no other actors are likely to take the lead in creating and maintaining the necessary multi-employer infrastructure.

Employers, for example, want capable workers lined up outside their doors, delivered by public schools, community colleges, and vocational training institutes. The example of construction, where nonunion contractors have lived off apprentice-trained workers from the unionized sector for decades, indicates that tight labor markets are unlikely to stimulate training (in other than organization-specific skills). Schools do not see their role as preparation for work, except in the most general sense. Educators, like government agencies, lack "inside knowledge" of skill requirements, work practices, and the mobility patterns and career objectives across occupations and industries. Rapid technological and economic change in the new economy aggravates this longstanding problem. Workers and employers are the two groups well positioned to grapple with career preparation. Policymakers may have to bring them together. This section points to examples of how this can be accomplished.

Perhaps the first task is to change attitudes toward worker associations, too often painted as old-style, obstructionist labor unions and too seldom as organizations that contribute to training, to work-related communication and learning, and to matching job seekers with job openings. Some managers understand unions' potential. The owner of a Delaware temporary agency, after first noting that no one in his industry develops what we have called interpretive capacities (and what he called "soft skills"), added, out of the blue (Aronson et al., 1998)

> What happened to the apprenticeships . . . ? Unions had the world by the you-know-whats and they blew it. They put all their attention in the wrong direction. Those apprenticeships are just wonderful. I see all that coming back. It would be a tremendous value in banking . . . the rebirth of the guilds. But in all industries, not just the typical old-boy networks—electricians, carpenters, plumbers . . . .

Technical Occupations. Like the Xerox employees profiled earlier, many technicians work in hierarchically structured settings that offer few opportunities for advancement. Their skills may be invisible to those outside the occupational community. Low status and modest pay hamper recruitment, training, and retention. Managers may skimp on training for fear of losing technicians to a competitor or, in a big company, to another division. Word-of-mouth helps technicians find new jobs, but the process is haphazard. Technical occupations, accordingly, seem ripe for strengthening of multi-employer career paths and worker communication channels.

New occupational associations have begun to form. The Society for Technical Communications has more than 20,000 members, most of them technical writers, editors, and illustrators. The society provides information on job openings and promotes economies of depth by publishing handbooks and manuals. (Typical publications bear titles such as *Guidelines for Beginning Technical Editors* and *Guide to Preparing Software User Documentation.*) The System Administrators' Guild, established in 1992, provides similar services to members who work with and oversee computer and information systems. In another example, the long-established Society of Automotive Engineers created an affiliate for mechanics, the Service Technicians' Society, largely because the sophisticated electronic systems found in new cars require skills, especially in diagnosis, quite unlike those needed to work on older vehicles.

Technological change has also been rapid in telecommunications. Moreover, while the industry has been growing, AT&T, which once had the most highly structured internal labor market in the entire economy, has been contracting. The Communications Workers of America (CWA) represents many workers at AT&T and the post-divestiture regional Bell Operating Companies. With intense new competition, these and other telecommunications organizations began relying heavily on outside contractors. Rather than let jobs go to lower-wage, nonunion organizations, CWA has established pilot Employment Centers in Los Angeles, Cleveland, and Seattle that place members in temporary assignments (duRivage, 2000). The employer of record may be a telecommunications organization or a temporary agency that acts as an intermediary, but in all cases workers are covered by a collective bargaining agreement that provides portable benefits and training.

CWA has also begun to organize workers in occupations that have not in the past been unionized (duRivage, 2000). In 1998, it chartered a new local union in Seattle—the Washington Alliance of Temporary Workers, or WashTech—formed by Microsoft temporary workers, who make up about a third of the organization's regional workforce. One-third of these temporaries have been on the job for a year or longer. Some have been in the same position for many years, with responsibilities indistinguishable from "regular" Microscoft employees. In June 1999, WashTech petitioned four temporary agencies for bargaining recognition on behalf of 18 Microsoft contractors.

WashTech's goals include parity in pay and benefits (sick pay, holiday pay, health care) for full-time "temporary" workers. In response to member requests, the association has begun a series of month-long courses on topics ranging from the Java programming language and database design to career planning. WashTech is now in the process of forming a cooperative through which workers could contract out their own labor, similar to CWA's Employment Centers. The association also speaks for its members on issues such as immigration quotas for programmers and engineers, which directly affect high-tech temporaries.

Clerical and Administrative Workers. Office employees in the semiautonomous work system once enjoyed the job stability if not the economic rewards of lower and middle managers. Although information technology (IT) and business process reengineering have destroyed many of these jobs, they also create demands for new software skills and for administrative and interpersonal abilities suiting the "delayered" office.

Some companies have reengineered effectively, often with participation by clerical workers alongside IT specialists and consultants. Others have failed abysmally, spending heavily on software and hardware that does not meet the organization's needs or proves unnecessarily difficult for workers to use. These inefficiencies have many sources. The most relevant source here is that too many office employees work and learn in isolation from one another. Organization-specific skills have not disappeared; the Wolf Organization's computer systems are nothing like those at Mount Rushmore Mutual. Still, many of the basic components of office work—setting priorities and getting the critical tasks done, dealing with vendors, planning meetings, and managing the bosses—are common to organizations of all types. Professionalizing the occupation by strengthening the infrastructure for learning and career development would generate better outcomes for workers, smoother operations for employers, improved service for customers, and higher performance in the economy as a whole. A Toronto case and several U.S. examples point the way.

The Toronto initiative, under way since 1993, is distinctive in encompassing the clerical occupation as a whole, rather than as a particular subset, such as displaced, disadvantaged, or temporary clerical workers, or those in a single industry (Aronson et al., 1999). A multistakeholder committee with representatives from six major employers (including Royal Bank of Canada, Bell Canada, and Manpower) provided the initial impetus, documenting the disordered nature of careers and training for clerical workers. The committee urged that career paths be constructed across organizations, with training programs leading to portable skills. They also recommended delivery of services to laid-off workers through community-based centers, rather than individual work sites. The first community-based Clerical Workers' Center opened in 1997, providing career counseling to over 1,000 displaced clerical workers in its first year. A "Training Network" brings together educators and trainers from public and private sectors. Network members are constructing an inventory of course offerings to determine equivalence and transferability and identify gaps in training that impede worker advancement.

In Philadelphia, a branch of Cooperative Home Care Associates (the home health agency discussed previously) offers training for entry-level clerical workers that embodies the interpretive problem-solving orientation of its health care programs. In New Jersey, the Communications Workers of America has implemented two-year apprenticeship programs for computer applications and computer support specialists. More than a hundred "at-risk" students have entered high school "Transition to Apprenticeship" programs. Apprentices will get the on-the-job portion of their training in libraries and public colleges where the CWA represents employees.

In California's Silicon Valley, the Temporary Worker Employment Project seeks to reorient the temporary clerical industry in a higher-wage, higher-skill direction (Benner & Dean, 2000). The undertaking includes a nonprofit temporary agency that takes less of a markup than for-profit agencies and pays workers a minimum of $10 per hour. With foundation support, the agency offers family health care at $50 per month. Course modules developed in collaboration with Mission Community College and the college's employer advisory panel will be part of a new Associate Degree program. The program will give workers immediate training in skills in demand in the local labor market while also building a foundation for advancement over the longer term. The project also supports an association of temporary workers, which fosters sharing of work experiences, and development of an advocacy agenda, including a code of conduct for temporary agencies. The code requires agencies to describe openings truthfully in a written job description, including the anticipated duration of the assignment. Agencies that endorse the code will be listed in a guide to good temporary agencies, giving them an edge in recruitment at a time of low unemployment in the region.

A NEW VISION OF THE LABOR MARKET

Given creative public policies, we believe a new labor market system could emerge based on the interpretive model, strengthened multi-organization career paths, and membership organizations that represent worker interests.[5] Table 3.6 shows what that system might look like—with fewer low-wage jobs and more staircase careers. The spread of multi-employer career paths would reinforce the tendencies of technological change and competitive pressures to break down old-style integrated organizations. In the new system, organizational boundaries would blur; distinctions in pay, status, and career opportunities—and between long-term and contingent workers—would diminish. Americans who began their work lives in "bad" jobs would

Table 3.6 Work Systems, Business Organization, and Career Paths, 2010

Work System	Business Organization	Career Paths
Entry-level (tightly constrained or unrationalized labor-intensive)	Small or large establishments with employment linkages to larger organizations or business networks	Advancement to semiautonomous jobs through organization-based, community-based, occupational, and industry-specific career pathways
Semiautonomous (expansion of interpretive approach to performance improvement blurs boundary with high-skill autonomous jobs)	Business networks widespread; some stable regional networks with dominant lead organizations (health care, large-organization retail, tele-communications); other networks more fluid, resembling the construction industry (managerial and administrative services, small organization retail)	Intraindustry and interindustry staircase careers—extended attachments at several organizations or networks; significant opportunity to move into high-skill autonomous jobs
High-skill autonomous	Business networks widespread; some decentralized "virtual" networks of professionals	Most across employers within occupation/ profession

Source: Reprinted from Stephen A. Herzenberg, John A. Alic, and Howard Wial, *New Rules for a New Economy: Employment and Opportunity in Postindustrial America,* Table 14, p. 147. Copyright © 1998 The Twentieth Century Fund. Used by permission of the publisher, Cornell University Press.

have access, through structured institutions, to good jobs. People would find it easier to escape low-wage, dead-end jobs. Once in a good semi-autonomous or high-skill autonomous job, workers could advance and deepen their skills within an occupation, industry, or business network, aided by established multi-employer career paths. Distinctions between single and multi-employer careers would blur. A nurse, for example, might start out in a home health agency, move to a nursing home and then to general-duty nursing in a hospital, and finally move up in the hospital to more specialized nursing or supervisory work.

Because multi-employer institutions would channel displaced workers into roughly comparable positions with other organizations, losing a job would not be the calamitous event it often is today. Employers would find it easier to adjust to changing market conditions without resistance or resentment from workers. Of course, the downsizing of an entire occupation or industry would still bring displacement that multi-employer institutions alone could not resolve. But where, as in banking today, some organizations shrink while others expand, the new institutions would help workers manage transitions. And by promoting both voluntary mobility and inter-organization communication among workers, they would improve economic performance.

APPLICATIONS

If the new economy is to generate better outcomes for all workers and for the nation as a whole—not just for Internet entrepreneurs and elite professionals—we will have to reinvent many of our institutions. That will take policy changes. We have not discussed those policy changes; but we have tried to show how that reinvention might begin "on the ground." Career consultants are among the best placed of all groups to begin taking the concrete actions called for. A new deal for a learning economy is not just a theoretical possibility, it is a practical objective.

This chapter should help career consultants relate to clients with a wide range of skills and experience. But working to better an individual's situation is only one step toward meeting the larger needs of society. We have also argued that our economic performance can improve, making possible higher wages and living standards for all. Economies of depth and coordination are good for workers and also improve the quality of services for consumers. Multi-employer institutions and membership associations for career development help individuals while contributing to the spread of knowledge and hence to widespread performance improvement. Whatever your role in this new economy—job seeker, career counselor, employer, or citizen—you can help make it work better. We offer the following exercises for reflection and action.

EXERCISE 3.1

ACTION STEPS FOR WORKERS AND JOB SEEKERS

- Understand your skills. What do you know and what can you do? What kind of training (formal and informal) do you have? Are your skills recognized by credentials or in other ways? Would another employer value them? What new skills should you seek?
- Look for ways to improve economies of depth. Who in your workplace can you learn from? Teaching others will increase the depth of your own skills and knowledge. Whom could you mentor? Extend your informal learning networks beyond your own workplace. Who outside your workplace deals with similar problems or does similar work? Can you learn from them—or help them learn?
- Look for ways to increase economies of coordination. Where do you see opportunities for better communication and coordination in your workplace? What would it take to capture these economies?
- Link up formally with those beyond your own workplace. What membership organizations exist in your field? Are you active in them?

EXERCISE 3.2

ACTION STEPS FOR CAREER COUNSELORS

- Keep the bigger picture in mind, alongside your responsibilities to individuals. What can you do to strengthen multi-employer institutions? How can you encourage organizational as well as individual learning?
- Guide workers eligible for public training dollars (for example, vouchers—Individual Training Accounts) to opportunities that connect to careers across organizations. What monies and programs exist in your community?
- Urge your clients to expand their personal networks for learning and advancement. What membership associations could they join? Who can you put them in touch with?
- In the industries or occupations you know best, guide clients first to employers that develop workers' skills and provide well-structured career paths. Who are those employers? Let the good employers know that you understand and value the training and career opportunities they provide.

EXERCISE 3.2 (CONT'D)

- Recognize that almost any job can be redesigned to improve quality, service, and professionalism. Help employers find opportunities for reorganizing work and raising the skill levels of their employees. Listen also to your clients' views of their jobs. Where do you sense new opportunities? How can you pass that information on?

- Show employers that good human resource practices translate into better business performance. For instance, giving employees portable skills and the chance to network outside the organization may reduce turnover, helping organizations keep their best workers. What statistics exist or what numbers and stories need to be gathered to back up those claims?

- Show good employers that it is in their interest to provide information on job quality. Lack of such information means that the best employers may not have the advantages in recruiting they deserve. Could you help produce more systematic information—for example, a list of employers that abide by an industry code of conduct, a "jobs with a future" handbook profiling good companies—that would steer workers to better employers, increasing market pressure for positive human resource practices?

- Develop your own networks with other counselors. Industries and occupations are changing too fast for any one person to keep up across the board. Who is in your network? What do they know that you don't?

- Join and participate in your professional association. Along with other benefits, it will help you understand how such groups improve economies of depth. In which organizations are you active and which should you join?

- Visit the construction apprenticeship program with the best reputation in your area. When you talk with the people involved, keep in mind that worker associations come in many types, not just traditional labor unions. What did you learn and what can you teach others?

- Support local multi-employer training partnerships, consortia, and "skills alliances," more of which now receive public support thanks to the 1998 federal Workforce Investment Act. What alliances exist in your area? Could you encourage others?

EXERCISE 3.3

ACTION STEPS FOR EMPLOYERS

- Reexamine the fundamentals of your businesses. Is your strategy based on quality and responsiveness to customers? How do you seek to achieve this?
- Redesign your work system(s) to improve quality, service, and flexibility. Can you create better jobs for your employees while also providing better service for your customers? Higher sales? Greater profits? Can you increase the capacities of your incumbent workforce, reducing the need to outsource?
- Ensure that information and knowledge flow upward to managers and laterally among employees, not just from the top down. Encourage work teams to trade insights and brainstorm. Invite communication of nonproprietary information outside your company. You'll be paid back as others reciprocate. What can you do to improve information flows in your organization and between organizations?
- Create well-defined career paths visible to your employees. Provide counseling (and training, including tuition refunds) for those seeking to qualify for higher-level positions. What paths and programs exist? How might they be supplemented?
- Establish peer recognition awards through which employees can recognize their colleagues (and you can recognize your best workers). How do you acknowledge your employees? How do your employees perceive that system? What else can you do, both formally and informally?
- Give employees, including your lowest-paid staff, time off to attend membership organizations or less formal networks. Pay their membership dues. Do you have a structure in place to encourage this?
- Participate in business or trade associations that work with high schools and community colleges to meet local labor market needs. Make sure these programs provide a foundation for lifelong learning as well as skills needed today. (Who knows what your business will need tomorrow?) How are you coordinating with and supporting groups focusing on education and training? What more can you do?
- Take the lead in forming a regional training partnership in your industry. Who do you know who will join you in these efforts?

EXERCISE 3.4

ACTION STEPS FOR CITIZENS

- Patronize businesses with good employment practices—for example, those that provide training and advancement opportunities, especially pathways out of dead-end jobs. Who are they? Who else needs to know about them?
- Make sure that local schools offer high-quality programs for students who may not be planning to attend college, along with a sound foundation for all students in basic skills (reading, writing, arithmetic). What programs exist? Which officials and policies support them?
- Recognize the dignity in all work. Acknowledge those who provide high-quality service. Hold up your end in interpretive dialogues, and not only with professionals.

REFERENCES

Aronson, I., de Wolff, A., & Herzenberg, S. A. (1999). *Careers in laboring and office occupations*. Harrisburg, PA: Keystone Research Center. (Report to the Russell Sage Foundation under RSF Project #8597-01.)

Belzer, M. (2000). *Sweatshops on wheels*. New York: Oxford University Press.

Benner, C., & Dean, A. (2000). Labor in the new economy: Lessons from labor organizing in Silicon Valley. In F. Carre, M. Ferber, L. Golden, & S. A. Herzenberg (Eds.), *Non-standard work: The nature and challenge of emerging employment relationships*. Industrial Relations Research Association Annual Research Volume. Ithaca, NY: Cornell/ILR Press.

Dresser, L. (2000). Building "jobs with a future" in Dane County: Lessons from Wisconsin. In F. Carre, M. Ferber, L. Golden, & S. A. Herzenberg (Eds.), *Non-standard work: The nature and challenge of emerging employment relationships*. Industrial Relations Research Association Annual Research Volume. Ithaca, NY: Cornell/ILR Press.

duRivage, V. L. (2000). CWA's organizing strategies: Transforming contract work into union jobs. In F. Carre, M. Ferber, L. Golden, & S. A. Herzenberg (Eds.), *Non-standard work: The nature and challenge of emerging employment relationships*. Industrial Relations Research Association Annual Research Volume. Ithaca, NY: Cornell/ILR Press.

Eaton, S. C. (1997). *Pennsylvania's nursing homes: Promoting quality care and quality jobs*. Harrisburg, PA: Keystone Research Center.

Fine, J. A. (1999). Unpublished doctoral dissertation draft, Department of Political Science, Massachusetts Institute of Technology.

Gapasin, F., & Wial, H. (1998). The role of central labor councils in union organizing in the 1990s. In K., Bronfenbrenner et al. (Eds.) *Organizing to win* (pp. 54–67). Ithaca, NY: ILR Press.

Herzenberg, S. A., Alic, J. A., and Wial, H. (1998). *New rules for a new economy: Employment and opportunity in postindustrial America.* Ithaca, NY: Cornell University/ILR Press.

Hoffer Gittell, J. (1996, September). *Coordination, control, and performance of interdependent work processes.* Harvard Business School working paper.

Horowitz, T. (1994, December 1). Mr. Eden profits from watching his workers' every move. *The Wall Street Journal,* p. A9.

Orr, J. (1996). *Talking about machines.* Ithaca, NY: ILR Press.

Rose, S. (1995). *Declining job security and the professionalization of opportunity.* Washington, DC: National Commission for Employment Policy.

NOTES

[1]This example is slightly modified from Herzenberg, Alic, and Wial, 1998, pp. 37–38.

[2]This example is slightly modified from Herzenberg, Alic, and Wial, 1998, pp. 38–39.

[3]This example is slightly modified from Herzenberg, Alic, and Wial, 1998, pp. 39–40.

[4]This discussion is based on training documents developed by the Philadelphia branch of Cooperative Home Care Associations. Many of the documents were prepared by Zara Joffe.

[5]Herzenberg, Alic, and Wial, 1998, chapter 8, contains detailed policy prescriptions that we believe could bring about the new vision of the labor market sketched in this section.

4

Integrative Life Planning*

A NEW WORLDVIEW FOR CAREER PROFESSIONALS

L. Sunny Hansen

Dramatic changes occurring in work, the workplace, and work patterns make it necessary for career and human resource development professionals to approach their work with a different mind-set than in the past. Changes in demographics, families, individuals, and organizations around the globe also contribute to this need. Experts from fields such as organizational management, sociology, business, economics, medicine, multiculturalism, futurism, and career development have described these changes and explored the potential impact on individuals and organizations.

This chapter approaches the topic of workplace changes and life planning from a career psychology perspective. Its purpose is to (1) identify aspects of the larger societal context in which these changes are occurring; (2) discuss important changes relating to work and other life roles; (3) suggest that our mission as career counselors and HRD professionals requires

*This chapter is based on the book *Integrative Life Planning: Critical Tasks for Career Development and Changing Life Patterns* by L. Sunny Hansen, San Francisco: Jossey-Bass, 1997.

us to put more emphasis on the needs of human beings with whom we work; and (4) present an integrative framework, Integrative Life Planning (ILP), for changing individuals and organizations.

THE CONCEPTUAL FRAMEWORK

The Integrative Life Planning (ILP) concept is a comprehensive, interdisciplinary framework to help people make life choices and decisions in the context of the 21st century. It is built around the assumption that societal changes require us to think more broadly with regard to career development and to help our employees, students, and clients do so as well. Six critical tasks or themes form the core of ILP:

1. Finding work that needs doing in changing global contexts
2. Weaving our lives into a meaningful whole
3. Connecting family and work
4. Valuing pluralism and inclusivity
5. Exploring spirituality and life purpose
6. Managing personal transitions and organizational change

This chapter describes what these themes mean and how they might be incorporated into the work of career professionals. Although several practical strategies are included, ILP is not a cookbook of "how-to" strategies; it is a conceptual framework for a new worldview for career development.

Several metaphors are important in Integrative Life Planning, the main one being that of quilts and quilters. Quilts represent the combination of pieces (patches) into a whole, signifying themes of connectedness and community. They are central to ILP. Metaphors combined with visualization are found in several of the ILP strategies at the end of this chapter.

For some time career professionals have realized that traditional approaches to career planning are not quite adequate for these times. In the first half of the 20th century, we used Frank Parsons's (1909) matching model—a logical, rational process of fitting people into jobs—a pattern of vocational guidance and counseling that continues to be used. In the second half, we learned about career development, primarily from Donald Super (1951, 1980)—that career is more than occupation, that it occurs over the life span, is developmental, changes over time, includes life roles, and is a process, not a single event. As we move into the 21st century, we are focusing on a view that is integrated and concerned with connectedness, wholeness, and community.

GLOBAL WORKPLACE CHANGES

A voluminous literature exists about global workplace changes and transitions, providing a context for understanding ILP. For example, economist Jeremy Rifkin (1995), focusing heavily on technology and global change, describes "the end of work," at least as we know it. He presents convincing statistics from around the world, especially Japan, Europe, and North America, about how workers have been replaced by robots, automation, and downsizing and how fewer workers are needed to produce goods and services. We are entering the Third Industrial Revolution (after the Industrial Age and the Information Age), which portends both good and evil.

Rifkin's conclusion (one that we have heard before) is that societies must move to shorter workweeks so that the available work may be shared. While many societies today are moving toward capitalism, the future trend is from a market to a post-market economy, with more time being given to the *Third Sector,* the nonprofit volunteer sector, where there is much work to be done among marginalized people and communities.

Peter Drucker (1995) proposes a theme similar to Rifkin's when he describes how we work in the 20th-century age of social transformation. He points out how knowledge has replaced muscle and also suggests, like Rifkin, that the United States is moving into a Third Sector—the nonprofit sector—comprising those organizations that take care of the social challenges of modern society. As this transition occurs, he believes individuals will be able to find worth in volunteer work in the social sector. He describes the challenges of the knowledge society as providing for the welfare of the majority, staying competitive in the world economy, and managing continuing transformation.

Hazel Henderson (1995, 1996), another economist and futurist, suggests that the world is engaged in "global economic warfare" and that we, the human race, are losing because we are not attending to human needs. She integrates the subjects of science and technology, the economy, and the environment and urges nations to find new indicators of societal progress other than the gross national product (GNP) or gross domestic product (GDP). She believes we can "build a win-win world" by identifying new cultural indicators, such as recognition of women's "caring work," and sees hope for the future, especially in the cooperation of multiple grassroots groups, such as nongovernmental organizations in the global economy.

Another "big picture" aspect of the changing nature of work is discussed by Agneta Stark (1995), a Swedish business and economics professor at the University of Stockholm. Like Henderson, Stark is critical of the absence of "caring work" (often "women's work") from assessments of national progress. She makes a strong case for giving greater attention and status to "caring work," such as kin-care, childcare, and other nurturing occupations. She points out, ironically, that whether women are working at home or working for pay, society regards them as "drainers" (people who *use* resources) rather than "sustainers" (people who *produce* resources).

British sociologist Anthony Giddens (1991) describes local and global factors that affect self-identity as individuals make life choices and engage in life planning. He characterizes today's world as chaotic, running out of control, in contrast to the beginning of the past century when people believed they would learn to control those forces as they learned more about themselves and the world. Three important trends in the current "risk society" are *globalization, detraditionalization* (the changing of traditions around the world), and what he calls *social reflexivity.* Social reflexivity is a concept used by sociologists to examine how societal transformations influence an individual's view of self in new contexts. When individuals have a different—or for them unusual—experience of the world, they learn to use that new information to see their world differently. They are forced to fit varied sources and kinds of information (for example, new lifestyle choices) into their lives. From a constructivist view of the world, they learn to use the new information to construct (or reconstruct) their own lives. From a sociological perspective, Giddens believes this reflexivity (or constant feedback loop) will help people write their own biographies, tell their stories, and live with uncertainty.

These views are somewhat similar to those of recent counseling theorists and psychologists who see career counseling as a means to help clients tell their life stories and reconstruct their stories as they would like them to be. They include those who see career as story (Jepsen, 1995), use narrative approaches to career counseling (Cochran, 1997), and use transformations in contemporary social life as a context for counseling (Peavy, 1998). Peavy, in particular, introduces the technique of life-space mapping as part of his sociodynamic approach to counseling. The Integrative Life Planning worldview seems to have much in common with Giddens's modernity and self-identity and with composing a life through storytelling.

According to futurist David Pearce Snyder (1996), the "workplace revolution" can be viewed as part of historical cycles. Such changes as reengineering corporations, reinventing institutions (government, corporations, health care, labor relations, and public relations), displaced workers, devolution of the industrial economy, downsizing, and wage deflation are natural consequences of the Information Revolution anticipated by futurists 30 years ago. Snyder recommends that we join the revolution and reinvent ourselves, or we may experience tremendous stress and pain. We need to recognize that we no longer have "a safe career" and that in the future we will all be innovators in helping to create solutions to local and global problems.

William Bridges's (1994) view of "the end of the job" or the "de-jobbed society" has us all selling our *d*esires, *a*bilities, *t*emperament, and *a*ssets (DATA) and learning how to live with uncertainty. He sees an uncertain world of contract and contingent workers in which each person must become an entrepreneur, work on teams, and find work to do, not just fit into a job description.

Douglas Tim Hall, organizational management consultant and professor at Boston University, suggests that managers and employees need to start putting more emphasis on *relationships* in the workplace, which he elaborates on in his book with the paradoxical title *The Career Is Dead—Long Live the Career: A Relational Approach to Careers* (1996). Essentially Hall says that the old career pattern—moving up a ladder or career path—is dead, but the new career, which he calls the *protean career,* is alive and well. It is in this direction we must move—helping employees change and adapt quickly, like the Greek god Proteus, to meet the needs of changing organizations and society. With the new psychological contract, we must get our work satisfactions and growth through relationships.

Hall and his associates draw directly from psychological theories of women's development called "self-in-relation" (Jordan, Kaplan, Miller, Stiver, & Surrey, 1991). They suggest that workers will need to develop skills of lifelong learning, teamwork, adaptability, valuing diversity, communication, and decision making. They will also need the "relational competencies" of self-reflection, active listening, empathy, self-disclosure, and collaboration to better understand themselves and others as they become self-directed, continuous learners in a dynamic and diverse workplace.

In addition to changes in the global economy, a number of demographic changes have put pressure on the workplace to pay attention to human needs. These include an increasingly diverse workforce with multiple family types, an increasing number of working women unevenly spread in career fields and still earning less than their male counterparts, and the dominance of dual-income wage earners. (See chapters 1 and 2 for more specifics.) Many human resource initiatives are addressing human needs through employee assistance, outplacement, coaching, work-life balance, and diversity management. Attention to employee needs for benefits such as childcare, kin-care, care for aging parents, and care for self is growing.

Peggy Simonsen (1997) provides a new integrated approach to career development in the workplace. Although she defines career in the narrow sense of job or occupation, she promotes a "development culture" in organizations using career development as a change agent. She integrates career development and organizational development into a learning system, emphasizing awareness of global workplace changes. She also highlights the importance of process, flexibility, and change, with career specialists (internal managers) and external career counselors as change agents.

All these global, workplace, and demographic changes indicate a coming together, an integration of knowledge from several disciplines. They create the context for ILP and lead to ILP's values and assumptions:

- Dramatic changes around the globe and at home require us to broaden our thoughts and practices about how we work with employees, clients, and students and to help them understand the changes as well.

- We need to help our clients develop skills in *integrative thinking* as contrasted with linear thinking. They need to understand the importance of holistic thinking as contrasted with reductionist thinking.

- Being aware of and prioritizing the critical tasks in one's own life are an essential part of human development.

- Focusing on the holistic process in our lives is necessary.

- A new kind of self-knowledge and societal knowledge is critical to understanding the contexts and themes of Integrative Life Planning.
- Recognition of the need for and commitment to change in people, organizations, professions, and society are essential to the ILP process. Change can occur at many levels.

THE SIX CRITICAL TASKS

Following is an in-depth exploration of the six critical tasks central to ILP, complete with discussion questions to help professionals and clients understand each task and integrate it into an organizational context. Hands-on exercises based on the tasks are presented at the end of the chapter.

Task 1: Finding Work That Needs Doing in Changing Global Contexts

The first task deals with global issues that signal work yet to be done to make society a better place. These ten seem especially important to me:

- Preserving the environment
- Constructive use of technology
- Understanding changes in the workplace and in families
- Accepting changing gender roles
- Understanding and celebrating diversity
- Reducing violence
- Promoting economic opportunity (reducing poverty)
- Advocating human rights
- Discovering new ways of knowing
- Exploring spirituality

Many writers have identified their own lists, and I urge career professionals and their organizations to identify their own issues. See, for example, the *Encyclopedia of Human Problems* with its 10,233 global challenges that confront humanity (cited in Johnson & Cooperrider, 1991).

Certainly there is a great deal of concern about the need to preserve the environment. Danish career counselor Peter Plant (1995) suggests we approach ecology through "green guidance" and advances the radical, yet sensible, idea that counselors should try to help people consider environmental implications when they are choosing work to do.

Using technology constructively has become a real issue, especially since the advent of the Internet. Technology challenges us to capitalize on its potentials while controlling its dangers. Issues of pornography (especially child pornography), violence, invasion of privacy, computer addiction, and the personal isolation brought on by relating to machines rather than people are very real.

Workplace and family changes are occurring around the world. Women's entry into work, recognized as one of the dramatic changes of the 20th century, has increased awareness of the connection between work and family. Those changes are causing a small revolution in gender roles (varying greatly across cultures, of course).

Around the world, violence against women (and men) continues with battering, domestic violence, and hate crimes based on race and sexual orientation. Witness Afghanistan, Kosovo, and our own deplorable crimes of violence against specific groups in the United States, such as gays and African Americans. Work to reduce violence is going to be needed for a long time (Hansen, 1999).

While diversity initiatives have increased opportunities for ethnic minorities, women, and people with disabilities, the backlash against affirmative action reminds us of the work yet to be done to achieve the dreams of equality. Lobbying for legislation and working on enforcement may be worthy work for some. We have begun to understand diversity and, in some cases, value diversity, but we are a long way from celebrating it. Diversity training in education and the workplace can help toward this goal, but the work that needs doing is endless.

The challenge of "discovering new ways of knowing" may be especially important to those who work in academic settings, but its implications are worldwide. The traditional empirical, quantitative ways of knowing are incongruent with some of the tasks of Integrative Life Planning. Qualitative research methods have been enhanced by the multicultural movement's emphasis on harmony, being, subjectivity, integrative thinking, and wholeness. Recognition of other ways of knowing than the logical positivism that

DISCUSSION/REFLECTION 4.1

CRITICAL TASK 1: FINDING WORK THAT NEEDS DOING IN CHANGING GLOBAL CONTEXTS

1. What is the work that needs doing in your organization? What is the work that needs doing in in the larger society to which you and/or your organization can contribute? How does this work relate to the work that has already been defined in your mission statement, work teams, and performance evaluations?

2. What kind of impact will changes in the global contexts have on employees in your organization and elsewhere—their attitudes toward work, the organization, and career? Their emotional and psychological health? What assistance are they being given in moving to a new kind of career planning and a protean career in which they are to expect change and expect to change themselves? To expect employability rather than employment?

3. What new talents do employees or clients have that have not yet been developed or used? How can the organization tap their creativity? What new possibilities are available? Who provides outplacement, coaching, or counseling when needed, and in what kind of circumstances? How does the organization help workers develop *career resiliency*?

dominates psychology and other social and behavioral sciences has begun but has a long way to go.

Theologian Matthew Fox, in *The Reinvention of Work* (1994), suggests the "good work" that needs doing will help sustainable development on the planet as well as enhance the human condition. "Bad work" (crime, drugs, prostitution, violence) should be eliminated.

ILP urges career and HRD professionals to identify their own human challenges and priorities. Discussion/Reflection 4.1 provides a series of questions to examine critical task 1—finding work that needs doing.

Task 2: Weaving Our Lives into a Meaningful Whole

The second critical task starts with identifying the different socialization of women and men for various life roles and the unique influences on (and barriers to) the life planning of each. Donald Super's (1951) broad definition of career and his Life-Career Rainbow (1980) present a useful context for both holistic life planning and roles/relationships of women and men. His lifespan model (Super & Sverko, 1995) includes the theaters of life (home, family, work, school, community) and life roles (child, student, parent, homemaker, worker, citizen, leisurite).

ILP looks at the whole person and asks to what extent work organizations facilitate holistic development—of mind, body, and spirit—and encourage attention to other life roles. Both men and women are beginning to feel that work cannot meet all their needs, and many are expressing a desire to balance work and other life roles—to see work within a life—and to become more integrated people.

Bakan (1966) defined two different ways of ordering reality: *agency,* linked with men, is objective, rational, analytic, fragmented, and competitive; *communion,* linked with women, is subjective, nurturing, holistic, cooperative, expressive. Substituting the terms *self-sufficiency* for agency and *connectedness* for communion, I agree with Bakan that both realities need to be integrated into the lives of both women and men. The ultimate goal is one of women and men sharing nurturing and provider roles. According to Hansen (1997), these equal partnerships occur when each partner

- Treats the other with dignity and respect
- Demonstrates flexibility in negotiating roles
- Enables the other to choose and enact roles and responsibilities congruent with the individual's talents and potentials as well as with the couple's mutual goals for work, the relationship, the family, and society

Today career professionals are beginning to recognize that what happens in one part of life affects other parts. These parts may include, besides the vocational role, the social, intellectual, physical, spiritual, and emotional roles. The connection of mind, body, and spirit is an important concept in ILP. Holistic system approaches are becoming more common, sometimes under the term *wellness,* recognizing the connection between the personal and career. A special issue of *Career Development Quarterly* (Subich, 1995) asked the question, "How personal is career counseling?" The responses, from well-known counselors and counseling theorists, were overwhelmingly "very personal" and attested to the connection between mental health and work issues.

DISCUSSION/REFLECTION 4.2

CRITICAL TASK 2: WEAVING OUR LIVES INTO A MEANINGFUL WHOLE

1. How does the organization recognize that employees are whole persons with multiple dimensions and try to foster that wholeness? What mentors and role models are available? How do they function in the 21st-century organization?

2. How does continuous learning take place, and what options are available to workers who want to learn to direct their own careers? How will employees learn how to work on projects and teams—not just typical "linear" teams (narrow decision making, conventional individual rewards) but "circular" teams (creative, open, democratic, group vision, open flexible environment) with common team goals and individual goals?

Weaving our lives into a meaningful whole includes a number of issues: awareness of female and male socialization, life roles, and the gender-role system; renegotiation of roles and relationships for equality; the connection of mind, body, and spirit; and the acknowledgment of personal issues in career counseling. Discussion/Reflection 4.2 will help you integrate your thinking about this task.

Task 3: Connecting Family and Work

The roles of women and men in work and family (all kinds of families) and the gender role dilemmas that arise as people move beyond their ascribed roles of provider and nurturer often cause considerable conflict and stress. These work-family dilemmas include attitudes toward childcare, importance of both work and family to both partners, task sharing, role salience, marital satisfaction, stress, social supports, decision making, and power, as well as suggested strategies for resolution in both family and work sectors.

BORN FREE, a national research and training program created in the late 1970s at the University of Minnesota, was developed to address some of these issues. It is based on the existence of a gender role system across cultures and the network of attitudes, feelings, and behaviors that result from the pervasiveness of gender role stereotyping in the culture. Three factors of major importance to the gender role system are the masculine and feminine stereotypes, the division of labor into "men's work" and "women's work," and valuing men more than women. The program attempts to *b*uild *o*ptions for men and women (within all cultures); *r*eassess *n*orms through which we have all been socialized; and *f*ree *r*oles of both women and men in work and family, through *e*ducational *e*quity (BORN FREE). Every culture ascribes certain roles to men and women, usually the unpaid family role to women and the paid work and provider role to men. Studies including both industrialized and developing nations have shown that these stereotypes exist across cultures.

Organizations can pursue a range of activities to help achieve balance between work and family. Hall (1990) suggests:

- Creating more flexible work arrangements
- Recognizing that both women and men may make similar kinds of career accommodations privately
- Creating greater corporate flexibility including varying forms of time out from a career—for example, in many Scandinavian countries family leaves are available to both women and men
- Making greater use of home-based work
- Viewing a person's work-family choice as flexible (not a one-time career decision) because family and career orientations change over time; multiple tracks with multiple entrances and exits are needed

Issues of family and work gained attention in the 1970s when Rosabeth Moss Kanter (1977) asked, "Why does family always have to fit around work? Why can't work sometimes fit around family?" Problems are exacerbated in the two-earner or dual-career family. Issues of balance, originally viewed as women's issues, are now being raised by men as well. Some suggest that instead of describing work-family issues, we should talk about work-life issues that include singles and couples with and without children. While a number of corporations and nonprofit organizations have work-family policies and task forces, the demanding work ethics and norms of corporations and other institutions (including universities) make family-friendly policies difficult to implement. Yet a recent study by Rosalind

DISCUSSION/REFLECTION 4.3

CRITICAL TASK 3: CONNECTING FAMILY AND WORK

1. What is the organization doing to be family friendly and help employees with work-family issues? Are work-family initiatives in place and integrated throughout the organization?

2. Is management or HRD staff diagnosing the organization to determine practices that inhibit work-family linkages and those that are facilitative? Is the organization using the strategy of "looking at work through a work-family lens?"

Barnett and Caryl Rivers (1996) provides a more positive picture, as illustrated by the title: *She Works/He Works: How Two-Income Families Are Happier, Healthier, and Better Off.* With the creation of virtual organizations where employees have greater freedom and control over their work hours, work tasks, and workplaces, some of these problems may disappear.

Connecting family and work is an increasingly critical task with many facets. Because the family-work connection so often has been overlooked or minimized, it is time to give it more central attention in workplaces. We need to help employees, students, and clients understand the relationships between the choices they make about family and work, or life and work, and help them implement those choices and decisions with maximum benefit to themselves, their families, and their communities. Discussion/Reflection 4.3 will help you examine this critical task.

Task 4: Valuing Pluralism and Inclusivity

The fourth critical task calls for an informed awareness of all kinds of differences—racial, ethnic, class, religion, gender, age, disability, sexual orientation, language, and regionality. Goals of this task are to help career professionals (1) gain an understanding of the meaning and implications of valuing diversity; (2) learn to understand their own biases and attitudes; (3) help their clients develop a worldview that allows them to function in a multicultural environment; and (4) utilize their knowledge to help diverse clients, students, and workers in educational and organizational settings.

ILP challenges traditional assumptions about career and career development. For example, traditional career planning assumes that people have choices—which isn't always true for people outside the opportunity structure. Career theories assume that people can have control over their lives, that "sense of agency." But this is not true of many who have been victims of personal or institutional bias, racism, or sexism. Many people from Eastern cultures have a different worldview from the Eurocentric view of most career theories. Self-actualization, a goal of much career counseling, may not be important to people whose career decisions are made jointly within the family or in a communal rather than individualistic culture. Traditional career-planning approaches often ignore the numerous economic and social barriers that ethnic minority members face in seeking educational and occupational opportunity. Much traditional career counseling focuses on occupational choice and ignores the multiple facets, including sociopolitical and psychological realities, of a person's life. See chapter 8 for more on multicultural career counseling.

Integrate is a widely used term in the multicultural and ethnic counseling literature. To integrate means to renew, to make whole by bringing different parts together. These parts can be different cultures. To integrate also means to bring people of different racial groups into free and equal association. The word may also be applied to an individual, as various traits, feelings, and attitudes are integrated within one person. To integrate also may mean to remove legal and social barriers, a mission of the larger society that is applicable to life and career planning.

Pluralism has been defined as "the quality or condition of being plural, or of existing in more than one part or form; the existence within a nation or society of groups distinctive in ethnic origin, cultural patterns, religion, and the like; a policy of favoring the preservation of such groups within a given nation or society; and the theory that ultimate reality has more than one true explanation" (Goralnik, 1979, p. 732). Pluralism seems to reinforce the value of difference, to recognize many parts, groups, experiences, and truths, and to establish a context for valuing diversity. It is a means for optimum human development.

Alvin Leung (1995) and Derald Wing Sue (1995) urge professionals to question the validity of current theories, techniques, and strategies and call for a pluralistic perspective in career counseling, including systems interventions with multiple rather than single strategies. Work with diverse populations may be more helpful if help is provided out of the office—in home or community settings—and if the helper roles are of ombudsperson, advocate, consultant, organizational change agent, and the like.

While multiculturalism is being defined broadly to include several dimensions of identity—especially race, ethnicity, class, and gender—gender factors often have been ignored in multicultural theory and practice. Although it is important for career professionals to understand that race is the most salient characteristic for most people of color, gender is a thread that runs through every culture and affects women's (and men's) development and options.

One issue regarding tradition and morality needs to be mentioned in relation to immigrants, refugees, and increasing cross-cultural populations. There is a tendency to assume that all culturally specific customs, values, social conventions, behaviors, and traditions are sacrosanct and to be respected. In these situations, the dominant group may abuse or harm other groups and show lack of respect for human dignity and freedom. Brazilian psychologist Elizabeth Gama (Hansen & Gama, 1996) addresses this well when she says, "There are certain behaviors and their associated values, beliefs, and attitudes that, although traditional or common among certain cultural groups, are morally wrong. And moral principles are universal and applicable across cultural boundaries" (p. 96). More specifically, Gama mentions the various forms of abuse that women are subjected to in many cultures: male domination in Latino and Asian cultures, domestic battering in the United States, restriction of women's freedom in many Arab countries, poor treatment of Untouchables in India, sale into marriage of young girls in several cultures, and the surgical clitoridectomy practice in some African and Arab cultures. With increasing numbers of immigrants and refugees entering the United States and the workplace, career professionals need to be aware of these cultural and human rights issues.

Hall and Parker (1993) introduce the concept of *workplace flexibility* to address diversity, meaning "attention to the 'whole' of the employee's life (including work-life issues and issues of difference) and investigation into creative ways of enhancing the fit between people and their work roles" (p. 7). They linked issues of work and family and diversity under the "workplace flexibility" rubric and found that more flexibility resulted in lower absenteeism, higher morale, reduced turnover, and improved productivity.

DISCUSSION/REFLECTION 4.4

CRITICAL TASK 4: VALUING PLURALISM AND INCLUSIVITY

1. How does the organization attend to managing diversity? How can people learn to better relate to each other in organizations, to manage difference? How does "relational growth" occur, and how is it facilitated?

2. How can the organization promote new kinds of flexibility for all employees? To what extent is flexibility being viewed as a strategic advantage? To what extent is multicultural organizational development training available for managers, HRD specialists, and all employees?

Interpersonal effectiveness has always been important on and off the job. Changing demographics of society and the workplace will make effectively dealing with difference within and across cultures a major task. We know that job loss in general is more likely to occur because of interpersonal problems than because of inability to perform the work.

A key aspect of diversity is learning how to deal with difference. Juan Moreno (1996), a diversity and equal opportunity director at the University of Minnesota, presents a wise credo about "entering the world of 'the other'" whether the different culture is inside or outside of the national boundaries. Below are a few examples from his dozen or so steps to help people cross boundaries or enter other cultures:

- Know ourselves before entering into cultural immersion experiences, then get to know others.
- Keep a sense of humor, laugh at ourselves, our uninformed behavior, our relative ignorance.
- Recognize that we are all "others" to somebody.
- If possible, leave the sandals of our own cultures at the doorstep.

Discussion/Reflection 4.4, above, focuses on encouraging this important critical task.

Task 5: Exploring Spirituality and Life Purpose

The fifth critical task links spirituality with meaning and purpose. A considerable body of literature has emerged on spirituality and counseling, but only in the last decade has spirituality become more widely associated with career. Some suggest that the interest began in the 1950s with the shift from psychology as pathology to psychology as positive human development, especially with the work of Abraham Maslow and Carl Rogers. The United States experienced a surge of interest in spiritual concerns in the early 1980s when concern about the materialism and self-centeredness of the national character heightened growing feelings of alienation. Topics such as purpose and meaning became more popular. In the late 1990s, there seemed to be a new openness to including spirituality in career and life planning, expressed in *Connections Between Spirit and Work in Career Development* (Bloch & Richmond, 1997).

While there are many definitions of spirituality, I define it as the core of the self that gives meaning to life, a higher power outside of oneself. It has been long ignored in our rational, logical, career decision making of the past, but many people, especially in Eastern cultures and many other racial/ethnic groups, consider it central to life.

Matthew Fox (1994) writes eloquently of spirit and work when he says,"Life and livelihood ought not to be separated but to flow from the same source, which is the spirit. . . . Spirit means life, and both life and livelihood are about living in depth, living with meaning, purpose, joy, and a sense of contributing to the greater community" (p. 1).

Along with the search for meaning, there has been a reexamination of our material values and the place of money in work and in life. Some of this is prompted by those in their 20s and 30s who are seeking more balance in life and who refuse to give their whole lives to their jobs. Much has been written about moving away from materialism—moving from the fast lane to the middle lane, changing the face of ambition, downshifting, and reinventing and redefining success.

Fox has been especially critical of the materialism driving our society. The primary value in life, he says, is "living life fully"—what I call *holistic development.* He criticizes our "work and spend" mentality in which advertising "stimulates our appetites and makes needs of wants"(p. 34). In his view, we need to alter employee incentives, improve wages for the lowest

DISCUSSION/REFLECTION 4.5

CRITICAL TASK 5: EXPLORING SPIRITUALITY AND LIFE PURPOSE

1. How do you define your spirituality? How does it affect your work? Do you see meaning and sense of purpose in your work? Can the work culture be changed to allow for expression of spirituality (as different from religion)?

2. What does "spirituality in the workplace" mean to you? How might it be explored in career counseling and/or human resource programs?

paid, encourage gender equality so that work at home is understood as work, preempt spiraling consumption, and establish time as a value in itself.

Work should be more spiritual, he observes, based on a larger meaning or purpose, not just to fill a job but to benefit society or the community by giving back with one's unique talents. His vision of the work role is where "mind, heart, and health come together in a harmony of life experiences that celebrate the whole person" (p. 2). Stressing the importance of preserving the environment, he suggests that we need to see the universe and the planet as the center of our work and understand the necessity of people doing good work to contribute to the wheel of justice and compassion in the world.

The issue of spirituality and humanitarian definitions of work may seem incongruous with the hard-driving competition of the workplace. The way career professionals deal with these issues will probably vary, but this important area of life and of Integrative Life Planning will become even more central in the future. You are invited to further explore this critical task in Discussion/Reflection 4.5.

Task 6: Managing Personal Transitions and Organizational Change

The sixth critical task focuses on managing personal, organizational, and social change and includes several practical models for helping people make transitions. Nancy Schlossberg has one such model in her book *Overwhelmed: Coping with Life's Ups and Downs* (1994). Schlossberg believes that understanding the transition process can help us better cope with transitions, especially if we learn how to

- Approach change (by identifying our roles, routines, assumptions, relationships, whose transition it is, and where we are in it)
- Take stock (of our situation, self, supports, and strategies for coping)
- Take charge (by selecting appropriate coping strategies, developing an action plan, and learning or profiting from the change)

She also has developed the concept of "nonevents"—those we had hoped for but that didn't occur, such as losing an election, losing a job, not getting pregnant, or not getting promoted (Schlossberg & Robinson, 1996).

Clients will need to be taught new models of decision making because, as California psychologist, H. B. Gelatt (1989) suggests, the old rational, logical, linear models of decision making are insufficient for the new millennium. Clients will need to become conscious of risks and risk taking, and of what he calls *positive uncertainty*. He defines it as "a personal plan for making decisions about the future when you don't know what it will be" and "a flexible, ambidextrous approach to managing change using both your rational and intuitive mind." It is a unique approach to decision making that helps prepare people for the uncertainty, instability, ambiguity, and complexity that may face them in the 21st century. For example, people are urged to "live with paradox, to not be afraid to change your mind, or to declare your interdependence." Another paradoxical term, *planned happenstance* (Mitchell, Levin, & Krumboltz, 1999), involves capitalizing on those events that surprise us but from which we can carve a positive response.

This task reinforces the multiple career decisions people will make in a lifetime, including those resulting from unanticipated or random events. It also highlights the importance of helping people become change agents in their personal, family, and organizational transitions. Rich resources on organizational development and systems change can be helpful in this process. A "change agent as process helper" assesses the institution as it is now and as we would like it to be, and then systematically follows the principles of organizational psychology to change it.

I believe we can be change agents in our own lives, in our interpersonal relationships, and in our institutions—local, national, or global. Identifying both the barriers to and facilitators of change can be helpful in

DISCUSSION/REFLECTION 4.6

CRITICAL TASK 6: MANAGING PERSONAL TRANSITIONS AND ORGANIZATIONAL CHANGE

1. What is the organizational culture or philosophy regarding personal development? To what extent does the organization treat workers as whole persons? Are employees given time off to do volunteer work, to contribute to the community? to have time for other parts of their lives? for self-care? In what ways does the organization demonstrate caring for its employees?

2. What are employees learning about being a change agent? The process of change? About managing and shaping change? What are managers and teams learning about and how are they enacting new styles of managing, leading, and performing?

implementing change process. We can also teach our employees, clients, and students to be change agents in the same way. To assist the transition and change process, see Discussion/Reflection 4.6.

SYNTHESIS AND APPLICATION

ILP is comprehensive, interdisciplinary, inclusive, holistic, and integrative. As a systems approach, it connects many parts of our lives with society. Career and HRD professionals are asked to select the tasks that are the most important or meaningful to them and their organization. Each task connects the various aspects of human life:

- Identity (ethnicity, race, gender, class, disability, belief, and so on)
- Dimensions of development (social, intellectual, physical, spiritual, emotional, and career)
- Life roles (love, labor, learning, and leisure)
- Social context (society, organization, family, individual)

Table 4.1 shows the shifts in our views when we apply Integrative Life Planning.

Table 4.1 Shifts in Views with ILP

Integrative Life Planning Means Moving From		
Thinking locally	to	Sharing globally
Planning for work	to	Planning for life roles and how they relate to each other
Focus on self-sufficiency only	to	Focus on self-sufficiency and connectedness for both women and men
Expecting stability	to	Expecting and managing change and transitions in both family and work
Monoculturalism	to	Multiculturalism and inclusivity
Dominant-subordinate relationships	to	Partnerships
Fragmentation	to	Wholeness and community

Although Integrative Life Planning is a very comprehensive "big picture" concept, there are ways to learn about it and use it with your students, clients, or employees. Discussion/Reflection 4.7 encourages your synthesis and implementation of the six critical tasks. In addition, possible activities are integrated throughout the Integrative Life Planning book (Hansen,1997), as well as in the exercise section of this chapter.

Action Strategies for Career and HRD Professionals

ILP offers a few specific strategies that career counselors and HRD professionals can use to help employees and their organization manage transitions and change:

- Become informed on work, workplace, and work pattern changes that exist now and are projected in order to help employees understand and prepare for them. Identify innovative organizations that are implementing some of the changes (for example, Starbuck's, Motorola, General Electric, Sun, Microsoft, Xerox, and Ben and Jerry's).
- Develop a global mind-set or worldview that will help you see the "big picture"; develop systems thinking; and understand, appreciate, and value diversity of all kinds.

DISCUSSION/REFLECTION 4.7

SYNTHESIS: IMPLEMENTING ILP THEMES OR TASKS

1. Where is your organization on the continuum of change with these indicators? How are they relevant or not relevant to your employees and setting? How would you prioritize these ILP themes or tasks for your organization?

2. After reading about ILP, which one or two critical tasks are most important for you? Which one or two are least important? Given your responses to these two questions, what are your next steps in achieving Integrative Life Planning in your own life? What steps will you take to use ILP in promoting the development of your employees, students, or clients?

- Help your organization move from fragmentation and separation to integration and holistic approaches in both the whole organization and the whole person.

- Support or develop workplace flexibility as an opportunity for the organization's strategic advantage. Apply this flexibility to work and family issues and to multicultural issues.

- Become familiar with different leadership models, which help organizations move from "command and control" to interactive leadership (Rosener, 1990) and leadership that hits "the connective edge," as described by Lipman-Blumen (1996), and that is cooperative and not always competitive.

- Help your organization develop a more humane psychological contract that takes human needs into account through such actions as reducing downsizing, recognizing workers as the most important asset, and finding new ways to reward surviving workers.

- Develop programs to help employees, students, clients, and managers acquire and maintain the skills they will need, including resilience, relational skills, technology skills, capacity for continuous learning, the ability to network and team, and the ability to take risks and learn from setbacks.

- Increase efforts to help workers find work (that needs doing), change work, and adjust to changing work patterns. Help them to be change agents in their own lives as well as in their own institutions and the larger society. Help them to live with uncertainty, but as "positive uncertainty" and to develop a "future sense."

- Help employees and clients in their search for wholeness, meaning, and purpose. Assist in their developing a sense of community and connectedness. Help the organization develop policies that will facilitate their becoming whole persons, allowing time for family and for community volunteer work.

CONCLUSION

Integrative Life Planning is strongly grounded in democratic values and a concern for social justice. The work of Brazilian reformer Paulo Freire and his "*conscientizacao*" is relevant here. Freire emphasized "the process of developing critical consciousness," stating that one of the purposes of education (and I would add counseling, career development, and HRD) "is to liberate people to awareness of themselves in social context" (quoted in Ivey, Ivey, & Simek-Morgan 1993, p. 113). In the new social context of work in the 21st century, there is much to be done.

With its new worldview, the Integrative Life Planning concept is comprehensive, interdisciplinary, and inclusive. It is a systems approach, connecting many parts of our lives and societies. Though created primarily for Western cultures, some of it may hold promise for global cultures as well. Career and HRD professionals in each culture will have to decide which of the interactive, connected tasks are relevant and applicable, depending on their own contexts, priorities, and worldviews. No psychologist, counselor, or career professional could be expected to absorb the entire ILP concept at once. Each will have to select those tasks/themes that are most important or meaningful at a given time and work with them, remembering that connectedness, wholeness, and community are central to the ILP concept.

ILP STRATEGIES/EXERCISES

The following strategies adapted from *Integrative Life Planning* (Hansen, 1997) are intended for use in classes, workshops, or training sessions. They are used with permission.

EXERCISE 4.1

FINDING WORK THAT NEEDS DOING IN CHANGING GLOBAL CONTEXTS (TASK 1)

This activity is designed to help participants in a class or work group begin to approach work and job search in different ways. Ask participants to consider the phrase "think globally, act locally" and identify two global issues and two local issues that need solutions (see page 129 for some examples). Then ask them to translate the issues they chose into specific tasks to accomplish on both levels. Discuss with one other person.

Global issues	*Specific tasks to do*

Local issues	*Specific tasks to do*

EXERCISE 4.2

SELF-SUFFICIENCY AND CONNECTEDNESS (TASKS 2 & 3)

This exercise is intended to help men and women gain a better understanding of the need for wholeness and balance in their lives. That women and men can be both self-sufficient and connected, or have *agency* and *communion*, as defined earlier in this chapter, is an important idea in Integrative Life Planning. Ask participants

- How do you define self-sufficiency and connectedness for yourself?

____
____
____
____

- Can you quantify on a continuum the amount of each you have at present?

____
____
____
____

- What do you see as optimum in a balanced perspective for yourself and your partner, spouse, significant other, or someone you work closely with?

____
____
____
____

- What factors promote self-sufficiency in men and women?

____
____
____
____

EXERCISE 4.2 (CONT'D)

- What factors are barriers?

- What factors promote connectedness in both?

- What are the barriers to connectedness?

- To what extent are these integrated in your life and in the life of your significant other (partner, spouse, coworker,etc.)?

- What compromises have you had to make along the way?

Have participants share their insights with one or two others and then discuss in the larger group how they feel about looking at these two aspects of their lives.

EXERCISE 4.3

LIFE ROLE PLANNING (TASKS 2 & 3)

This strategy is designed to help participants understand the importance of life roles, not just job roles.

Ask participants to take an 8 1/2" x 11" piece of paper, draw a line across the middle, and draw five circles above the line and five circles below. In the upper circles, have them indicate which five roles currently are most important to them (numbering them by rank). In the lower circles, have them do the same, indicating which roles they think will be most important in the next 15 or 20 years. Ask them to examine their circles in light of the following questions:

- What are the expectations associated with each role?
- How important are the roles at different life stages?
- How much of your time, energy, and talents do you give to each role?
- What is the impact on significant others of the way in which you carry out your roles?
- How do these roles affect your relationships with your significant other (if you have one)? Your children (if you have them)?
- Where do leisure, volunteer, and service roles fit in?
- Are the roles flexible or rigid?
- How are the roles different if people marry at 20 years of age versus 30 or 35? How might they be different for gay or lesbian couples?
- What happens to the roles when people retire?
- How can awareness of role options help you in life planning?

EXERCISE 4.4

DEALING WITH DIFFERENCE (TASK 4)

Understanding attitudes, behaviors, and feelings when you enter a culture different from your own is the purpose of this activity. In your work group or team, read Juan Moreno's *On Entering the World of "the Other."* (See page 138 in this chapter or pages 266–267 in Hansen, 1997, for more on this.) As leader, guide the members through a visualization in which they imagine each step of the experience.

Think of a time when you entered a culture very different from your own (or a culture you would like to visit).

- What was it like for you?
- Where did you go?
- Who was there to meet you?
- What was it like in the new place?
- Were there any language barriers?
- How was it different from your own location?
- What did you like about what you found there?
- What barriers did you encounter?
- What were the people like? similar to you? different from you? accepting? hostile? friendly? neutral?
- What did you to do to try to understand this new culture?
- How long did you stay?
- You are about to leave this culture now. What did you learn about your own culture?
- How did it feel to be back home?
- How did you feel about the experience?

EXERCISE 4.5

FINDING OUR CORE (TASK 5)

This activity uses visualization and metaphors to increase participants' awareness of spirituality and meaning in their lives. Many people associate spirituality with the core of the person, providing deep integration or wholeness.

- Have participants think of a symbol that represents the core of who they are, the thing that motivates or drives them, and draw it on 3 x 5 card. For example, a person who is very achievement oriented might draw a ladder; a person who is nurturing and caring might draw a heart.
- Ask participants to form pairs and discuss with each other what their symbol is, why they chose it, what it means to them, and so on.
- End the activity by sharing with others in the group and discussing commonalities, differences, and what each learned from the experience.

EXERCISE 4.6

DREAMS AND HOPES (TASKS 2, 3, & 5)

The goal of this activity is to help participants visualize and articulate their dreams and hopes of the past, present, and future. Dreams, like fantasies, often come true.

In a workshop setting, have participants envision their past, present, and future and draw three circles to see how they fit together.

- Ask participants to identify three dreams they have for the next 10 to 15 years: one for their own future, one for the kind of work organization they would like to be part of; and one for what they want their society to be like.
- Have them assume they are on a cloud overlooking their own life and workplace. Invite them do their visioning from the perspective of the various life roles they are likely to have: work, study, family, leisure, and community activity.
- After they have imaged each, ask them to write down what is happening in each of these areas.
- Have them meet in groups of four to discuss the strategy, commenting on what they learned, which of the three dreams was most important to them, how they were related, and so on. Remind them to share only what they feel comfortable discussing.

EXERCISE 4.7

PERSONAL TRANSITIONS AND RISK TAKING (TASK 6)

The purpose of this activity is to facilitate thinking about what a risk is and to better understand the risk-taking process. As leader, share three big risks you have taken in your own life, preferably at different life stages. Then ask participants to

Write down an important risk you have taken related to your career development at three different life stages. Describe the risk.

Risk 1: ____

____

Risk 2: ____

____

Risk 3: ____

____

Ask yourself the following questions about each of the three risks. Then talk about your risks with two other people in your group.

- How big was the risk?
- In what way was it a risk for you? for others in your life?
- Who or what supported you in the risk? blocked you?
- What were the consequences of the risk? short range? long range? positive? negative?
- If you could, would you take the same risk today?
- Of the three risks, which was the greatest risk and why?

Discuss one of your risks in a group of three.

After sharing, have participants think about the meaning of the activity for them. What did they learn or discover? What did it tell them about themselves? Have them apply this to risks in their work setting.

EXERCISE 4.8

INHIBITORS AND FACILITATORS OF CHANGE (TASK 6)

The purpose of this strategy is to help workers, clients, and employees become aware of the need for change in their personal life or their organization and of factors that limit their ability to effect change. The change agent worksheet below suggests that a change agent may identify a short-range goal or a long-range goal and then list examples of personal change, interpersonal change, and organizational change that are challenging. Participants should identify the inhibitors (barriers) to the changes as well as the facilitators. Also indicate criteria needed for accomplishment. In groups of three or four, participants may offer suggestions to each other on how to reduce the inhibitors and increase the facilitators.

Short-range goal: ______________________________

or

Long-range goal: ______________________________

Effecting Positive Change in My System

Three Levels of Possible Change	**Barriers**	**Facilitators**	**Criteria for Accomplishment**
1. Personal change—myself			
2. Interpersonal change—with partner, spouse, students, friends, coworkers, etc.			
3. Institutional change—school, college, agency, business, etc.			

Source: Adapted from *Integrative Life Planning: Critical Tasks for Career Development and Changing Life Patterns* by L. Sunny Hansen. Exhibit R.1, "Change Agent Activity Worksheet," p. 310. Copyright © 1997 by Jossey-Bass Inc., Publishers. Used with permission.

EXERCISE 4.9

LIFE-PLANNING INFLUENCES (TASKS 1–6)

The purpose of this activity is to help participants reflect on different parts of their life in context, using a quilt as a metaphor.

Give each participant a different colored square or piece of paper and ask him or her to think of it as a piece of his or her own quilt of life, with the following instruction: Think about the various influences on your life and career (using "career" in the expanded sense of life roles).

- In the upper left corner, write what you believe are the two most important challenges facing society or your organization today (for example, low morale, interpersonal conflict, violence, poverty, and so on).
- In the upper right corner, write down which one or two of the six domains of human development are most important to you (social, intellectual, physical, spiritual, emotional, career). Then write one or two that are least important.
- Think about all the progress that has been made in the relationships between women and men in this society. In the lower left corner, write the most important remaining tasks to be done. How might this be different in another culture?
- In the lower right corner, think of interpersonal and diversity issues present in your own organization. Which one most affects you and needs to be worked on?
- In the left middle, imagine yourself 10 or 15 years from now. If you were to make a change in what you are doing in your career or life pattern, write down what that would be.
- Finally, in the middle right of your square or paper, draw a symbol that represents the core of who you are—what motivates you, your own personal metaphor (for example, a river, a ladder, a heart, and so on) and what it means.

Share your piece corner by corner with two or three other people, bringing in only what you feel comfortable sharing.

Process the activity with the whole group, asking, "What did you learn from this experience? What commonalities did you find in the group? What differences?" Then point out that the pieces of all the members, when put together, represent a unique quilt of the life patterns of the participants in the organization.

EXERCISE 4.10

CIRCLE OF LIFE (TASKS 1–6)

The purpose of this activity is to gain a better sense of the connective themes of Integrative Life Planning. The circle of life is an important symbol of Native American and Native Alaskan culture. It is an ILP synthesis and an opportunity for reflection in your own circle of life. Before creating your own circle, it may be helpful to refer to Figure 5.1, Integrative Life Patterns, as seen on the following page, for a synthesis of the ILP concept.

Ask each participant in the workshop or class to complete his or her own circle of life as shown in Figure 5.2, on page 197.

If possible, participants should discuss their own circle with a significant other or partner and explain the various meanings of its components. The act of completing their own circle should put them in touch with the larger circle that is the globe and the global and local needs that exist in it—that is, the work that needs doing. The circle of life is the framework of ILP that informs participants about their own lives in terms of their commitment to their own organization and the larger community.

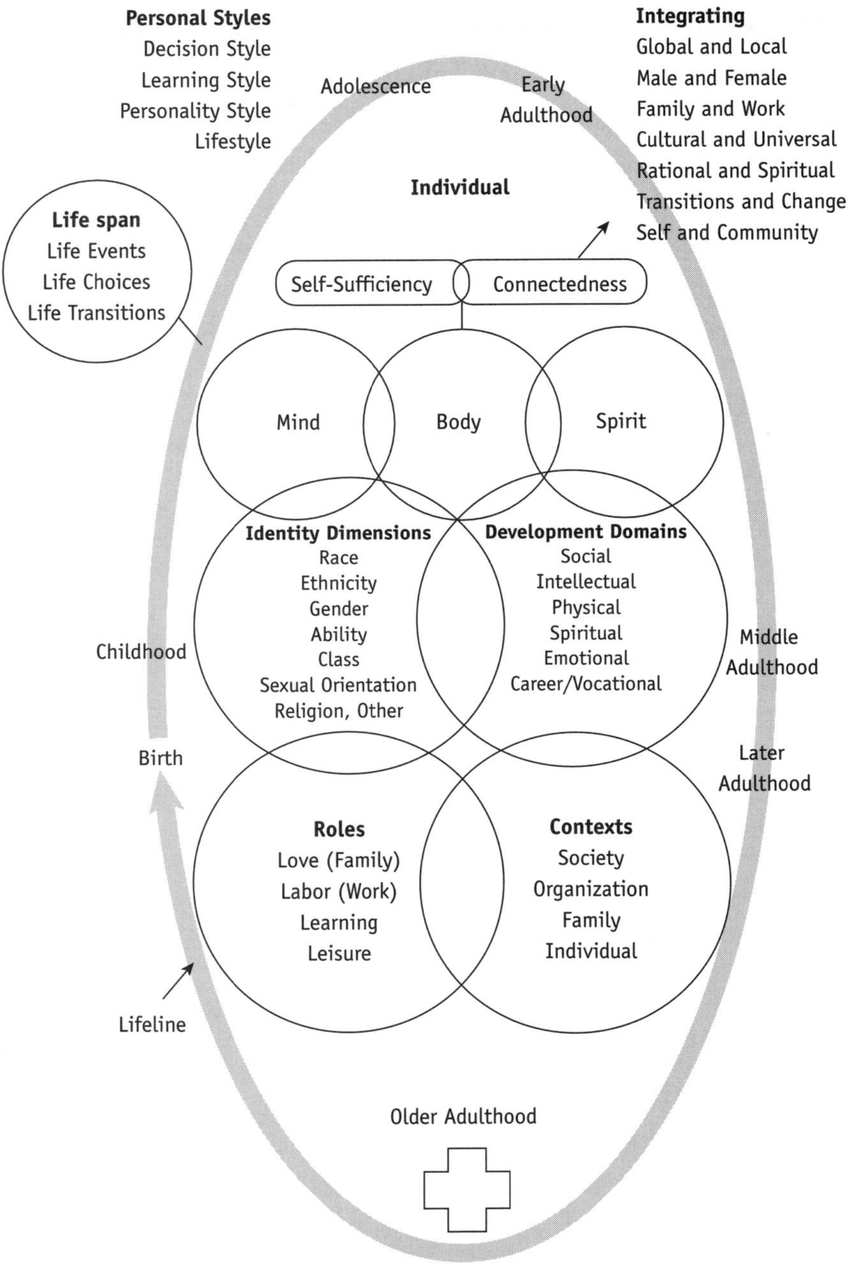

Source: Adapted from *Integrative Life Planning: Critical Tasks for Career Development and Changing Life Patterns* by L. Sunny Hansen. Figure 9.1, "Integrative Life Patterns," p. 264. Copyright © 1997 by Jossey-Bass Inc., Publishers. Used with permission.

Figure 4.1 Synthesis: Integrative Life Planning

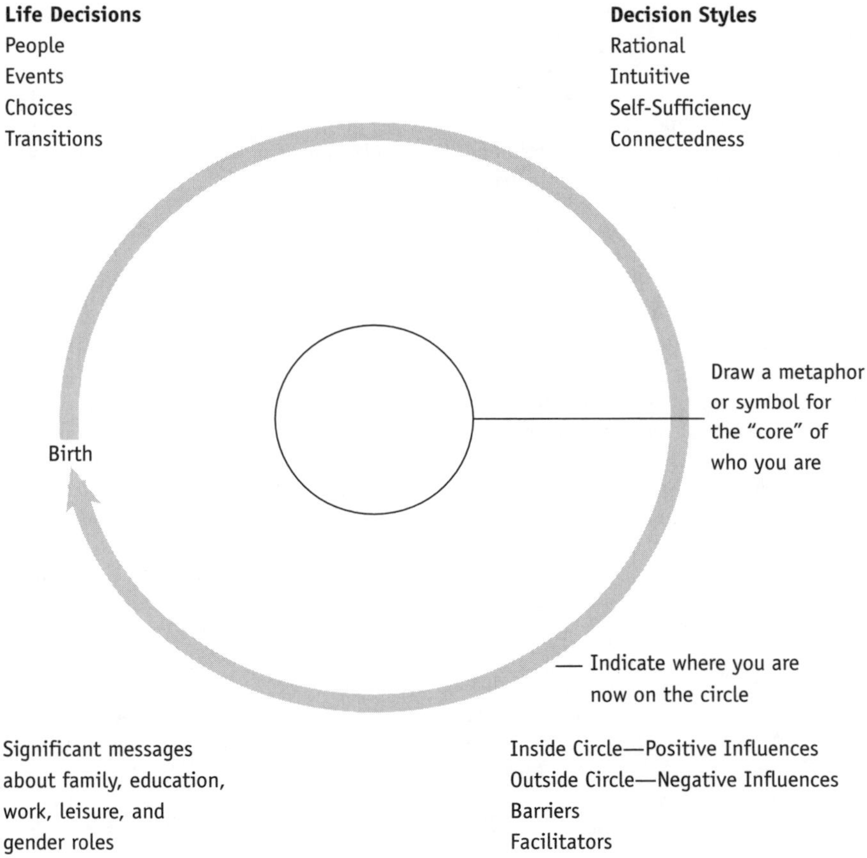

Source: Adapted from *Integrative Life Planning: Critical Tasks for Career Development and Changing Life Patterns* by L. Sunny Hansen. Figure 9.3, "The Circle of Life," p. 283. Copyright © 1997 by Jossey-Bass Inc., Publishers. Used with permission.

Figure 4.2 The Circle of Life

REFERENCES

Bakan, D. (1996). *The duality of human existence: An essay on psychology and religion.* Skokie, IL: Rand McNally.

Barnett, R. C., & Rivers, C. (1996). *She works/he works: How two-income families are happier, healthier, and better off.* San Francisco: HarperCollins.

Bloch, D. P., & Richmond, L. J. (Eds.). (1997). *Connections between spirit and work in career development.* Palo Alto, CA: Davies-Black.

Bridges, W. (1994). *Job shift: How to prosper in a workplace without jobs.* Reading, MA: Addison-Wesley.

Cochran, L. (1997). *Career counseling: A narrative approach.* Thousand Oaks, CA: Sage.

Drucker, P. F. (1995, January 2 & 4). How we work: The age of social transformation (Parts 1 & 2). *Minneapolis Star Tribune.*

Fox, M. (1994). *The reinvention of work: A new vision of livelihood for our time.* San Francisco: Harper.

Gelatt, H. B. (1989). Positive uncertainty: A new decision-making framework for counseling. *Journal of Counseling Psychology, 36*(2), 252–256.

Giddens, A. (1991). *Modernity and self-identity.* Stanford, CA: Stanford University Press.

Goralnik, D. B. (Ed.). (1979). *Webster's new world dictionary.* Cleveland, OH: William Collins, p. 732.

Hall, D. T. (1990). Promoting work/family balance: An organization-change approach. *Organizational Dynamics, 18*(3), 5–18.

Hall, D. T. (Ed.). (1996). *The career is dead—Long live the career: A relational approach to careers.* San Francisco: Jossey-Bass.

Hall, D. T., & Parker, V. A. (1993). The role of workplace flexibility in managing diversity. *Organizational Dynamics, 22*(1), 5–18.

Hansen, L. S. (1997). *Integrative Life Planning: Critical tasks for career development and changing life patterns.* San Francisco: Jossey-Bass.

Hansen, L. S. (1999, June). Gender-based advocacy for equity and nonviolence. *Counseling Today,* pp. 36–38.

Hansen, L. S., & Gama, E. M. P. (1996). Gender issues in multicultural counseling. In P. B. Pedersen, J. G. Draguns, W. J. Lonner, & J. E. Trimble (Eds.), *Counseling across cultures* (4th ed., pp. 73–107). Thousand Oaks, CA: Sage.

Henderson, H. (1995). *Paradigms in progress: Life beyond economics.* San Francisco: Berrett-Koehler.

Henderson, H. (1996). *Building a win-win world.* San Francisco: Berrett-Koehler.

Ivey, A. E., Ivey, M. B., & Simek-Morgan, L. (1993). *Counseling and psychotherapy: A multicultural perspective* (3rd ed.). Boston: Allyn & Bacon.

Jepsen, D. (1995, June). *Career as story: A narrative approach to career counseling.* Paper presented at National Career Development Association Conference, San Francisco.

Johnson, P. C., & Cooperrider, D. L. (1991). Finding a path with heart: Global social change organizations and their challenge for the field of organizational development. *Research in Organizational Change and Development, 5,* 223–284.

Jordan, J. V., Kaplan, A. G., Miller, J. B., Stiver, I. P., & Surrey, J. L. (1991). *Women's growth in connection: Writings from the Stone Center.* New York: Guilford Press.

Kanter, R. M. (1977). *Work and family in the United States: A critical review and agenda for research and policy.* New York: Russell Sage Foundation.

Leung, L. A. (1995). Career development and counseling: A multicultural perspective. In J. G. Ponterotto, J. M. Casas, L. Suzuki, & C. Alexander (Eds.), *Handbook of multicultural counseling* (pp. 549–566). Thousand Oaks, CA: Sage.

Lipman-Blumen, J. (1996). *The connective edge: Leading in an interdependent world.* San Francisco: Jossey-Bass.

Mitchell, K., Levin, A. S., & Krumboltz, J. D. (1999). Planned happenstance: Constructing unexpected career opportunities. *Journal of Counseling and Development, 77,* 115–124.

Moreno, J. (1996, February). *On entering the world of "the other."* Paper presented at Diversity Dialogues, BORN FREE Center, University of Minnesota, Minneapolis.

Parsons, F. (1909). *Choosing a vocation.* Boston: Houghton Mifflin.

Peavy, R. V. (1998). *SocioDynamic counselling.* A constructivist perspective. Victoria, BC: Trafford Publishing.

Plant, P. (1995, August 7–10). *Internationalisation: Economy & Ecology.* Paper presented at the Sixteenth International Congress of the International Association of Educational-Vocational Guidance, Stockholm, Sweden.

Rifkin, J. (1995). *The end of work: Technology, jobs, and your future.* New York: Putnam.

Rosener, J. B. (1990). Ways women lead. *Harvard Business Review, 68*(6), 119–125.

Schlossberg, N. K. (1994). *Overwhelmed: Coping with life's ups and downs.* San Francisco: New Lexington Press.

Schlossberg, N. K., & Robinson, S. P. (1996). *Going to plan B: How you can cope, regroup, and start your life on a new path.* New York: Simon & Schuster.

Simonsen, P. (1997). *Promoting a career development culture in your organization: Using career development as a change agent.* Palo Alto, CA: Davies-Black.

Snyder, D. P. (1996, March/April). The revolution in the workplace: What's happening to our jobs? *The Futurist,* pp. 10–13.

Stark, A. (1995, August 7). *Women in a postindustrial society.* Paper presented at the Sixteenth International Congress of the International Association for Educational-Vocational Guidance, Stockholm, Sweden.

Subich, L. M. (1995). How personal is career counseling? *Career Development Quarterly, 42*(2), 129–131.

Sue, D. W. (1995). Multicultural organizational development: Implications for the counseling profession. In J. G. Ponterotto, J. M. Casas, L. Suzuki, & C. Alexander (Eds.), *Handbook of multicultural counseling* (pp. 474–492). Thousand Oaks, CA: Sage.

Super, D. E. (1951). Vocational adjustment: Implementing a self-concept. *Occupations, 30,* 88–92.

Super, D. E. (1980). A life-span, life-space approach to career development. *Journal of Vocational Behavior, 16*(3), 282–298.

Super, D. E., & Sverko, B. (Eds.). (1995). *Life roles, values, and careers.* San Francisco: Jossey-Bass.

part TWO

Implications for Career Planning

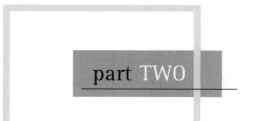

5

Informed Opportunism

CAREER AND LIFE PLANNING FOR THE NEW MILLENNIUM

Judith A. Waterman

While the fundamentals of work and life planning endure, the context in which we apply those principles has shifted—we live in an accelerated society with rapid, sometimes radical changes. What primary challenge does that accelerated world pose for individuals and the career counselors who serve them? Simply this: The individual must learn to cope with the idea that "the only stability possible is stability in motion" (Gardner, 1964). Career counselors must help clients work with the fact of change as the only true constant—and help them see the patterns in seeming chaos. Many of the conventional tools of the trade, including batteries of assessment and discussion techniques, still play a crucial role in helping clients meet their career and personal life challenges. What's different is the degree of flexibility required for both counselors and clients. To navigate this terrain, we must act as *informed opportunists*[1,2] combining accurate information with a flexible, opportunistic approach to our careers. We need to know opportunity when we see it and how to make it happen.

The conventional wisdom that opportunity knocks only once is not operative in this new world of work; it may knock many times and we have to be ready to recognize it.

Traditionally, career professionals have dealt primarily with people in work crisis, or with people wanting to plan for some change like retirement. Informed opportunism works well for these purposes, but it excels in enabling smoother travel in the topography of today's unexpected career challenges and uncertainties. These days, with relatively few exceptions, careers are not secure. And seldom do they follow well-defined paths. Informed opportunism helps us anticipate and prepare appropriate responses to impending change. The concept has a distinguished history.

Bill Hewlett, one of the founders of Hewlett-Packard (HP), wrote about it in 1983, in a book called *Inventions of Opportunity: Matching Technology with Market Needs*. HP was built on a series of surprises instead of solid, long-term product plans. The capacity to quickly turn technological surprise into a new product that, in turn, generated a market need was one of HP's most potent strategies. It's not a result of careful planning, but the outcome of informed opportunism. In a fast-changing, unpredictable world, the best plans are sets of rich information on one's own business and its markets—combined with the ability to move quickly to take advantage of opportunity. This holds true for individuals as well as companies. In fast-changing times, we need good information about ourselves, job markets, and possible opportunities as well as a mind-set that enables us to move swiftly. In the new millennium, career counselors will need to guide clients through relentless change, a flood of information, and swirling opportunity.

The steps to career planning based on the concept of informed opportunism are relatively straightforward:

- Understanding career realities
- Self-assessment
- Synthesizing the data and setting priorities
- Acting—then keeping the process moving

To see how these notions fit the informed opportunism model, let's look at the dilemmas faced by several people. To protect privacy, their names (and details not critical to their stories) have been changed.

- Like many other 27-year-olds, Sheila Masterson was a restless soul. A product manager at a small company based in northern California, she earned a decent salary, yet felt a vague sense of unease about her work. She attributed most of it to her upbringing and prior work experience. As with many of her latchkey peers, Sheila had been accustomed to letting herself in when she came home from school, fixing herself a snack, and starting her homework before either parent returned from work. During the 1980s and 1990s, she also watched many relatives lose their long-held corporate jobs. In fact, Sheila lost her first job after college when her company merged with another. Her second job gave her a taste of fast-paced life at a start-up company, where she learned much even as the firm withered and died. A third job gave her opportunities to stretch her potential and increase her skills. But when the product manager position came along at another company, offering a bit more money and better stock options, Sheila instantly hopped. Still, in a matter of months, restless feelings arose once again. She knew something was missing, but what?

- Marge Franklin, a 46-year-old human resources manager, had worked for most of her career at a single large corporation. With her two children grown and gone, Marge and her husband looked forward to retirement. Another 8 to 10 years at their respective firms would put the Franklins in a very comfortable position, with pensions and lifetime health insurance coverage. However, as Marge's company began to downsize, talk of a plan to outsource all human resources services ran rampant. A gnawing fear ran through Marge. After all, she'd spent her working life specializing only in human resources, and within one particular company. Nearly a decade had gone by since her company had last asked her to attend a class or receive training; focused on staying lean, the firm left it to employees to brush up their job skills. Despite her years of experience, Marge felt like a has-been. Would it be all downhill from here?

- Bob Elliott had lived in the San Diego area all his life. After high school, he attended San Diego State University, earned a degree in marine engineering, and took a job with a local industrial firm. Bob and his wife, Debbie, a schoolteacher, had three children and owned a home in southern California. On most weekends the family could be found at the beach, surfing, snorkeling, and playing volleyball with relatives and friends.

Bob's roots in the area ran deep. However, the company at which he worked as a midlevel manager had been taken over by another firm. The culture and political climate of the combined operations changed radically. Accustomed to orderly and logical work processes, Bob viewed the new senior managers as a freewheeling lot who often acted without much thought or study. He felt lost in this environment. Through a friend, he heard that a Denver firm was looking for someone with his background. Bob applied and, to his surprise, was offered a job with greater responsibility and pay. In many ways it was a wish granted, but with it came a host of considerations. Debbie had an excellent teaching position and was treated like a school treasure. With friends and relatives nearby, childcare had never been a problem. And Denver was a long way from, and a mile higher than, southern California's beaches. Should he make that climb?

UNDERSTANDING CAREER REALITIES

The starting point for Marge, Sheila, and Bob, and for most of us, is to examine the dynamics of the new millennial workplace. To remain employable and to lead satisfying lives, each of us must take responsibility for seeking experiences and job assignments that keep our skills up-to-date, our enthusiasm peaked, our contacts current, our attitudes realistic but optimistic, and our lives in harmony.

The old deal, where employer and employees pretended a career was pretty much for life, is dead. Even the corporations that once made explicit long-term employment promises—such as AT&T, IBM, Hewlett-Packard, and Motorola, to name just a few—cannot keep that vow. Baby boomers might be the only generation that mourns the passing of job stability. A good portion of today's workforce, in fact, has never experienced the world of "stable" careers. Look at Sheila Masterson, well into her fourth job before the age of 30, feeling antsy to move on and not feeling that this is at all unusual. Today, the majority of us assume that we'll have multiple jobs and even multiple careers. We tend to accept the notion that responsibility for career development and work-life balance rests solely with us as individuals. But a lot of us don't understand how to cope with that charge.

Numerous employee surveys suggest that one of the things workers most want from employers is help with career issues, with answers to the following questions:

- Am I in the right job?
- Are my skills of real value to the organization?
- Where is the company going and how can I remain valuable?
- What other positions might fit my needs and skills well?

Had Marge Franklin's firm invested in this arena and the training it implies, she would have felt much more in control of her destiny during downsizing.

The more savvy employers realize that career self-reliance doesn't mean leaving employees completely on their own. Some organizations have instituted various types of career assistance programs, including in-house or external training programs, college reimbursement programs, mentoring systems, and career centers, some of which are run internally and others by independent organizations. One difficulty for a firm with multiple offices is extending services across locations. A solution seems to be the "virtual" career center—a computer-based system with programs in self-assessment, career planning, job postings, and other organizational information.

An example is CareerSteps,[3] a career assessment and development software product that is distributed to individuals over the web. Both Hewlett-Packard and VISA International, the world's leading consumer payment system, use this product. They take pride in efforts to be responsible partners with their employees, instead of parents. VISA[4] feels that this program sends a clear signal to employees that it wants them to stay with the company and to grow, progress, and succeed.

Here we see a true partnership emerging between the company and the individual, one that obviously benefits both. Career professionals and individuals need to remain aware of such in-house initiatives. They provide exciting evidence that career and life planning have finally become a hard business issue.

Career self-reliance, or career resilience as it is sometimes called, does not mean free agency. In the best of worlds, a strong bond between individuals and an organization can be powerful. If lost, the employer suffers excessive turnover, which can be a real cost disadvantage. One study (Saratoga Institute, 1998) finds that the cost of losing and replacing a salaried employee is 50 percent higher than the cost of keeping that individual on board.

The bond is beneficial for employees, too. Few really want to move continuously, and if a company gives a good reason for loyalty, most prefer to stay. Shifting jobs within a corporation could be a better step toward career-life satisfaction than jumping to a different ship. This, of course, assumes that the company itself is demonstrating loyalty—in the form of integrity, fairness, a mission that goes beyond just making a buck for the shareholders, and the willingness to invest in career help.

Another upheaval in the millennial job market is a sharp rise in entrepreneurial efforts. There has been tremendous growth in individual and small businesses. Today, more people are working for themselves—as contractors, consultants, or founders of new enterprises. While self-employment has always been around, flattening of corporate structures, outsourcing of services, and phenomenal productivity increases in the economy opened the door for more entrepreneurs. Some folks are born to self-employment while others are frightfully ill-suited to such a career option. Unfortunately, some jump on the bandwagon primarily because it is the popular thing to do.

Trends are a powerful influence on career choice, perhaps too powerful. During the financially expansive 1980s, venture capital, investment banking, law, and management consulting promised six-figure salaries and a seemingly limitless future. In the 1990s, the Internet explosion and the rise of "dot-com" businesses unleashed more entrepreneurial spirit than all the combined gold rushes in history.

We all need to understand such trends and to have some knowledge of today's job market and career realities. This is a great place to start the informed part of informed opportunism. But knowing what's going on out there, important as it is, isn't enough to make well-informed career decisions. Too many of us rely solely on our impression of what's hot and end up in jobs that feel cold.

Career strategist Lili Pratt[5] has worked with executives in transition as well as with MBA graduates looking into new careers or making that initial choice. She says that these people often focus on trends and market information—and forget about who they are as individuals. They choose the "hot" careers exalted by their peers and the current market, those with high visibility and steep learning curves. However, in the first 18 months of their new jobs, Pratt states, "virtually everyone goes through a metamorphosis. The reality bears little resemblance to what they anticipated, and many are disappointed." These individuals have it partly right: They did get informed, but only on the market. They also need information about themselves.

Of course, understanding career realities is not exclusively a millennial issue. Bob Elliott's decision about Denver could have been just as tough at any time in the last half-century. Many of today's career and life dilemmas are identical to those of the past. Questions of "Where do I live?" and "What do I do?" and "How will I pay the bills?" are fundamental to the human condition. So is the inner urge to learn, grow, and experience different environments, which can stimulate us to alter our path and to change careers of our own volition. At most points in life's passage, problems and obstacles are likely to appear.

Many of these factors are subtle. Others are as blunt as a pink slip. But I would argue that the fast pace of change can be made less difficult and traumatic through informed opportunism. The next step is to become well-informed about yourself.

SELF-ASSESSMENT

Accurate, unbiased self-knowledge is the cornerstone of the process of informed opportunism. Knowing who we are and what makes us tick is at the base of effective work and life planning.

We are different people at age 40 than we were at 20. There are differences in our attitudes when single, married, divorced, and remarried. Having children can change our perspectives in a massive way. Although some of us can hold rock-solid values through a lifetime, others see values shattered by experience and adopt new ideals. As we experience new life phases, roles, and conditions, our needs and priorities may change. Thus, self-assessment and continuing reassessment are critical to career and life planning.

Using Tests in Assessments

While there are numerous ways to gather assessment information, many career professionals use testing inventories[6] as tools for exploring career and life options. I believe they're invaluable—not necessarily as predictors of what we should or shouldn't do, but for the thoughts and discussions they generate. Tests and assessments often bring up important personal or professional issues that might not otherwise surface. And they frequently generate or verify ideas about work issues or possible paths of action.

Most people have taken a personality or interest test of some sort. Sometimes they have had a bad experience in the process, and this has given testing a bad rap. The problem is complex. Some tests, the ones we often see in pop magazines, are too simplistic. Others, such as the popular *Myers-Briggs Type Indicator®* (MBTI®) instrument (see Myers, McCaulley, Quenk, & Hammer, 1998), though validated via mountains of research, measure only one aspect of the person (in this case, personality type); hence they provide information that taken by itself is limited. Those who interpret the test instruments may not have a deep understanding of tests, their limitations, their intent, their norms, and their strengths, and thus can easily misread the results. For instance, the venerable granddaddy of interest tests, The *Strong Interest Inventory®* instrument (see Harmon, Hanson, Borgen, & Hammer, 1994), has, on the surface of things, "told" more than a few of my clients that their interests resemble those of a military officer or an enlisted person. A high score on these scales does not necessarily mean one should sign up for boot camp, but it does indicate an interest in working in a structured and organized environment. Thus, a test is only as dependable as the person interpreting it.

Obviously, test results are not always correct. They can vary because clients misinterpret or misread several questions, find certain wordings offensive, answer questions based on the way they would like to be rather than the way they are, or take them at a time when they are just "not themselves." Career counselors as well as clients should always question the validity of any one instrument, and should typically administer or take multiple tests. That way they can regularly compare the results of one test against those of others. Do they confirm one another? Do they correlate with the person's life experiences and personal opinions? Or do they bring up discrepancies for further investigation? Remember that, for many career tests, there is no such thing as perfectly "normal," or one clear-cut answer. As in physical measurements of, say, cholesterol levels, assessments have ranges that suggest one thing or another. It's up to the counselor and the client to figure out whether those ranges demand action or feel healthy.

A skilled counselor questions results and combines scores to look for patterns. This process helped Sandra Grey confirm a dream. In her mid-30s, an active volunteer, wife of a doctor and mother of two teenage boys, she attended a series of career and life planning sessions as part of a small group. Her explicit purpose was to decide whether she should attend law school. Sandra's *Strong Interest Inventory*® results suggested that she might not be suited to law school. Her scores revealed just an average interest in the subject of law and politics, but very high interests in social service and public speaking. When her interests were compared with those of practicing lawyers, she showed only midrange similarity. However, when compared with social workers, guidance counselors, speech pathologists, and elected public officials, her scores were very similar.

Ironically, as the counseling sessions progressed, the group discussions only intensified Sandra's desire to go to law school. The profession met an image she'd come to hold dear and reinforced her belief that a law degree would enable her to contribute to the social good she so valued. Guided by her interest inventory results, she specialized in a side of law that suited her. Today Sandra Grey is a successful county public defender.

Most career counselors agree that examining interests is an integral part of self-assessment. While many of our interests change, *core interests* generally remain stable. Thus, it's important to pay attention to them when deliberating career and life alternatives. Consider James Darwell, the director of finance at a well-known publishing house. He had begun his college education in mathematics, found that field too abstract, changed his major to American literature, and, finally, graduated with a business degree. He worked as an editor before becoming a CPA. Neither job was completely satisfying. James remembers continually looking for some way to integrate his numerical, business, and literature interests and recalls turning down a number of job offers because they lacked the composite integration he wanted. When an accounting position at a publishing firm opened up, however, he aggressively went after and got the job. While time has added new interests to his portfolio, those basic themes—math, literature, and business—have remained the same. He's just combined the trio in different ways. James Darwell is a great example of informed opportunism—taking advantage of opportunities that fulfill his interests and motivations and saying no to those that don't.

Like interests, aptitudes are a fundamental of self-assessment and many can be defined through testing. They are the basis for understanding where we function most comfortably, frequently giving us a competitive advantage. Aptitudes include such things as muscle coordination and the abilities to quickly generate many ideas, see differences in small detail, and visualize three-dimensionally. Aptitudes remain with us throughout our lives—to be called on, developed, and used at will. While an experienced counselor can often assess a mature client's aptitudes quite easily, younger people and adults with limited exposure may be a real challenge. A referral to specialists in aptitude testing may be in order. One such organization, the Johnson O'Connor Research Foundation,[7] gives a battery of tests that do an exceptional job in assessing a wide range of innate aptitudes.

David Ransom,[8] director of Johnson O'Connor in San Francisco, relates one of his most interesting experiences—testing identical triplets. Now in their mid-30s, the triplets were only 19 at the time he tested them. All three scored only in the fifth percentile on their visual clerical efficiency, a test on how easily a person processes printed material. In fact, the boys had scores that were nearly identical across the board. A decade and a half later, one of the triplets had taken a job as an administrator in an insurance company. "It was just torture for him," says Ransom. The man had obviously forgotten his Johnson O'Connor results. "There can be other reasons for dissatisfaction," says Ransom, "but undue stress for many people might simply be the lack of particular aptitudes that are needed for the work they are trying to do."

Interests also temper aptitudes. While using natural aptitudes gives us a chance to excel, it is far from the only criterion in a career choice. There are many people who can do something well but do not really want to make it their work. One example Ransom cites is a person who has extraordinary visual efficiency with paperwork, but who is also very good at producing a flow of ideas. Despite the paperwork aptitude, this individual might have no interest in doing clerical work. His or her main interest, instead, might be producing ideas. This person might find an outlet in investment banking or some kind of market research—jobs that need some paperwork efficiency, such as scanning data quickly and accurately, but that focus on finding ideas in the data taken in. So, although a test might characterize paperwork as a strong aptitude, an individual might align with another aptitude that more closely fits his or her interest. In the end, interests usually win out over aptitudes.

The *Fundamental Interpersonal Relations Orientation–Behavior*™ (FIRO-B™) instrument is a useful test that focuses on interpersonal behavior (Waterman & Rogers, 1996). Consider Byron Steele, who had chosen his present job three years ago after taking the Johnson O'Connor aptitude tests. At first he was happy, but soon, no matter how hard he tried to make the job work, he grew less content. He visited a career counselor, who combined his Johnson O'Connor results with tests and techniques that explored his interests, values, and personality. Byron's FIRO-B scores revealed a big discrepancy between the persona he showed others and his inner needs. He scored in the high range for *expressed inclusion,* indicating that outwardly he was friendly, gregarious, and social. However, his fairly low *wanted inclusion* score suggested that on the inside he was a rather private person. To perform well and to feel his best, Byron needed a fair amount of time to work and think through ideas on his own, yet he also needed to use his considerable people skills. Unfortunately, his friendly manner caused people at his office to frequently stop and chat, and even offer to collaborate on work that Byron preferred to do independently. He felt guilty not responding to their sociable and cooperative gestures, so the vicious cycle, and his discontent, continued.

Byron tried to alter his behavior, but impressions are hard to change. His coworkers, his boss, and his company continually misinterpreted his social needs. Byron grew more and more frustrated. Finally, he switched to a new firm and moved from product marketing to market research, which better suited his interaction style, and where he is much happier. He changed the external circumstances and not himself, which is a path that's usually much easier to follow.

Other tests and other attributes often provide important clues to career and life satisfaction. An administrative assistant at a shipping firm, Maria Davis sensed that she would enjoy being a manager, although none of her friends or family had ever been in management. Her company suggested that Maria consider its management training program, but she hesitated. She wanted to be certain that management was an appropriate choice for her. The *California Psychological Inventory*™ (CPI™) instrument (see McAllister, 1996) proved especially helpful. Maria's "dominance" score was a 76—very high. It revealed that she was assertive, forceful, and self-confident, typically a leader who liked to get things done. Other high scores on this test showed that she had a strong drive for achievement and was enterprising, dependable, and outgoing. Such characteristics did not surprise Maria; what amazed her was how much higher her scores were than those of most people. Personality attributes as strong as Maria's are double-edged swords; they can be a great asset or a tremendous weakness. The intensity of her scores told Maria that she needed to use these powerful characteristics. And yet, their strength warned her that in a management role, she could easily become too overbearing and could quickly lose the support of subordinates. She immediately entered her company's management training program, reenrolled at a local college, and finished her degree in economics. Three years, a degree, a marriage, and a baby later, she is the manager of the same department where she'd served as an administrative assistant. Although it requires her mindfulness, she usually tempers her "bossy" traits and is generally viewed as an excellent manager.

Additional Tools for Assessment

Other tools besides tests are also helpful in the quest for self-knowledge. These include biographical interviews, card sorts, video interviews, motivated pattern exercises, looking for patterns in favorite experiences, and something I call "needs, wants, and wishes."

Naturally, with the passage of time, we change and grow. Yet the most dependable place to look for what will likely motivate us in the future is in our past. Just talking with an individual can uncover clues. This technique is nothing more than a simple interview concerning a person's past. Most of the time I start with such an interview before even considering other evaluation approaches. In fact, the interview usually helps me decide what self-assessment techniques I want to use—or whether my client can already clearly articulate who she or he is.

A good biographical interview can bring to the surface the qualities most central to motivation and satisfaction.

- What did the client take pleasure in or not enjoy learning about, participating in, and doing in school?
- What did the client like and dislike about paid and nonpaid jobs, avocations, and other activities?

These experiences not only show patterns of motivation that existed in the past, but also reveal clues to what might be fulfilling in the future.

A corollary technique that can lead to great insight and that individuals find inherently intriguing is called "favorite experiences." I have clients review their memories, either verbally or in writing, and pick a handful of favorites from different times in their lives. The idea is then to probe those favorites to see what they have in common and what they reveal about motivations. The concept underlying the technique is that past is prologue. This technique is based in part on Bernard Haldane's (1988) idea that the clues to personal excellence can be found in our achievements. It is grounded in favorite life accomplishments and produces profiles that ring true to our backgrounds.

One client chose two memories from his junior high school years: finishing second place in a tough ski race and getting an *A* in his first algebra course. What did these seemingly disparate events have in common? It turned out that he had unusually high needs for accomplishment and recognition, needs that hadn't really been fulfilled in his life. What made the two events stand out was that both achievements and their proximity in time made him feel like he was "somebody" in the eyes of others. This helps explain why this man's first job didn't fit. He was an assistant physicist in a research lab, a position that fit his interest and aptitudes in math and science perfectly. But he was frustrated. What he realized after the "favorite experience" exercise is that, immersed in a research lab where he was surrounded by Ph.D.'s, he had no chance to stand out. And for this person, the need to be in situations where he could distinguish himself was strong.

One of the main things to look for when people describe their favorite experiences is body language. When people are talking about an experience they've loved, their whole countenance lights up. Conversely, they may be talking about something they "should have loved"—or something that other people think is important—but the body droops and the face loses its animation, even if they say all the right things about those activities. Sometimes clients aren't convinced of the power of their body language, let alone the predictive power of past experiences. In many instances, I videotape interviews about these favorite times and then review the tapes carefully. What I'm looking for is not what I may have missed or the snippets that add up to patterns, but those precious moments when the person is relating a story with real animation and enthusiasm. I edit these gems into a short tape and show it to the client. It's just another way of conveying self-assessment information, but in an extremely compelling and very personal way.

Career professionals sometimes use techniques similar to the "favorite experiences" one to look for *motivated skills*—skills that enliven us and bring satisfaction. When we use them, time flies. We get energy from their use. We sometimes find excuses to use these skills, even when reason (or the boss) tells us that there are other things we should be doing at that moment. However, our *marketable skills*—skills that we can do well enough, that are needed in the market, and that we get paid for using—may be different from our motivated skills. Marketable skills can rescue us, sustain us, give us work, even serve as stepping-stones to get to positions where we can use more of our motivated skills. The ability to articulate our marketable skills, in addition to our motivated skills, serves a meaningful purpose.

To gain a solid and realistic sense of our marketable skills, we can employ a simple but effective exercise. We just list them—simply write down the variety of things we can get paid for doing. Ask clients to think about all their previous jobs, both paid and volunteer (as well as other life experiences like keeping the family books or organizing the family vacations) and then write down everything they did in those positions, no matter how significant or trivial the task. This marketable skills list can include aptitudes, personality traits, talents, abilities, and attitudes that could be of use to an employer.

I encourage clients to consider both great and not-so-great work experiences. Even a bad experience can be a good way to learn about ourselves, and may point toward a positive new direction. In fact, trying various jobs with the conscious intent of learning from our successes and mistakes is an example of what behaviorist Karl Weick (1979) calls "retrospective sense making." He urges that it is our most powerful tool for guiding the future.

Robin Holt[9] argues the same point for people who have no idea what they want to do. She tells them just to do *something* that has an appealing element to it. "Then keep careful notes about what you've liked and not liked, where you've been successful and not successful, and what skills you enjoyed or didn't enjoy using. Use the experience as a learning process to build on—and to work toward getting it right."

Another way to mine critical self-assessment information is through a gamelike technique. Card sorts, for many clients, are a nice change of pace from tests, long interviews, and paper-and-pencil exercises. In fact, during the development of CareerSteps, the developer, MindSteps, found that even on a computer screen, people liked arranging cards into piles better than other organizational systems.

A typical card sort involves a deck of cards with different skills described on each. In this exercise, we group the skills according to how well we can perform them, and how much we would like to employ them. The aim is to get us thinking about which skills motivate us, which ones are marketable, which aren't, and which ones we definitely do not wish to market.

Card sorts also can be used to help us understand which interests, values, environments, and the like particularly motivate us. (See chapter 6 for more on values card sorts.) Take the case of Joe Adams, who came from a family of steelworkers. Unlike his two brothers, he'd gone to college, graduated with honors, and received his MBA from a well-regarded business school. He spent some time working at the White House and then joined a prestigious management consulting firm. Joe's self-expectations were on track. And yet, after two years of consulting, he felt empty.

Joe visited a career counselor. Through discussions and particularly a values card sort, he found a nugget of insight. He identified more with labor than with management, even though he saw himself in a professional role. Joe's answer to the dilemma was to connect with labor union officials. Eventually, he left the large firm and established his own consulting practice, concentrating on labor issues and often serving as an arbitrator, where his feel for both union and management perspectives was uniquely valuable and satisfying.

Just as the past provides clues to self-satisfaction, so do thoughts about the future. Considering our needs, wants, and wishes frequently brings personal issues to light that other techniques miss. I ask clients to consider questions like the following:

- What would you do if you knew you had only five years left to live? or only one year?
- What feels most important in your life right now? What do you feel is missing?
- What things are you proudest of?

- What would you like to change?
- What do you feel you really need in the way of money, support, time, and resources to make your life work the way you would like?

Such questions evoke responses that bring out what a person thinks is necessary or desirous to fulfill her or his life.

For instance, a client, Frank Conover, found deliberating his needs, wants, and wishes to be the most influential part of his job choice. Because of personality and value differences with his partner, Frank had severed his partnership in a two-person educational Internet business. He knew he was in the right field because he fervently wanted to improve education for children, and he believed the web was the way to do it. Frank decided that the factors determining which companies he would apply to were their size (larger than ten people, but still what he called a small company) and their providing web-based technology solutions in the field of education.

For some people, a singular need, want, or wish stands out far above the rest in making career and life decisions. It could be the types of people they work with or a short commute; or perhaps it's being in a certain city or rural setting. Karen Karsten, for example, worked with a career counselor who tested her interests, values, and motivated skills and helped her confirm the career areas for which she seemed well suited. However, it was the exploration of her personal needs, wants, and wishes that took the doubt out of which job she would choose. Karen was pregnant with her second child and unless her job included flexible work hours and the ability to work from home part of the time, she was not interested—no matter how well it otherwise suited her interests, skills, values, and personality.

There is, to be sure, no one best test or method of career counseling. Some counselors use standardized tests; others don't. Counselors also have different views on how much advice to offer clients. Some take a completely hands-off approach. Others believe they owe their clients quite a bit of nudging. My own style is a bit of a mix. While it's not my place to tell a client what to do, I think I contribute by holding up a mirror and saying, for example, "How does that fit with your motivated skills?" If I have a strong opinion, I say so, but I keep the roles clear. I'm the advisor; the client is the decision maker.

SYNTHESIZING THE DATA AND SETTING PRIORITIES

At this point, we have a pretty good general idea of what's going on in the job market and a great deal of objective information on who we are as individuals. And, of course, we know a lot about our current job and life outside work. In this stage of informed opportunism, our aim is to examine how well our work and our life outside work fit with who we are. The idea is to pick the big issues. What doesn't fit so well? How can we change that?

The initial challenge in this part of the process is to whittle down the mound of information we've gathered about ourselves and to mold the data into something that's workable and realistic. I work with my clients to examine all the assessment information and draft a list of characteristics (perhaps 20 or 30 items) that most define their personal satisfaction. The list may include such diverse items as strong personality characteristics that need accommodating, situations that are most stimulating or gratifying, the amount of money needed for the lifestyle they desire, and skills they take delight in using. Then I ask my clients to study their lists. We discuss the items and compare their importance. When they have synthesized these data and selected 8 to 12 items that most influence their personal satisfaction, the draft has evolved into what I call a "personal satisfaction scale." This is a tool for measurement: We can gauge our probable satisfaction with any situation by comparing the characteristics on our personal satisfaction scale with a situation's likelihood of accommodating them.

This personal satisfaction scale specifies the various main qualities that bring enjoyment to work and life for each of us. One person's ultimate items might include such things as financial security, feeling like an expert, and using analytical skills to improve results. Another's might include being a member of the team that makes the important decisions, affiliating with respected organizations, and having the chance to develop a relationship with a potential marriage partner.

The personal satisfaction scale is closely related to the ideas of passion and purpose. Some career professionals believe finding passion and uncovering purpose are the central issues for career guidance. Fredrick Hudson of the Fielding Institute asks, "What is our central developmental task at this point in our lives?" Hudson implies that this task keeps changing with time. Career counselor Howard Figler[10] agrees with the importance of purpose. "The issue of purpose has always been at the forefront of my mind; people being able to embrace purpose and shape it and live it and make it the center of their career," he explains.

The personal satisfaction scale represents passion or purpose but it articulates qualities with additional detail. This individualized metric becomes the basis for examining differences between where or who we are and where or who we'd like to be. It can be used to gauge potential satisfaction as possibilities present themselves or as a guide to forge fulfilling options. Clients tell me that when life seems a little sour, unless the cause is personal relationships or poor health, using their personal satisfaction scale can help them decide what's wrong and can suggest ways to restore satisfaction.

When the personal satisfaction scale doesn't mesh with reality, the question becomes, "What doesn't measure up?" The most obvious analysis compares our current job or one we're considering with our personal satisfaction scale. We reflect on which qualities are well matched, which are unfilled, and what about the position might be altered to make it more pleasing. Our personal satisfaction scale can address whether a job choice suits us well or whether one position is better than another.

The process of thinking about what does and doesn't measure up may focus on a single issue or it may generate a list of questions, ideas, and possible opportunities.

The list might include such things as

- Job choice
- The imbalance between work and the rest our of lives
- The support of others for our plans
- Skills or information we need to acquire in order to remain career resilient
- Creating an opportunity that fits
- Personal qualities we need to better our chances of improving performance or achieving desires

Of course, focusing on too many of these issues at one time only dilutes our endeavors. It is better to choose a few major priorities to concentrate on for the next week, the next month, and the next year. And by "few," I mean one, two, or three—not dozens.

When Pamela Andrews, an unhappy executive recruiter, compared her work to her personal satisfaction scale, she realized that, despite disliking her job, she actually liked her profession. Her company no longer stood for the quality work that she relished. "Quantity driven, not quality driven" is how she described her employer. She understood at some level the need for quantity, but producing quality had always been a core value for her. Her personal satisfaction scale let her see that her employer didn't measure up. She decided to find a different place to work.

Through her self-assessment, Pamela had a good idea about the size of company in which she would most likely flourish. She knew what kind of clientele she wanted to serve. And two of her most significant motivational delineators needed fulfillment in her new work environment: her value of quality and her style of operation. Informed as well about the market and her specialty, Pamela was ready to look for or create an opportunity. She joined a small recruiting firm with a quality reputation that specialized in finding senior-level executives who could lead turnarounds at troubled companies.

The personal satisfaction scale can also point toward an entirely new focus. Remember Sheila Masterson, the young woman we met early in this chapter who changed jobs frequently? In her fourth full-time job at a relatively tender age, Sheila clearly adapted to change with an attitude befitting the new millennium. And yet, to her, the business world was no more than a means to fill up the hours of a day, earn spending money, and keep her parents from worrying about her. Until now, work simply didn't inspire much passion.

Sheila found that what really sparked an interest was not business but historical things that had endured for centuries. This rang a "favorite experience" bell. In school, she'd taken several archaeology classes, which provoked her deep interest. She loved watching television documentaries about ancient Egypt, Middle Eastern civilizations that had vanished, and excavations of Incan monuments. She'd gone into business mainly because it seemed like the thing to do.

A little more research provided Sheila with the information she needed, at least in terms of what personally interested her. She also started researching the job market in the area of adventure travel and nonprofit organizations that coordinate volunteers who help out on excavations and other research projects. When a northern California university advertised for a business manager to run its archaeological volunteer program, Sheila was quick to match information with opportunity. She has now held that job for three years, and, as of this writing, has no interest in moving to yet another job anytime soon.

When careers are chosen for inappropriate reasons, or when internal or external factors change sufficiently, dissatisfaction typically ensues. The personal satisfaction scale would indicate that current work and life arrangements don't measure up on one or several critical dimensions. This describes Bob Elliott, who had gotten the offer to move to Denver but was disheartened. Taking the job in Denver, he sensed, could cause far more serious problems than it would solve. He considered the money, prestige, and perks of the Denver job. He thought about his discomfort with the new management of his current company. And then he saw why he couldn't accept the offer. Bob's individual and family roots were too deep in the San Diego soil. Relocating the children would be difficult for them. His wife would also need to find another job, one she might not like as well. They'd all miss the beach, the close proximity to extended family and old friends, and much more. His personal satisfaction scale helped him see his true priorities.

That still left Bob with a problem. There simply weren't many jobs for marine engineers who were middle managers. But he and his career advisor didn't focus on ferreting out other potential careers. Instead, they assessed which motivated but unused skills Bob might additionally employ. Their list included making and maintaining contacts, leading teams, and taking responsibility. They also examined why the more freewheeling environment of the new management made him so uncomfortable and explored how he might better deal with it.

By personality and profession, Bob liked order. The new managers had this industrial firm going off in several different directions, looking for new business and areas in which to invest. Bob and his counselor considered a way to bridge the gap. Bob would ask his new management if he could run an autonomous team that seeks out new business. That way he and his company might have the best of both worlds: a group that could function with the orderly and methodical approach that fit Bob's needs yet focused on something that met the new leaders' vision.

The company management appreciated Bob's experience, including his wealth of contacts in the southern California region. He might be the perfect individual to start a spin-off business. His supervisors appreciated how he had taken charge of his own career development. Despite a few months of uncertainty, Bob was back on track at work. He stayed in San Diego with his company. By focusing on the information that was truly important, he created a win-win situation for himself and his company.

In this chapter we've concentrated on the importance of finding key issues or gaps and brought focus to the task of getting one's life in better harmony. The personal satisfaction scale helps point us in the right direction. This gives us the information we need to choose our priorities and focus in the months or years to come. What's next?

ACTING—THEN KEEPING THE PROCESS MOVING

By now we ought to be well on the way to true resilience. With all the information we've gathered and winnowed, we can quickly tell the difference between swamps disguised as opportunity and wellsprings of success.

Development Plans

The next step is to construct a proactive plan for development. We may only need a development plan geared to growth where we now work or we may need a strategy that more broadly addresses our total work and life plan. Many companies require development plans that are okay to use as a format. However, old-style development plans are often tailored to company needs and seldom accommodate an individual's desire for growth and learning. If we're equipped with good self-information, however, we can use development plans as vehicles for matching individual needs with those of an organization.

From a company's perspective, such a tailored plan should bring the process alive and take it as far from routine bureaucratic needs as possible. From the boss's point of view, the development plan should make discussions with an employee far more productive. And from an employee's point of view, the plan is a way of saying, "I understand company needs; here's what I want to do next, and this is how I think it fits with organizational needs." It's not a document of demands, but a platform for productive discussion. Career planning services such as those offered by Sun Microsystems and the CareerSteps software make development planning the last stage in the process.

Résumés

Another part of taking action includes polishing up the résumé. It sounds a bit odd in conjunction with the notion of development planning, but the idea of writing and revising a résumé applies whether we want to stay with our job and company or leave. Inside an organization, a résumé can be the basic document for selling ourselves to a team we'd like to join, to get into desired projects, or to just experience the sense of a different kind of contribution. Besides, it's smart to have our résumé ready–just in case. These are fast-moving and unpredictable times.

Both the résumé and development plan should pay particular attention to what we referred to in the self-assessment section: both our marketable and motivated skills. Unfortunately, far too many people write résumés highlighting only those skills they used in previous jobs, even though that's no longer the work they want to do. It's like jumping out of the frying pan into just another frying pan. Résumés and action plans need to emphasize the skills that fit the job we want, not the one we had.

Informational Interviewing—Low- and High-Tech Ways

Beyond the résumé and development plan, many career counselors suggest what they call "informational interviewing" as a part of making opportunity happen. Armed with the new knowledge of what you'd like to do next, the idea is to get out and talk with people who are in jobs similar to the kind you aspire to.

The case of Betsy Cope, a well-respected and very senior administrative assistant in a large corporation, illustrates this process at work. After several years of finding her job as an administrative assistant draining, Betsy decided to consult a career counselor. Her assessment results said, among other things, that she needed to work with her hands, outdoors if possible. Her interests most strongly correlated with those of an electrician.

With the counselor's help, Betsy prepared an informational interview outline containing questions she might wish to discuss with various people in her company. Its purpose was to help her learn more about the work they did, to find out whether it matched her own interests, and to determine what new skills it would take to get into a job like theirs–from her very foreign area. Sample questions on Betsy's outline were

- What are the education and experience requirements for this job?
- What skills do you need to perform it well?
- What are its basic duties and responsibilities?
- What's the pay range for a job like yours?
- Where would you expect this job to lead you?
- What are your normal working hours?
- Is flextime or independent contracting a possibility?
- What do you like best and least about your work?
- What are the pressures of your job?
- What kinds of problems or challenges does your department face?
- What other jobs are similar to yours?
- Who else should I talk to about this or similar types of work?

Outline in hand, Betsy met first with the manager of her company's facilities maintenance division, then toured several company factories to see if any of the work there appealed to her. Although she felt at home in all departments and liked the kinds of people she met, no particular jobs caught her eye at first. But, in her discussions, she discovered that the facilities maintenance group, a predominantly male division, was looking for more women. This was certainly an opportunity she never would have predicted, but one that she knew was exactly right for her.

Betsy arranged for a number of interviews with different facilities maintenance people and her discussions confirmed her new knowledge about herself—the work done by electricians seemed fun and right for her. The problem now was that Betsy had none of the education or skills to work as an electrician. But opportunity continued to strike. The division manager, a proponent of diversity in the division, suggested that Betsy enter a union-sponsored apprenticeship program for electricians. With her company's support, Betsy also enrolled part-time at a two-year college to build the knowledge she would need for her new career. Within a year, she made a lateral move from "class 17" administrative assistant to "class 17" mechanical technician. These days she says, "I'm incredibly happy. I wear jeans and I'm outdoors a good part of the time."[11]

One company turned the informational interviewing process into an enjoyable experience using its internal computer system and a process called "AskMe." Anyone who wanted to be an AskMe resource would register with the company's HR department. His or her name, complete background, picture, and anything else he or she wanted to add about his or her career or personal background would go on the AskMe system, which any employee could access.

This made it easy for employees to obtain information about any jobs in the company, assuming that most other employees had signed up as AskMe resources. An employee such as Betsy Cope could call anyone, anywhere in the company, including the CEO (who'd also signed up), to arrange an informational interview. While some managers resisted this system initially, fearing both the time drain and the loss of their own people, most soon grew to enthusiastically support it. They found that the interviews were interesting (most people enjoy talking about themselves), and they got far more exposure to people across the company, including those they might eventually want to hire, than they would have any other way.

Behavior and Attitudes

Obviously, it was not only Betsy Cope's actions, but her manner that helped achieve her goals. If she had "turned off" her new contacts by the way she acted, her informational interviewing process might well have fizzled or missed its mark. Often it's not so much what we do but how we do it that makes our actions successful.

Betsy's attitude also promoted her success. Psychologist Albert Bandura[12] notes that in order for people to contend with new situations like careers, they need a resilient belief in themselves—which he calls *self-efficacy*—especially concerning the things they are trying to learn and do. This means they must be optimistic instead of realistic, and they must persevere in the face of difficulties. When people are only realistic, they believe they can do only what they have done before. The realities of life include failures, adversities, setbacks, and inequities; realists simply succumb to these.

Bandura's research indicates a direct relationship between people's attitudes about acquiring skills and the way they deal with taxing situations.

"Those who believe that ability is an inherent, innate, or inherently fixed attribute are the ones that are very threatened by failure, because that indicates they're dumb," he explains, "whereas with those who really look upon complex decision making as an acquirable skill, errors don't have any negative value." These people can learn from their mistakes how to master a particular activity. Given a choice of doing something in which they look good or something where they can expand their knowledge and competencies, they prefer expanding their competencies.

Marge Franklin, the HR professional about to be downsized out of her long-term employment, exemplifies the concept of changing her attitude and then using that new approach to make opportunity happen. At the outset of the impending change in her life, Marge was selling herself short. Like many other baby boomers, she believed the popular fiction that only kids raised on video games could flourish in the high-tech world. She didn't realize that her innate intelligence and vast experience would help her master new tasks far more rapidly and comprehensively than most 22-year-olds. With her judgment clouded by fear, she could not even begin to envision a different path.

When Marge prepared an inventory of her skills and aptitudes, she was astonished. It covered three pages, single-spaced. In nearly 25 years of corporate employment, even in the same human resources department, she'd worked on more than a hundred different initiatives. These included such disparate tasks as designing a new payroll system, developing an introductory class for new hires, and assisting in launching a quality initiative. When she joined the company, IBM Selectrics were the typewriters of choice. Since then, Marge had learned to use seven separate computer systems, as each new technology generation replaced the old. What's more, she could handle any business software program on the market. In fact, because her firm used the Internet and an intranet system for business, Marge was completely conversant with the web. She began to feel more qualified as she realized she had spent her entire career continuously learning. And even though she had no intention of leaving her secure place of employment, she composed an impressive résumé centered around the skills she loved to use.

Marge drafted two plans of action—one to further her development within her company and another outside of her company. Her plan B was to become an independent human resources consultant. She interviewed a number of people already in the profession as well as some businesspeople she knew who might want to buy such services. She listened carefully to their opinions and decided whether the option seemed appealing. When her company offered incentives for employees to leave, Marge decided to take the package. At this point, she knew there was little to fear. She was informed. And she embodied the concept of informed opportunism.

Marge set up a consulting firm, knowing that in a rather brief period of time, her former employer would need human resources help. What's more, she began pulling in other clients—young firms with young employees who were impressed with her technical skills and the experience and wisdom she brought to their problems. She earned more money than she had in her corporate job, easing her fears about funding a retirement. And she also knew that she could consult on a part-time basis in the future, as long as she was willing to keep learning. Marge had found that her personal satisfaction scale emphasized continuous learning and staying abreast of technology. Her central marketable skill, of course, was in applying these to the human resources field that she knew so well. She moved to action with a plan for course correction as needed.

Continuing the Process of Informed Opportunism

Putting together a development plan and an updated résumé is actually the next-to-last step in this process. Everything is changing fast and often unpredictably. As each of us goes through life, we also change. New interests develop as new needs, wants, and wishes evolve. These lead to new motivations and perhaps the need for new skills, a new avocation, a new venue, a different job. Thus, it is helpful to repeat the process at least once a year or whenever a new opportunity comes up. Remember, this process includes

- Understanding career realities
- Self-assessment
- Synthesizing the data and setting priorities
- Acting—then keeping the process moving

Repeating the process won't be as time consuming the second, third, or fourth time. Much self-assessment work doesn't vary over time. But as time goes by, even if no new job is proffered, new discrepancies may arise between our personal satisfaction scale and what's happening in our lives. Therefore, the big issue for this year may be different from last year's. That's why it is wise to keep assessing, keep learning, and keep revising that development plan. Informed opportunism is a continuing process of self-renewal. I can think of few things that are more important.

As Richard Bolles says about the career and life planning process, "What tools I'm trying to teach you are tools for a lifetime. You probably won't have to use all of them all at once as you're doing now, but you'll surely be using some of them almost every month for the rest of your life. Things have to keep changing."[13] Bringing together information and opportunity gives us a way to more flexibly respond to the challenges of career and life planning in the new millennium.

EXERCISES: IN PURSUIT OF INFORMED OPPORTUNISM

Note to the Individual Doing Career Investigation

The following exercises can be done without professional assistance. However, you may find it helpful to discuss your results with a career professional who is more objective and informed about career and life planning or to take a battery of tests under a career professional's supervision.

Note to the Career Counselor

The following exercises are intended either for individual or group work. A comprehensive program for career and life planning includes more than these exercises cover. The purpose of the exercises is to help your clients recognize opportunity when they see it and know how to make it happen.

- What can they learn from the important decisions in their past?
- What motivates and satisfies them?
- How do they use their talents?
- How can they enhance their chances of making good decisions?
- How might they put the concept of informed opportunism into practice?

EXERCISE 5.1

INFORMED OPPORTUNISM IN YOUR LIFE

Purpose: To help you focus on how you have responded to change in your life, how you have made important decisions, and what you might learn from the past.

1. List the significant changes that have occurred in your life.

2. Answer the following questions as a way of analyzing your life changes. (You may do this through reflection, writing, or discussion.)

   Was the change anticipated?

   Did you exert any control over the change? If so, how?

   Did you gather information about the situation(s) before you made the change; for example, in a career change, did you have information on the company's reputation, the job's comparative pay and benefits, the proximity to your preferred sports and hobbies?

   Did you consider how the change might motivate and satisfy you—for example, how well it fit with your interests, skills, values, personality, and wants?

   Did you think about the probable effect that the change would have on you or those important to you?

   Was your personal style effective in dealing with the change?

   What were the positive and negative results of the change?

   What can you learn from this experience, and what might you do differently the next time?

3. Process your results. Now return to the questions above and consider whether you see any patterns in these situations.

4. Summarize what you have learned from this exercise.

EXERCISE 5.2

BUILDING YOUR PERSONAL SATISFACTION SCALE AND SETTING PRIORITIES

While some people know themselves well enough to succinctly articulate the 8 to 12 attributes that compose the essence of their personal satisfaction, most do not. This exercise helps you create your own personal satisfaction scale. It highlights the main qualities that spark enjoyment in your work and life. Conducting a thorough self-assessment (through analysis of previous experiences, self-appraisal exercises, tests, discussions, and personal insight) can significantly assist you in this process.

- To create your scale, first make a long list of your attributes—for example, skills you enjoy using, skills that come most naturally to you, strong interests, important values, significant personality qualities, your self-concept and self-image, environments where you feel and function at your best, your needs, wants, and wishes. Don't worry about being selective now. It's best to come up with 20 or 30 items on this first pass.
- Now you need to decide which of all these pieces of information are important enough to influence your career and life planning. Just keep thinking about, comparing, and discussing these qualities until you have cut the list down to between 8 and 12 items. When you've pruned it this much, you have your personal satisfaction scale.
- Look over your scale and contemplate how your present work and personal life measure up to these items. Which items on the scale seem in sync with your life and work, and which do not? Choose one or two discrepancies for your concentrated effort over a designated time period.

EXERCISE 5.3

UTILIZING YOUR PERSONAL SATISFACTION SCALE

This exercise shows you one way to use your personal satisfaction scale in examining an important issue or gap in your life. Describing the process can be cumbersome, so examine the following example to better understand how to use this technique.

1. Select an issue or gap in your work or personal life that you wish to examine.
2. Identify various options you might consider in responding to the issue you selected and list them as alternatives a, b, c, and so on.
3. Assign a weight (numerical value of 1, low, to 10, high) to each of your personal satisfaction items according to their importance to you.
4. Rate how well each of your alternatives fits with each of the items on your personal satisfaction scale (from 2, "very good fit," to –2, "very poor fit"). The way you define and rate these items is subjective. No one but you can judge how well the items fit with the alternatives. When you make your comparisons, the need for additional information may become apparent. If, when you use your scale, the resulting conclusions don't feel right, it means the items you chose for your scale need further editing or additions.
5. Multiply the weight of each item by the number that represents how well it fits with each alternative; then total the column that shows the scores for each alternative. (You seldom find the perfect choice, but your scale can help identify what important information you may be missing and which alternatives are better than others. It can also pinpoint components of a choice that will be unfulfilling for you.)

The accompanying example (on page 193) illustrates how one man evaluated two job possibilities by numerically rating them against his personal satisfaction scale. We see that "sales rep in a musical instrument distribution company" seems a better choice than "owning and managing own music store." However, one of the items on the scale, "Be a central part of my community," was not a particularly good fit with the sales rep. This reminds the man that he will need to find avenues in his personal life or create ways through his work to progress toward making a prominent place for himself in his community.

Key: 2 = Very Good Fit 1 = Fairly Good Fit 0 = Neutral −1 = Poor Fit −2 = Very Poor Fit

Personal Satisfaction Items	Weight (10 pts. tops)		Alternative A *Sales Rep. in Music Dist. Co.*			Alternative B *Own & Manage Music Store*		
1. *Interface personally with people to give them quality service*	*10*	×	*2*	=	*20*	*2*	=	*20*
2. *Time flexibility and independence*	*10*	×	*2*	=	*20*	*−2*	=	*−20*
3. *Be a central part of my community*	*9*	×	*−1*	=	*−9*	*2*	=	*18*
4. *Use music knowledge background*	*8*	×	*1*	=	*8*	*1*	=	*8*
5. *Enough money for present lifestyle*	*8*	×	*2*	=	*16*	*−1**	=	*−8*
6. *Have significant responsibility with authority to execute it*	*7*	×	*2*	=	*14*	*2*	=	*14*
7. *Less congested geographic area*	*6*	×	*2*	=	*12*	*2*	=	*12*
8. *Move around—not at desk all day*	*5*	×	*2*	=	*10*	*2*	=	*10*
** for some time*			Totals:		*91*			*54*

Source: Reproduced by special permission of the publisher, Consulting Psychologists Press, Inc., from *New Directions in Career Planning and the Workplace,* 1st edition, by Jean M. Kummerow, Editor.

EXERCISE 5.4

TAKING ACTION

You have thought about what measures up to your personal satisfaction scale and have carefully chosen one or two priorities for concentration. This exercise focuses on developing a plan of action based on those priorities.

Consider the following list of suggestions. Choose the ones most appropriate to your situation or create your own list. Schedule these on your calendar.

- Arrange for assistance with your communication skills.
- Seek honest information about your attitudes, working style, skills, and effectiveness. Take positive steps to respond to this input.
- Discuss your possible options and decisions with people who are important to you or to the success of your new path.
- Prepare an informational interview outline—questions you might discuss with people who are doing or who are familiar with the kind of work that you are considering. Then talk to these people.
- Construct a résumé aimed at the work you would like to be doing. Emphasize your motivated skills, but, if needed, use your marketable skills as stepping-stones. Circulate your résumé (preferably in person) to anyone who might have ideas, information, or influence for you.

REFERENCES

Publications

Bandura, A. (1997). *Self-efficacy: Exercises of control.* New York: Freeman.

Gardner, J. W. (1964). *Self-renewal: The individual and the innovative society.* New York: Harper & Row.

Haldane, B. (1988). *Career satisfaction and success: How to know and manage your strengths.* New York: AMACOM.

Harmon, L. W., Hansen, J.-I. C., Borgen, F. H., & Hammer, A. L. (1994). *Strong Interest Inventory: Applications and technical guide.* Palo Alto, CA: Consulting Psychologists Press.

Hewlett, W. (1983). *Inventions of opportunity: Matching technology with market needs.* Palo Alto, CA: Hewlett Packard Company.

McAllister, L. W. (1996). *A practical guide to CPI interpretation* (3rd ed.). Palo Alto, CA: Consulting Psychologists Press.

Mitchell, K. E., Levin, A. S., & Krumboltz, J. D. (1999, Spring). Planned happenstance: Constructing unexpected career opportunities. *Journal of Counseling and Development, 77*(2), 115–124.

Myers, I. B., McCaulley, M. H., Quenk, N. L., & Hammer, A. L. (1998). *MBTI manual: A guide to the development and use of the Myers-Briggs Type Indicator* (3rd ed.). Palo Alto, CA: Consulting Psychologists Press.

Saratoga Institute. (1998). *Human resource financial report.* Santa Clara, CA: Saratoga Institute.

Waterman, J. A., & Rogers, J. (1996). *Introduction to the FIRO-B* (3rd ed.). Palo Alto, CA: Consulting Psychologists Press.

Waterman, R. H., Jr. (1987). *The renewal factor: How the best get and keep the competitive edge.* New York: Bantam Books.

Weick, K. E. (1979). *The social psychology of organizing* (2nd ed.). Reading, MA: Addison-Wesley.

Interviews

Bandura, Albert, David Starr Jordan professor of social science and psychology, Stanford University. Interview on September 23, 1989.

Bolles, Richard N., author of *What color is your parachute?* Interview on September 20, 1989.

Figler, Howard, author of *The complete job-search handbook* and coauthor (with Richard Bolles) of *The career counselor's handbook.* Interview on May 6, 1999.

Holt, Robin, director of corporate services, alumnae resources. Interview on April 27, 1999.

Krumboltz, John, professor of education and psychology, Stanford University. Interview on October 19, 1989, and November 3, 1998.

Pratt, Lili, partner in M2, San Francisco, California, and career strategist at Stanford Business School, Career Development Office. Interview on October 5, 1989.

Pulley, Mary Lynn, president of Linkages.com. Interview on May 5, 1999.

Ransom, David, director, San Francisco office of Johnson O'Connor Research Foundation. Interview on April 30, 1999.

Resources

Hornaday, A. (1997). How do you know when it's time to go? *Fast Company Magazine—Handbook of the Business Revolution,* 34–39.

Peters, T. J., & Waterman, R. H., Jr. (1982). *In search of excellence: Lessons from America's best-run companies.* New York: Harper & Row.

Pulley, M. L., & Deal, T. E. (1997). *Losing your job—reclaiming your soul: Stories of resilience, renewal, and hope.* San Francisco: Jossey-Bass.

Super, D. E., & Nevill, D. D. (1989). *The values scale* (2nd ed.). Palo Alto, CA: Consulting Psychologists Press.

Waterman, R. H., Jr. (1987). *The renewal factor: How the best get and keep the competitive edge.* New York: Bantam Books.

Waterman, R. H., Jr. (1994). *What America does right.* New York: W. W. Norton.

Waterman, R. H., Jr., Waterman, J. A., & Collard, B. A. (1994, July/August). Toward a more resilient workforce. *Harvard Business Review, 72*(4), 87–95.

NOTES

[1]I use the term "informed opportunism" to refer to people's personal lives. Robert H. Waterman, Jr., originally coined it in reference to organizations in *The renewal factor.*

[2]Similar to yet distinct from the concept of "informed opportunism" is the theory of career counseling called "planned happenstance," Kathleen E. Mitchell, Al S. Levin, and John D. Krumboltz (1999). Interview with John Krumboltz, November 3, 1998.

[3]CareerSteps is a product of eProNet, a firm based in San Mateo, CA.

[4]From original MindSteps web site.

[5]Interview with Lili Pratt, October 5, 1989.

[6]While career professionals often refer to these sorts of inventories as psychometric assessments, I will be referring to them by the more common term, "tests."

[7]Johnson O'Connor is an example of a high-quality aptitude-testing firm.

[8]Interview with David Ransom, April 30, 1999.

[9]Interview with Robin Holt, April 27, 1999.

[10]Interview with Howard Figler, May 6, 1999.

[11]Based on an example given in *What America does right,* Robert H. Waterman, Jr. (New York: W. W. Norton, 1994).

[12]Interview with Albert Bandura, Stanford University, September 23, 1989.

[13]Interview with Richard N. Bolles, September 20, 1989.

6

Beyond Balance to Life Quality

THE INTEGRATION OF WORK AND LIFE

Betsy Collard and H. B. Gelatt

Once upon a time there was work and there was life. They were separate, independent parts. You did your work "there" (usually at the office) and you lived your life "here" (usually at home). As work became a larger and larger part of life, we called it career. Still, work and life were viewed as separate as evidenced by the term used to define the current career crisis, *work-life balance.*

When it becomes apparent that we are spending too much time at work, and not enough time with life, it is logical for us to want to balance the time more evenly. That view made sense in a world that progressed in linear, predictable patterns. But today we live in a white-water world.

Technology is rapidly removing all barriers as to where, when, and how we work. In the new global work world, it is increasingly possible to work anywhere, anytime, any way. The workplace is becoming as virtual as it is fixed to a physical place or time. To continue to think of work and life outside of work as separate will be not only increasingly difficult but progressively disabling. Pursuing a strategy of balancing work and life perpetuates the idea of separateness and reinforces imaginary boundaries in a world that is becoming more open, more interconnected, and boundaryless. In such a world, seeking balance, equilibrium, and stability may be counterproductive. People need a different approach to dealing with the impact work and technology are having on their lives. They need to leave behind the notion that the amount of time and energy devoted to "work" needs to balance the time and energy devoted to "life" and to focus instead on life quality. That is the central theme of this chapter.

The career development profession will serve clients best by moving to a more encompassing, holistic view of work, career, and life. Although a number of counselors address whole-life issues with their clients, as a profession we still frequently focus on assessing work skills, work interests, work values, and career issues. Our self-assessment processes need to include more of the whole-life issues we will focus on in this chapter.

How can career counselors help clients enhance the quality of their lives when changes are so constant and multifaceted? How can they help clients achieve a more holistic and integrated perspective about their lives?

A great deal has been written about work-life balance and how to create a more fulfilling, satisfying life. (See Suggested Reading at the end of this chapter.) Our intent is not to replicate the excellent work that has been done in this area, but to build on it by discussing four new ways for career counselors to approach the work-life issue.

- **Reframe the work-life issue in terms of life quality.** In a world that is increasingly characterized by blurry or nonexistent boundaries, the issue is not how to balance work and life but how to enrich the overall quality of life. Reframing the conversation with clients is much more than semantics—it changes how they view the issue and the strategies they might develop. It changes the focus from *work* to *life* and from *balance* to *quality.*

- **Identify the two components of life quality.** Generally when people think about improving the quality of their lives, they think about how to prioritize the way time is spent. They focus on the quantity of time devoted to different activities. But life quality is determined by two components: what individuals do (how time is spent) and their personal experience (thoughts and feelings). What people do on a daily basis certainly is a big contributor to the quality of their lives, but how they experience what they do is even more important.

- **Pay attention to the "inside" barriers to achieving life quality.** Identifying the mental barriers that may be standing between a client and a new approach to life is often neglected in career counseling practice. But in many cases, these internal barriers can be powerful—almost insurmountable—roadblocks on the path to enriching the quality of clients' lives. Just as counselors need to help clients develop their definitions of quality of life, so must they help them uncover the internal obstacles that may be in the way.
- **Question the common wisdom of "simplify."** Common wisdom says people should simplify their lives in order to focus time and attention on what is important to them. Sometimes the opposite is also sound advice. Sometimes doing more, but more of something different, can bring individuals a greater sense of control over their lives and enhance life quality.

Each of these four ideas will be discussed in some detail. There are questions for reflection on how to incorporate these ideas into a career counseling practice and additional practical exercises that can help clients achieve a new perspective on the work-life issue at the end of the chapter.

REFRAMING THE WORK-LIFE ISSUE

That most Americans long for a more meaningful and satisfying life is no secret. "Yearning for balance" is a common theme of studies inquiring about life satisfaction. Respondents feel their daily activities do not reflect their true priorities. They want less stress in their lives and more reassurance that their lives are making a difference.

Typically, the reaction to such complaints would be to look for ways to cut back on work and bolster the time commitment to other life activities so that the two sides of the balancing scale—representing work and life—would be level. Reframing the work-life issue so that the focus is on finding meaning and satisfaction through quality rather than quantity opens up an entirely different conversation.

Career counselors have many tools to help clients assess and improve their work situation. Broadening the counseling goal from improving work quality to enhancing life quality causes career counselors and clients to ask different questions, seek different strategies, and develop different skills. Life quality becomes the major career development issue and more traditional career counseling objectives—self-assessment, expanding skill sets, identifying values, and defining the elements of meaningful and satisfying work—become secondary, support efforts.

Just as holistic health eliminates mind-body and physical-mental dichotomies, a holistic approach to life quality blends work and personal life, social and spiritual life into a whole-life quality perspective. It requires a shift in perspective for both counselor and client to see things differently and, therefore, to do things differently. It is a broader, more ambitious agenda, but one with the potential for more significant, longer-lasting results.

The metaphor of a symphony orchestra may be helpful in describing the synergy of life quality. There are dozens of musicians playing different instruments in a symphony orchestra. When they all play together, in tune and in sync, the music is beautiful. The result of the whole orchestra is more powerful than the notes being played by any one musician. But producing beautiful music cannot be achieved by giving each instrument in the orchestra equal time or emphasis. Each musical score achieves its brilliance by the contribution of different instruments at different times, in context with contributions of other instruments, according to the requirements created by the composer and arranger.

What would music sound like if the composition were created from the viewpoint that the music from the brass section should be in equal "balance" with that from the strings? Or if every oboe sound had to be countered with an equal measure of timpani booms? Only a few gifted composers could follow these guidelines and produce music enjoyable to play and to hear, and their task would be much more difficult.

Creating and arranging a life composition is similar to writing for a symphony. Each individual is the composer, arranger, conductor, and performers rolled into one. There will be times when one part of the life orchestra needs to be quiet while another section takes center stage. The oboe and timpani may not share equal playing time. The balancing scale will be off-kilter, but the resulting music will still be beautiful. Because it is impossible to sit down and write a composition for life from start to finish, the performance is always a work in progress. The musical score will need to be continuously recomposed and rearranged with emphasis on different instruments at different times.

Career counselors need to help clients look at the quality of their lives now and think about how they would ideally like their lives to be. The symphony metaphor may help individuals move away from the idea of balance and ask themselves more questions about the holistic quality of their lives.

IDENTIFYING THE TWO COMPONENTS OF LIFE QUALITY

The quality of people's lives is determined by two components: what they do and how they experience what they do. Many career counseling sessions focus on the first component but pay little attention to the second.

The Doing

A typical first step in getting to know clients is to ask them to describe their daily activities and how they would like to spend their time along several different dimensions—the content of daily activities (what), the environment (where), the relationships (who), and the motivation (why). With the what, where, who, and why of daily activities identified, the counselor may then suggest a number of enrichment strategies that will help clients change part or all of their daily activities so that they are more meaningful and satisfying. The values-driven work instrument developed by the Career Action Center (1996) is helpful in examining the "doing" component of life quality. It focuses on different aspects of "doing"—the what, where, and who elements—in addition to core intrinsic values. It asks clients to evaluate their work values in terms of the content of their work (what), the environment in which it is done (where), and the people with whom it is done (who).

Perhaps the most common strategy used by counselors is to explore the life quality issue along the time dimension. This dimension suggests that we look at how much time the various activities of our lives consume. When we spend too much time doing one thing (work) at the expense of another (life), we try to reprioritize how our time is spent. The strategy for balancing work and life has been to count up the time spent at work and the time spent at nonwork, and then try to reduce one and increase the other. This is called time management. But time management focuses on the *quantity* of what we do; it does not pay attention to how we experience what we do, which is a major factor in the *quality* of our lives. Conventional time management strategies are helpful. People learn to spend time differently; they do different things, which means they stop doing other things. However, time management is a linear strategy because time is linear. It is not a holistic, integrated strategy; it is incomplete.

The Experiencing

While it is fairly commonplace for career counselors and clients to focus on the first component of life quality, the doing, few spend enough time on the second component, individuals' experience regarding daily activities: How do they feel about what they do, where they do it, who they do it with, and why they do it? Both components must be acknowledged if life quality is to be improved.

The process of quality-of-life enrichment is like the process of stress reduction, but in reverse. Intense deadline pressure, for example, is a "to do" that causes stress. How the individual experiences the pressure of deadlines—exhilaration, panic, excitement, fear, energy, paralysis—raises or lowers the stress level. Like cholesterol, there's "good" stress and "bad" stress, and the difference between the two comes from the individual's reaction to external factors, not from the activities themselves.

If someone says, "My work is stressful," or "My life is boring," the tendency is to look for solutions outside of the individual. The advice might be to modify the work situation so that it isn't stressful or to add new activities to a life so that it isn't boring. But if the perspective is different, if the comment is "I experience my work as stressful" or "I experience my life as boring," the conversation has an entirely different slant. Then the focus is on how people can change their thoughts and feelings in order to increase the richness of their life quality experiences.

Whether the goal is to reduce stress or enrich life quality or both, the key is to pay attention to both the outside components (what people do and what happens to them) and the inside components (how they experience what they do and what happens to them).

"To control attention means to control experience, and therefore the quality of life," says Mihaly Csikszentmihalyi (1997). Attention, it seems, is an underutilized but powerful resource. What we pay attention to is what we experience. What we don't pay attention to, we don't experience—it is not part of our life. Two people walking along the same wooded path will see different things. One will think the path is in lovely shade, the other that it is dismally dark. One will look down and notice tiny buds about to burst into flower, while the other will scan treetops in search of unusual birds. One will be impatient about the condition of the trail; the other won't even notice that it is rough in spots. They are walking the same way, through the same environment, and maybe even with the same motivation, but they are having quite different experiences.

The first component of life quality, the doing, is determined by what activities are engaged in, day in and day out. The second factor, the experiencing, is determined by what the individual pays attention to and how the individual sees and interprets what is noticed. To live is to experience and to experience is to pay attention. There is an old joke that asks, "If a tree falls in the woods and the media's not there to cover it, did anything really happen?" No matter what happens to people in the "doing" part of their lives, if they don't pay attention, they don't experience it, and it cannot add to or detract from the quality of their lives.

Since these are the only two components of life quality, for individuals to enrich their life quality they can (1) change what they do—do more, do less, do something differently, (2) change how they experience what they do—pay attention to different things and/or pay attention to things differently, or (3) do both.

A holistic strategy for life quality means focusing on "experience management" as well as time management. We create our quality of life by what we pay attention to and how we pay attention.

> We notice what we notice because of who we are.
> We create ourselves by what we choose to notice.
>
> —Margaret Wheatley

ADDRESSING THE "INSIDE" BARRIERS TO ACHIEVING LIFE QUALITY

Many people consult career counselors because they feel the quality of their lives isn't what they want it to be, and they attribute their dissatisfaction to work and life being "out of balance." Counselors help clients identify career and life goals and develop a strategy to move toward these goals. This movement seems clear and straightforward, yet most clients find it very difficult to do. But counselors are dealing with human beings, most of whom find it very difficult to change. There are many reasons why, but one major reason is the number of barriers that may exist inside the client. Most people are the opposite of the little engine that chugged, "I think I can, I think I can." Instead, inside of an individual's mind and heart are perceived and real barriers that may say, "I don't think I can, I know I can't."

All too often, counselors and clients spend a great deal of time assessing and planning for change, but almost never enough time identifying potential internal barriers and ways to overcome them. When potential barriers go unexamined, they usually remain insurmountable and prevent clients from moving forward.

Just as life quality is in the eye of the beholder, so are the barriers. Everyone has a different set of reasons why they think it will be difficult (or impossible) to achieve their goals. At the top of the list are all the external, practical "realities" that could prevent individuals from achieving the lives they dream of—financial resources, family obligations, health limitations, meager opportunities, and so on. But, in reality, it is not these practicalities that stand in the way of achieving life quality. What makes change so difficult are the internal obstacles that usually go unexamined.

These internal barriers can be the most powerful roadblocks on the path to enhancing the quality of life, but once an individual has pushed past them, tremendous progress can be made. Convincing clients to do this work, however, can be a challenge. They come to career counseling sessions because they think they want a different job or to change fields, and they do not always easily see that personal insights will help them achieve career goals as well as improved life quality. Even though clients may be resistant to "looking inside," providing ample time in the counseling process to discuss potential barriers is one of the most important services counselors can offer a client.

One way to start the conversation about internal barriers is to ask clients to list all of the possible barriers that might be standing between themselves and success, however they define "success." Have the client identify and describe the most significant barriers in as much detail as possible. Getting all the possible roadblocks down on paper is helpful because a concrete list of specific items can be discussed one by one. Together, counselor and client can then brainstorm possible strategies for overcoming each identified obstacle (see Exercise 6.1, on page 215).

Many clients have a number of barriers. Some they are well aware of (usually external factors); others they may not realize they have (usually internal factors). The following are some of the most common internal barriers that individuals may harbor in their subconscious.

Barrier 1: Not Knowing What's Important to Them

Many people don't know what's really important to them as individuals and what they really want out of life. They are unclear about their priorities and uncertain about what they value most. They haven't invested the quiet, reflective time needed to make these discoveries.

Assessment tools, especially those dealing with values, are used by most career counselors to help clients develop an understanding of what is most important to them. It is commonly assumed that a person's work values and life values are the same or, at the very least, congruent. While this is probably most often the case, it is important to recognize that it is not true 100 percent of the time. For example, a client may place aesthetics as a high life value but at the same time not feel it is important in the workplace. Another client may be very organized and value that at work but prefer a personal lifestyle that is more spontaneous and free-form. Yet another client may place spirituality as a very high life value but not feel it is important or appropriate in the workplace. The examples could go on and on, but the point is that counselors need to question clients about how their life and work values are or are not related.

A twist on this barrier would be individuals who may think they know what is important to them, but don't. The popular admonishment "Be careful what you wish for because you might get it" suggests that this experience has happened to many people. They think they know what they want and then discover, usually after they have worked very hard to achieve it, that it wasn't what they expected or that it doesn't provide the meaning and satisfaction they sought.

Counselors frequently help clients "test" out what is important to them through a visioning process. They ask clients to envision and describe the life quality they want and then explore that vision with them. Such an exercise can help clients clarify and refine what is really important to them.

Whether clients think they know what is important to them or admit they haven't a clue, it is important for counselors to emphasize that being uncertain, unclear, or incorrect is a normal part of the journey of life. Being unable to clearly articulate life goals or quickly summarize a vision of life quality should not be thought of as a failing. It takes an accumulation of life experiences and time and attention in private reflection to know what one wants to experience in life.

Viktor Frankl pointed out that no one can answer the question "What is the meaning of life?" in general terms or in the abstract. The definition of the meaning of life differs from person to person, from day to day, and from hour to hour. What matters, Frankl says, is not the meaning of life in general, but rather the specific meaning of life in a given moment. Meaning does not come from the theoretical or hypothetical, as in the name of some abstract value, but from what is valued moment to moment.

The same is true of quality of life. What matters is not so much the quality of one's life in general, but the quality of life in a given moment. The more moments of life quality individuals can accumulate, the more they will experience an overall enriched quality of life.

Barrier 2: Being Comfortable with Problems

Some clients have trouble creating the life they want because they have difficulty moving out of the comfort zone where they live day to day. People get accustomed to problems and can forget that life doesn't have to be that way. Even with serious problems, it can seem easier to live with the current situation than to take action to change. John Galbraith put it this way: "Given a choice between changing and proving it isn't necessary to change, most people get busy on the proof." It often takes serious trauma (loss of a job or a loved one) or a life-threatening crisis to nudge people to consider major life changes.

Making choices and taking risks to improve a situation can generate considerable anxiety. It often means giving up something, and human beings don't like to do that. Letting go of something that has worked or been comfortable, and replacing it with something that is unknown and uncertain, is uncomfortable. There is an old saying that explains this well: "The certainty of misery seems better than the misery of uncertainty."

Raising this issue of being comfortable with one's problems can help clients develop the confidence they need to move forward. Certainty is comfortable—it feels safe. Uncertainty is uncomfortable—it feels scary. But in a comfort zone it is harder to learn, to grow, and to develop. Learning takes place when the comfort zone is left behind and something new is presented as a challenge. Every counselor has a pocketful of stories about clients who experienced dramatic career success and improved quality of life after a job loss, downsizing, forced change of location, or some other traumatic event. "Being fired was the best thing that ever happened to me" is a common declaration. So the role of the counselor in helping clients overcome this barrier is convincing them to recognize the borders of their comfort zone and push to challenge themselves in new ways.

Barrier 3: Getting Stuck in an Achievement Mentality

It seems to be human nature to want to have it all. People today have incredibly high expectations—they want to earn a certain amount, live in a certain area, achieve a certain level of responsibility, see that their kids get into a certain college, and "leave a legacy" for the next generation. But an achievement mentality can be a barrier to life quality because the tendency is to measure "success" in terms of accomplishment, often financially or careerwise. A focus on financial success and career success is not bad, but they can become so all-important that, if left unexamined, they can impair a person's vision about what really constitutes a quality life.

An achievement orientation is so prevalent in today's world that many people believe the only way to achieve a quality life is by scaling a series of mountains. Each peak is checked off as an accomplishment, with the thought that the more check marks there are, the better the quality of life. In this view, career success is achieved by climbing up the corporate ladder. But, as career counselors have been told by Beverly Kaye, "Up is not the only way." In fact, it has been said that *doing* is not the only way. "Doing" is the Western philosophy approach to life quality, while "being" is central to Eastern philosophy. Many people are familiar with the mantra "life is a journey, not a destination," but few actually make the thought the baseline for their daily lives.

Having an objective or interest in doing is not a barrier—but being overly attached to it is. When people have a specific goal in one area and are on their way to accomplishing it, they've made an investment of time and energy that they don't want to give up. The result seems to be within reach, and they don't want to be sidetracked until it is completed, even though the goal may not improve life quality. They don't want to let go. An achievement mentality focuses too much on the accomplishment—on the next step up the ladder, on doing, and on the destination. As Angeles Arrien puts it, "Be open to outcome, not attached." Quality of life is not where you are going, it is what you are creating. Being and becoming happen simultaneously.

People can be shocked out of an achievement mentality by personal trauma or life crisis. Helping clients explore the achievement barrier, before crisis, can be extremely helpful in getting closer to work-life quality. The life wheel tool used in coaching is one way to get clients to look at their desired life quality and the gap between that and today's reality (see Exercise 6.2). It can open up discussion about the "yes, but" barriers that an achievement mentality raises.

Barrier 4: Having No Time for Reflection

Complaining about a lack of time is one of the most often mentioned barriers to taking action to improve life quality. Getting clear on priorities, making choices, and changing behaviors take time and energy. The irony is that in today's world, with all of the technological advances to help us do work and home chores faster with less effort, most people are too overwhelmed with pressures from work and family to find the time that reflection, planning, and redirection require.

Clients lament, "If I only had more time," but seldom do they say, "If I only had more time I would spend it in thoughtful reflection." Reflection is basically the process of introspection or self-examination of one's thoughts, feelings, beliefs, and point of view. It is paying attention to one's way of seeing. Personal reflection, although gaining popularity in recent years, is still generally thought of as something done on weekend retreats or practiced for a lifetime by monks.

If the idea of finding time for a weekend of reflection seems difficult, the idea of finding time for *active reflection* in daily life seems outrageously improbable. People don't realize that just the opposite is true. It is far easier to find reflection time in small bites every day than it is to clear a "free" weekend in a jam-packed calendar. And it can be more effective. Quality of life, we have said, involves what is done day in and day out and how those activities are experienced on a daily basis. Life quality is made up of many small activities and experiences and is built, one day at a time, by paying attention. This is also called *mindfulness*.

Talking about active reflection and mindfulness may be uncomfortable territory for some career counselors and/or career clients. The strategies that emerge from this new approach to enriching life quality are not typical career counseling strategies. Reframing, for example, requires letting go of some thinking habits or standard operating procedures that may have become impediments to enriching life quality. Challenging untested assumptions, confronting mental barriers, and reexamining conventional wisdom are not what clients are expecting when they sign up for a career counseling session.

This is not to say that traditional career counseling strategies are no longer appropriate. They continue to have a valuable role in helping people move ahead. But given the situation of the world of work in this era of change, the career counseling profession needs to broaden its approach to helping clients in a way that involves holistic strategies and includes an individual's whole life.

One strategy to help clients overcome the time barrier is to brainstorm small steps, requiring small amounts of time that can be worked into a hectic schedule and can help the client move forward (see Exercise 6.3). A question like, "What is one small step you could take to improve the quality of your life today?" focuses on a small action step and on the here and now. A small step can seem manageable and can help break the logjam of "yes, but" barriers a client might raise that prevent taking action.

Barrier 5: Holding onto an Old Paradigm

Perhaps the largest barrier to overcome in enriching the quality of life is holding onto old beliefs and attitudes without even realizing that this is being done. As we discussed earlier, people's personal paradigms determine what they pay attention to and therefore what they experience. The greatest breakthroughs with clients often arise out of explorations about the attitudes and beliefs that are shaping their experiences.

An individual's paradigm is made up of the basic attitudes, beliefs, and ways of seeing that are the underlying foundation of how this person approaches life, work, relationships, the past, and the future. Is this person an optimist or a pessimist? Is the glass half full or half empty?

Does this person honor the rational or the intuitive? A client, for example, who approaches life issues from the logical side—using only facts without considering feelings, hunches, or intuition—is playing the game with only a partial deck of cards. But will he or she recognize that? Some people think of themselves as captains of their ships, while others are always looking for someone else to take control of the wheel. All of these questions and more help to uncover an individual's paradigm.

Everyone tends to think within his or her own paradigm. Every brain is full of "can'ts" and "shoulds" that, when discussed and reflected on with a counselor, can be reframed so that other options are possible. But without the prodding and probing, the individual may stay locked into a perspective, unable to see any other point of view.

Counselors can anticipate a poor reception from clients seeking work or a change of careers who are asked to think about their paradigm. It may not seem like career counseling. But it may be exactly what some clients need to do. Stephen Covey, in *The 7 Habits of Highly Effective People* (1989), tells us, "It becomes obvious that if we want to make relatively minor changes in our lives, we can perhaps appropriately focus on our attitudes and behaviors. But if we want to make significant, quantum change, we need to work on our basic paradigms" (see Exercise 6.4, on page 218).

QUESTIONING THE COMMON WISDOM OF "SIMPLIFY"

What strategies can counselors use to help individuals improve the quality of their lives, especially in the relationship between their work lives and their personal lives? How can counselors help clients see how they can move from the life they have today to one that more closely resembles their ideal?

Common wisdom suggests that once the elements of a quality life are defined, the way to achieve it is to simplify and focus time and attention on what is deemed important. It's the less-is-more philosophy that presumes that if life is simplified, there will be more time to appreciate what is really important. The strategy is, "Do less of this so you have more time to do more of that."

Stephen Covey's work is well known in this regard. He encourages people to look at their lives in terms of what is important and not important, and urgent and nonurgent, and then recommends a focus on what is important and nonurgent. Many people have found this formula helpful in prioritizing and focusing on that which is most central and important for them.

"Voluntary simplicity" is a concept that has been around for a long time and is now suggested as one of the top ten trends of the new millennium. It is a proposal for just plain simple living. It usually involves decisions about how to spend time and money. Simple living has been likened to Arnold Toynbee's principles of civilization growth called the Law of Progressive Simplification: *The ability to transfer increasing amounts of energy and attention from the material side of life to the psychological, cultural, aesthetic, and spiritual side of life* (quoted in Levey & Levey, 1998, p. 256).

Simplicity is common wisdom. But sometimes uncommon wisdom and unconventional strategies may be what's needed. Here are four uncommon strategies to consider.

Do More, but Do Something Different

Less is not always better. Sometimes taking on something that the individual has a personal desire to do will make the more routine and stressful easier to handle. A client who is feeling that her life is completely overextended, for example, takes on organizing a Habitat for Humanity housebuilding project because it is something she wants to do. It means more work, later hours, and less time for other parts of her life, but it also makes her work and the other parts of her life seem somehow more manageable. Why? Because she has added to her overall quality of life by participating in an activity that she values and finds enjoyable.

How often do people think they cannot do one more thing, attend one more class, go to one more event, work out one more time—only to find that after they have forced themselves to go they feel refreshed and reenergized about other parts of their lives? Sometimes people are too tired and too overextended, and they need to cut back. But other times, doing something more, and different, is exactly what is needed to feel less tired and more in control of life.

Career counselors can help clients see that sometimes cutting back is not the only answer. It may be that they need to do more, especially more of something different, in order to get a new perspective and to change their paradigm.

Do More of Something You Don't Like

Sometimes doing more of something you don't like brings you a greater sense of control and improves your life quality. Two examples illustrate this point. A woman's job requires that she give presentations before large audiences. She has little experience with public speaking, does not think she is very good at it, and strongly believes that every presentation is adding more stress to her life, not adding to its quality. But as she continues to fulfill the requirements of the job by giving presentations, she becomes more comfortable with speaking, learns how to be more effective, and, over time, comes to enjoy it greatly. What was once a work-life stressor is transformed into a work-life enhancer that adds to the quality of her work life.

Another client feels his health is suffering because of the stress he feels at work and at home. Although his schedule is demanding and he has never enjoyed exercise, an alarmingly high blood pressure reading convinces him to join a gym and enroll in a program that requires exercise sessions three times a week. The thought of working out is not motivating, but the goal of better health is. After a year of exercising regularly, not only has he reached his goal—lower blood pressure and better health—but he has come to enjoy his time at the gym for its own sake, not just as a means to an end. This individual has enriched the quality of his life and gained an increased sense of control by doing more of something he originally did not like.

Do the Same, but Do It Differently

Sometimes we can make the quality of our lives considerably better just by doing the same things differently. The client who is extremely stressed by a long commute in heavy traffic comes to a counselor about changing jobs. He loves his job, but hates the commute. He has recently purchased a house, so moving closer is out of the question. He is sadly beginning to believe that his only solution is to quit his job and change fields since there are few opportunities for his current career in the rural area where he lives.

The client and counselor explored a number of options that would allow this individual to do the same, but do it differently. Telecommuting was quickly eliminated because the client works with medical patients who must be seen in person, but the idea of changing the structure of the client's work day was intriguing. Together they developed a proposal to the client's employer that would change his work week to four 10-hour days. The employer agreed, and the client now has every Friday off. Not only did he cut back on the number of days he commutes, but coming in earlier and staying later puts him on the road when there is less traffic. By doing the same thing but doing it differently, the client has kept a job he loves and enhanced the quality of his life.

Do More of Something "Unimportant"

Common wisdom says to focus on what is important and let go of the rest. That may be good advice for achieving a specific goal, but it ignores the fact that often things categorized as "unimportant" or "insignificant" shape the way we feel about life. Sometimes the small things that we do to indulge ourselves add to our life quality and make us feel good at the end of the day. Sipping a cup of tea in a rocking chair, watching an old episode of *I Love Lucy*, filling in a crossword puzzle, or browsing through a pile of mail-order catalogs, not to order anything, but just to look—can help people relax and repair. These small things may be insignificant, but they are not unimportant because of the enjoyment they provide and their contribution to life quality. See Exercise 6.8 on page 227 for more on enjoyment of little things.

Do the Same, but "See" It Differently

What you focus on is what you experience. A client who worked for a very bureaucratic government agency found it tedious to maintain detailed records of her caseload. After a while, all she could focus on was the dreaded paperwork and she began to "hate" her work. It took several conversations with a career counselor before she recognized that her disgruntlement was being caused by the record keeping, not by the job itself. Through a self-assessment, she validated that her current job was aligned with many of her values and interests. She acknowledged that she liked the people she worked with and felt very good about the contribution she was making.

When it became clear that this job was actually a good fit for her, the client and counselor then discussed how she might approach the record-keeping task differently. The client calculated how much time was actually spent doing the task (much less than she would have guessed) and how much time and energy she spent resisting the task. They discussed why it was important to have detailed records—their function and how incomplete or late data could affect others in the organization. The realization that co-workers were relying on her record keeping was the catalyst this client needed to have a new viewpoint about the necessity of the task. She was able to reframe her attitude and make the paperwork a more manageable part of her job.

Simplify? Change? Do more? Do it differently? Do what you like? Do what you dread? Do it with a new attitude? It is always important for career counselors to remember that there is no one right way to approach improving the quality of life. At different times, different approaches make sense. The danger is in thinking too narrowly about possible strategies. No option should be off the table until it has been thoughtfully considered.

SUMMARY

This chapter has explored the issue of work-life balance and expanded it to a more holistic view of overall life quality. We have stressed how it's not simply what you do that contributes to the quality of your life, but also how you experience what you do. We have urged career professionals to spend more time on the internal barriers that prevent clients from taking action to improve their life quality and we have provided "uncommon wisdom" about ways in which life quality can be enhanced.

We believe that, as we move into the 21st century, this more holistic view of life quality will drive career development. Integration and synergy between work life and "nonwork life" can help to achieve life quality in a world that is full of change and instability. Counselors need to broaden their scope and move beyond focusing just on clients' work lives or careers, to focus on life quality and examine the relationship that work life has to total life. Counselors can then help clients develop strategies and overcome barriers for improved life quality while providing support for this lifelong process.

EXERCISE 6.1

EXPLORING LIFE QUALITY

Can you describe what quality of life looks like to you?

What are the ingredients?

How does that view differ from your life today?

What role does career success have in your definition of life quality?

What other aspects of your life contribute to its quality?

Which are especially important?

EXERCISE 6.2

EXPLORING WHAT YOU DO

Is what you are doing enjoyable because of the content?____________________

If so, what is the content?

____

____

Is what you are doing enjoyable because of the environment?_______________

If so, describe the elements that are especially satisfying.

____

____

Is what you are doing enjoyable because of the people you do it with?_________

What is it about those people and your relationship that makes them especially enjoyable?

____

____

____

Who are the people?

____

____

What is the nature of the relationship?

____

____

Is what you are doing enjoyable because of the reason you are doing it?

____

What is that reason?

____

EXERCISE 6.3

EXPLORING WHAT YOU PAY ATTENTION TO

1. At this very moment

   Begin by mindfully observing the world around you. Let your attention notice the breeze or lack of it, the light or darkness, the sounds or silence, the movement of objects, the "everything" (rocks, buildings, mountains, pavement) that is out there.

   Next shift your attention inward and notice everything that is happening within you (breathing, pulse, senses, feelings, attitudes, beliefs, physical and emotional reactions).

2. Ask yourself

   What outside and/or inside stimuli do you usually pay attention to?

   ___

   ___

   What outside and/or inside stimuli do you usually *fail* to pay attention to?

   ___

   ___

   Is there a pattern in your life history of "seeing and not seeing"?

   ___

   ___

3. What have you been paying the most attention to in your life this week?

   ___

   ___

4. What elements of your experience are calling for greater attention?

   ___

   ___

EXERCISE 6.4

OVERCOMING BARRIERS TO LIFE QUALITY

What are the restraining factors in your life that prevent you from achieving an enriched quality of life? What keeps you from getting what you want?

- Identify your goal—what is it you want to do to improve your life quality? I want to (your goal)

  ____

- List as many barriers as you can think of that might prevent you from achieving your goal.

  ____

- Put a star next to the 2 to 3 top barriers—the things that are most likely to make achieving your goal difficult.
- Discuss these potential barriers with a counselor or friend and brainstorm all the things you could do to determine if they can be overcome. Write those possible action steps next to each barrier.
- Circle the 1 to 3 action steps you could take to overcome those potential barriers.

Barriers	*Possible action steps to overcome barriers*
1.	
2.	
3.	
4.	
5.	

Develop an action plan: List the barrier you want to work on, the action you will take to test out that barrier, and by when you will do it.

Barrier	*What you will do*	*When you will do it*

EXERCISE 6.5

THE LIFE CIRCLE

- Think of all the different components of your life: your work, personal growth, leisure, relationships, spirituality, family/friends, finance, health, physical environment. Circle those listed above that are a part of your life and add any more below.

- Imagine that the circle below is a pie. Divide this pie in proportion to the percentage of time you spend on each component and label each section.

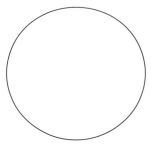

- Look at the life circle you have created. Think about the various components that make up the circle and their relationships to one another. Put a plus (+) by the areas you are satisfied with. What area(s) do you want to focus on to improve the overall quality of your life? Note those with a minus (–) sign.

- List all the things you might do in that area to improve the quality of your life.

- Describe one specific action you could take that would improve your satisfaction with this area of your life. Make it as specific as possible. What is the action? By when will you take it?

Action step *Date completed*

EXERCISE 6.6

ONE SMALL STEP: IMPROVING THE QUALITY OF YOUR LIFE ONE STEP AT A TIME

Sometimes it's difficult to move ahead to improve the quality of your life because it seems the changes required are too big, the obstacles too great. Major changes are most often not accomplished in giant leaps, but in a series of small steps. This simple exercise might help you move ahead.

1. Identify *one major thing* that you could do that would significantly improve the quality of your life (for example, reduce my stress level, change jobs, get more exercise).

2. What is *one small step* that you could take today that would contribute to that goal? (For example, I could get up from my desk and walk outside for five minutes to give myself a break; I could talk with a friend who knows about jobs in other areas; I could walk up the stairs rather than taking the elevator.)

EXERCISE 6.7

PRACTICING PARADIGM SHIFTING

One of the major barriers to enriching quality of life has to do with the way we see things. Old ways of thinking, outdated attitudes, unconscious beliefs, and untested assumptions can get in the way of attempts at changing our lifestyle or enriching our quality of life. We keep doing things the same way because that's the way we see things. Sometimes we need to work on our basic paradigms, our basic way of seeing things.

The following exercise can help you practice changing the way you see things. Here are six pairs of contradictory statements reflecting beliefs or attitudes about living life. Practice paradigm shifting by supporting each statement—giving reasons why each might be true.

1. The way I see things is the way things are.

____

____

The way I see things is the way I see things.

____

____

2. Experience is the best teacher.

____

____

Open-mindedness is the best teacher.

____

____

3. A realistic point of view is advantageous.

____

____

EXERCISE 6.7 (CONT'D)

An optimistic point of view is advantageous.

4. Who I am is defined by who I think I am.

Who I am is defined by my relationships.

5. My cultural conditioning is responsible for my beliefs.

I am responsible for my beliefs.

6. "The unexamined life is not worth living."—*Socrates*

"The unlived life is not worth examining."—*Max Lerner*

EXERCISE 6.8

A BIG LIST OF LITTLE THINGS

Life quality often is enriched by the little "unimportant things" that we don't pay much attention to. Make a long list of all the little things you love to do. The list should be big (to give you many enriching options), but the things should be little (to make them easier to include in your life). A sample list is provided below to help get you started.

A Stimulus List

- Eating an ice cream cone
- Taking a long shower
- Spending time in nature
- Reading for enjoyment
- Cooking
- Eating out
- Having coffee with a friend
- Reading mail-order catalogs
- Having a fire in the fireplace
- Checking out a new store
- Browsing in a bookstore
- Meditating
- Keeping a journal
- Listening to music
- Watching sports on TV
- Building, constructing, crafting . . .
- Being alone
- Spending time with an animal

Your Personal List

______________________	______________________
______________________	______________________
______________________	______________________
______________________	______________________
______________________	______________________
______________________	______________________
______________________	______________________
______________________	______________________
______________________	______________________
______________________	______________________

You might want to keep this list handy so you can refer to it from time to time. When you're feeling stressed or like your life is out of sync, remember the list and refer to it. Remember, little things that you like doing, done on a regular basis, contribute to enriching the quality of your life.

SUGGESTED READING

Bloch, D. P., & Richmond, L. J. (Eds.). (1997). *Connections between spirit & work in career development: New approaches and practical perspectives.* Palo Alto, CA: Davies-Black.

Explores the concept of meaning in work in the first half of the book and then offers career professionals practical tools for helping clients achieve their goals to connect spirit and work.

Career Action Center. (1996).*Values driven work.* Cupertino, CA: Author.

A values inventory, card deck, and facilitator's manual for counselors to use with clients to identify work values along different dimensions. The instruments help individuals identify and prioritize their values in terms of work content (the what), work environment (the where), and work relationships (with whom).

Covey, S. (1989). *The 7 habits of highly effective people.* New York: Simon & Schuster.

This a book about powerful lessons in personal change. Covey presents a holistic, principle-centered approach for solving personal and professional problems. The principles provide individuals with strategies to adapt to change and to take advantage of opportunities to create change.

Covey, S., Merrill, A. R., & Merrill, R. R. (1994). *First things first.* New York: Simon & Schuster.

Though dealing with time management and efficiency, the authors emphasize relationships and effectiveness, rather than results and efficiency. The authors have developed a "principle-centered" approach to time management that focuses on what is important to a person rather than what is urgent.

Csikszentmihalyi, M. (1997). *Finding flow.* New York: Basic Books.

The psychology of engagement with everyday life. A more readable version of *Flow* (1990), with emphasis on quality of life. Presents data about the "structures of everyday life" from creative research called the Experience Sampling Method.

Gelatt, H. B. (1998, Winter). Self-system-synergy: A career development framework for individuals and organizations. *Career Planning and Adult Development Journal, 14*(3), 13–23.

Describes an integrating framework for looking at career-life development through the life span. The holistic approach doesn't throw out what we have but incorporates the best of current concepts and techniques with a renewed emphasis on what has been neglected.

Guterman, M. S. *Common sense for uncommon times.* (1994). Palo Alto, CA: Consulting Psychologists Press.

Presents a model called "generative balancing, which is the will and capacity for creating success, finding meaning, and renewing ourselves daily and over the long haul." Includes a series of interviews with a diverse group of people who discuss their struggles with balancing and how their learned lessons can move them forward.

Hall, D. T. (Ed.). (1996). *The career is dead, long live the career.* San Francisco: Jossey-Bass.

A relational approach to careers, Chapter 1, "The Protean Career: Psychological Success and the Path with a Heart," and Part 2, "Relational Influences on Career

Development," are especially relevant, but the entire book is of interest to career counselors.

Handy, C. (1998). *The hungry spirit: Beyond capitalism—A quest for purpose in the modern world.* New York: Broadway Books.

"Money is the means of life and not the point of it," Handy states in the preface. With this book he hopes to persuade individuals to find a balance between the need to live comfortably and the need to find balance and meaning in our "consumer/consuming" society.

Hansen, L. S. (1997). *Integrative life planning: Critical tasks for career development and changing life patterns.* San Francisco: Jossey-Bass.

Integrative Life Planning (ILP), which incorporates many aspects of individual, family, and organizational life, consists of six critical tasks: finding work that needs doing, holistic career development, connecting family and work, valuing pluralism, exploring spirituality and life purpose, and managing personal and organizational transitions. (See also chapter 4 of this book for a synopsis of ILP.)

Hudson, F. M., & McLean, P. D. (1995). *LifeLaunch: A passionate guide to the rest of your life.* Santa Barbara, CA: Hudson Institute Press.

Designed as a workbook to be read slowly and then pondered, each chapter has a set of questions to consider from a personal viewpoint. Topics include patterns of change, defining one's "passions" and values; personal roles, seven stages of life, need for continuous learning, planning and vision, and developing "staying power."

Levey, J., & Levey, M. (1998). *Living in Balance.* Berkeley, CA: Conari Press.

Presents a dynamic approach for creating harmony and wholeness in a chaotic world. It offers a synthesis of ancient wisdom traditions such as mindfulness with cutting-edge research on peak human performance and effective, easy-to-implement tools.

Patton, W., & McMahon, M. (1998). *Career development and systems theory, a new relationship.* Pacific Grove, CA: Brooks/Cole.

This textbook is written by two career education and career counseling practitioners from Australia. Chapter 8 is an excellent summary of the issues and elements of general systems theory. The book also reviews previous career theories in relation to systems theory.

7

Values

A KEY TO MEANINGFUL WORK

Mark Guterman and Terry Karp

Values have always been integral to the career development process and are likely to be even more important in the years ahead. Virtually all career development practitioners work with clients' values to provide clarity about guiding beliefs and to help clients determine priorities and set personally meaningful goals. No matter how this is done, the question, "What is most important to you?" is fundamental in the career development process. This chapter examines why values are important in the changing world of work and provides a definition of values. It includes techniques for helping clients find and clarify their values as well as suggestions on integrating values into the career development process. The chapter explores typical issues, questions, and conflicts that might occur as clients work with their values and provides suggestions for dealing with these challenges.

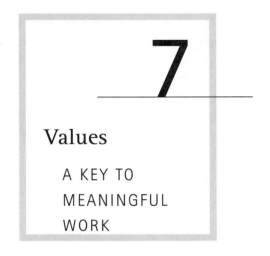

Increasing numbers of people of all ages and at all career stages are wrestling with finding meaning in their lives. There are several reasons for this heightened search. First, individuals are changing jobs and careers more frequently, and thus have more opportunities to use their guiding principles in making meaningful career decisions. These more frequent job changes are occurring partly because of changes in the global economy with downsizing, outsourcing, and the elimination of middle management positions. Job security with one employer is no longer a given. Increasing numbers of individuals are finally understanding the need to manage their own careers and to view changing employers in a more positive light.

Second, people are increasingly motivated, both by necessity and by desire, to continuously develop their skills. Many people now want to work in learning environments where they can improve and expand their marketable skills. Working with old technology, using archaic skills, or simply stagnating in one place can lead to an inability to find new opportunities in the future. People are more willing to leave a company to gain new skills and to go where they can use their talents and abilities in meaningful ways. However, sometimes, even though workers want to expand their skill sets, the often frenetic pace of work prevents this learning or puts incredible pressure on individuals to learn "just enough" to finish the project on time. Organizations tend to rely on people to continuously use their most developed and strongest skills. Sadly, this often results in an inability to acquire cutting-edge skills, and can lead to job burnout.

Third, definitions of success are no longer so linear, clear, or obvious, with the result that more people are creating personal definitions of success linked to their values. Success can no longer be solely measured by the proverbial climb up the corporate ladder, partly because those ladders are disappearing. From our vantage point, we have observed a shift in societal values in response to these changes in the world of work. Our society increasingly is embracing the values of success, prestige, and dedication associated with excessively long working hours. After all, people who are so busy all the time must be extremely important! There is a growing concern among individuals who wish to lead a more balanced life, allocating their time more evenly between work, career, family, and self-development. (See chapter 6 for more on work-life balance.) In fact, many of our clients are refusing promotions or resigning from high-powered careers in favor of pursuing other careers perceived to be more rewarding based on individual criteria of meaning and success, not a societal definition.

And fourth, spirituality and the search for meaning are being seen as a part of work, not separate from it. "Meaning" is becoming a significant and important factor in career decision making. Individuals frequently mention the need to get more out of their work than a paycheck and seem to have higher expectations from work and career than ever before. Thus, values clarification processes are critical in assisting clients with understanding their personal definitions of meaning and success. The process should enable individuals to have a deeper sense of what brings meaning to their lives, and allow them to be mindful of how certain career decisions may affect the rest of their lives. It can assist individuals with making mindful choices regarding possible conflicts around the need and desire to learn, the requirements of the organization, societal pressures, and a desire for success.

WHAT VALUES ARE

The quality of clients' values clarification experiences is dependent on them obtaining clarity and understanding of the meaning of their values. A first step in values clarification is to define the term *values*. While most career practitioners believe values are a key component in the career decision-making process, they do not all agree on the definition of values. We believe the following:

- **Values are guiding principles of life.** Values provide grounding in the key career question, "What is most important to me?" and, as such, can provide a solid foundation on which to base decisions and actions.
- **Values are not situational.** These guiding principles are who we are and do not change from work to nonwork lives; they are pervasive and enduring.
- **Values influence decisions and actions.** Values act as key criteria in choosing meaningful work and nonwork activities.
- **Values can be ordered by relative importance.** Values can be prioritized as to which are more important but cannot be artificially placed in an absolute hierarchy.

Research by Shalom Schwartz (Schwartz, 1992: Schwartz & Bilsky, 1987, 1990), a professor at Hebrew University in Jerusalem, has shown that values are based on needs—both the needs of the individual and universal human needs. In fact, research shows that values represent, in the form of conscious goals, three universal requirements of human existence to which all individuals and societies must be responsive.

- **Physical/biological survival needs of individuals.** Basic needs of shelter, food, clothing, and so on must be met before attempting to fulfill "higher-level" needs or desires.
- **Requirements for social interaction.** Humans need to interact with each other in some basic ways. Personal values are based upon how strong the need is and the type of personal fulfillment achieved by the interaction.
- **Survival and welfare needs of groups.** Our values may reflect the universal need to perpetuate our society or community in personally meaningful ways.

Schwartz derived 10 value categories from these universal requirements to test his theory about the universality of values. His data confirmed that people in many cultures implicitly distinguish these 10 types of values when evaluating the importance of specific values as guiding principles in their lives. Therefore, it appears these values have universal meaning. Later in this chapter we will present a card sort instrument, *ValueSearch* (Karp & Guterman, 1997a, 1997b), based on Schwartz's work.

Since we believe that core values are truly guiding principles of life, the ability to express those values is crucial for career satisfaction. Thus, the significance of the values will be constant regardless of whether the individual is considering life or career decisions. Clarity about values should provide insights on ways to obtain greater meaning from work. Therefore, it is our recommendation that you encourage clients to think of their entire life, not just their work life, while going through the values clarification process.

However, some people believe that work and life values are justifiably separate and, perhaps, should include different sets of values. Some may be unable to identify their values by considering their whole life. When this occurs, the initial focus should be on their work-related values since it is a career decision under consideration. If time permits, it may also be insightful to identify nonwork-related values. Some individuals may not feel any conflict or stress as a result of this dual perspective. However, the career counselor may choose to explore the client's perspective on splitting work and life values. Does the client feel tension as a result of this polarization of his or her values? Do value conflicts need to be explored? Can strategies be used to reconcile potential value conflicts? Other career-related issues may surface during these discussions that the client may wish to explore more deeply.

Another values issue for some clients is difficulty in determining which values are truly theirs and which are simply a result of internalizing other people's or society's expectations. Some, consciously or unconsciously, adopt the values of the organization where they work. The challenge in this situation is to devise a strategy that helps clients identify and choose their most important values.

One such strategy is based on our original premise that values influence our behavior and decisions. Therefore, assisting clients with identifying their true values means having them consider whether the value has been a factor in a recent decision or chosen behavior. For example, one client in sales couldn't decide whether "competition" was a primary personal value or the result of the culture in his organization. His company promoted competition within his department through weekly sales contests with significant prizes to the winners. The client was encouraged to evaluate his motivations during a recent sales contest. Ultimately, he realized his drive to succeed was based on the positive feelings associated with his personal achievement rather than a desire to be better than his coworkers.

The strategy above focused on the question, "Is the person living life consistent with his or her values?" An affirmative answer probably means the value is truly important to that individual. Understanding a negative answer is a bit trickier. Many people are unable to express their values due to life-work circumstances beyond their control. In fact, they may be seeking assistance as a direct result of this reality. One client worked in a company whose culture and corporate values were diametrically opposed to his. His coping strategy was to attempt to internalize the values of the organization. After a while, his health began to deteriorate and his relationship with his spouse became strained. However, the only reason he came to career counseling was to get job search assistance as a result of being downsized. For this client, the most poignant part of the values clarification process was reconnecting with his true values and making the commitment to find work where they could be expressed.

METHODS TO HELP CLIENTS FIND AND DECLARE THEIR VALUES

There are many ways to assist clients in this endeavor, such as beginning with questions as basic as, "What is most important to you?" or, "What most deeply motivates you?" in regard to decisions they may be facing. Several additional techniques that we have found very useful are listed below.

Journaling

Journaling is a technique often used in the career counseling process. It is a way for clients to document their experience and note how they feel at the time of writing. It also teaches them a way to work through issues they are facing. By keeping a journal, clients practice expressing what is real and important to them. They also can use previous journal entries as a means for reflection and gaining perspective on their work and life. Journaling can be as simple as keeping a diary or it can be used as a method to work through problems and issues.

One specific journaling technique is to have clients hold a "dialogue" with a particular value. For example, clients can be asked to choose a value they are ambivalent about or one they think they want but are not able to express currently. They are then instructed to write a dialogue with that value. They are told to not censor themselves while writing, to write continuously, and to not overthink while they are writing. One client held a dialogue with "security" and, in reflecting on his experience, realized for the first time that this value was not really his, but one his parents had given to him. He went on to say how he believed that holding this value so tightly had kept him from taking advantage of many enticing opportunities that had come his way. He was able to understand the power his values held over him and gained clarity about how he might want to change in the future.

Defining Moments

Many career counselors use lifeline exercises in their work with clients. A lifeline is a time line drawn to illustrate work history, key decision points, and other details relevant to the client's work life. A variation of the lifeline is an exercise called "Defining Moments." Clients are asked to reflect on their lives and make note of any event or time in their life they would describe as a defining moment–anything that helped shape them into the person they are today. These defining moments are not limited to work, nor are they limited only to the positive experiences in their life. The counselor can explore with clients underlying themes, transition patterns and styles, and how their values may have changed or evolved over time.

One client described a defining moment when she was 13 years old. She was an aspiring ballerina and had been dancing seriously since she was 7. During a major show, she took a fall that disrupted the entire performance. Though she wasn't hurt seriously, the embarrassment took its toll. Within six months she had stopped dancing altogether. In recalling this event some 25 years later, she was struck by how strongly she still identified as a ballerina. We explored this pull, which helped her to understand her values as she worked through ideas for a new career direction. She decided to go back to school for a graduate degree in drama therapy, and now uses movement, music, and psychodrama to help children and adolescents with their fears and anxieties.

Genogram

A genogram is a brief history drawn to resemble a family tree. It includes immediate family such as parents, grandparents, siblings, partner, and children, and any others who may have had influence in the client's life. The client draws a diagram (genogram) that notes (1) his or her relationship to each person, (2) that person's work, (3) the messages he or she received from that person about work, and (4) the values that individual imparted to him or her. The client can then use the genogram to explore his or her feelings about work and values to better understand how he or she might be experiencing guilt or conflict, or living according to someone else's values. The genogram can be discussed with others if you are in a group setting. Typically, some clients will be struck by the gap they discover between the messages they received growing up and how they feel in the moment. Others may acknowledge that much of their work life has been guided by "shoulds." For example, one young man wanted to be a writer and poet, but instead became an attorney because of his parents' strong belief in prestige and security. The genogram and subsequent discussions allowed him to come to grips with this reality and gave him strength to pursue another career direction.

Visual Representations of Values

Another way to help clients understand their values is through some sort of visual representation or a values metaphor such as a symbol, picture, word, or feeling that captures the essence of their most important values. For example, one client drew a large "V" at the center of a career map. Inside her "V," she listed her top values and what they meant to her. Her values became a visual anchor for her goals and development plans. In another example, a group of students created a "values collage," pasting pictures and other illustrations of their values onto posterboard. Some have created sculptures, mobiles, and comic books during this process. The technique is even more powerful when participants then get up in front of the group to "declare and claim" their values. These visual representations have been used as frequent references in the career decision-making process.

Card Sort Techniques

A frequently used tool in values clarification is a card sort instrument. Although there are many on the market, we'll discuss the one we created, *ValueSearch* (Karp & Guterman, 1997a, 1997b, 1997c), based on Schwartz's research. Our experiences with *ValueSearch* will serve to illustrate how to work with clients in the values clarification process. We want to be clear, however, that any values instrument, well used, can help your clients to find and declare their values.

ValueSearch consists of 60 values words. See Figure 7.1 for the list of values. Clients begin the process by sorting the 60 words into four categories: Always Valued, Often Valued, Sometimes Valued, and Never Valued. After clients sort the *ValueSearch* cards, they are asked to identify their top 10 values. Ten is an arbitrary number, so clients should be allowed to "keep" the values they simply cannot give up. Some clients wind up with more than 10 and a few have less.

The next step is for clients to write a personal definition for each of their top values—a few specific words or phrases that capture the meaning of that value for them. This step is necessary because simply choosing value words from a list is not sufficient to obtain clarity and understanding of the

Accomplishment	Adventure
Affiliation	Artistic Expression
Authority	Autonomy
Balance	Beauty
Challenge	Community
Competence	Competition
Contribution	Control
Cooperation	Creativity
Curiosity	Diversity
Duty	Faith
Family	Friendship
Fun	Harmony
Health	Helpful
High Earnings	Honesty
Humility	Independence
Influence	Integrity
Justice	Knowledge
Leadership	Learning
Love	Loyalty
Meaning	Moderation
Nature	Obligation
Pleasure	Predictability
Recognition	Respect
Responsibility	Risk-Taking
Self-Discipline	Self-Restraint
Service	Spirituality
Stability	Status
Structure	Team Work
Time Freedom	Trust
Variety	Wisdom

Source: Copyright © 1999 by Karp & Guterman. Used with permission.

Figure 7.1 *ValueSearch* Values List

meaning of an individual's values. Many times, values are subject to varying interpretations. Thus, words tied to values may have unique meaning based on each individual's life experience, and it is important to hear what those unique definitions are.

The definition process can be done in session or as homework. There are advantages and disadvantages to each. By having clients define their values in session, you can watch how they approach this task and make note of any issues or difficulties that come up. For example, one woman, when asked to define her values, had a difficult time. When asked what the difficulty was, she spoke of feeling disconnected from both the words themselves and the emotions associated with them. This gave the facilitator valuable insight into further work with the client. However, defining the words in session may take valuable process time and clients may feel under pressure to write a quick definition. The advantage of sending the assignment home with clients is that they can take more time with the definitions, even using a dictionary or thesaurus to help them out. This allows for deeper reflection, as well as more time to internalize the words and their meaning. With this approach, in the next session, the counselor should ask clients to share their definitions, as well as any feelings or insights that arose while writing.

To add to a client's ownership of the process, we encourage clients to add words not on the list that are important to them. Whether using our list of 60 *ValueSearch* words or your own favorite values instrument, no list is complete or exhaustive. It may also be that clients have preferred words to describe a particular value. Encourage them to substitute words they like better or are simply more comfortable with. Giving clients this option of adding or substituting words personalizes the process and makes it more meaningful.

As the clients define and understand what their values mean, a number of questions need to be addressed:

- Do the clients take ownership of their values? In other words, are they able say to themselves, "These really are my values!"?

- And, if owned, are they freely chosen or are they what the client believes *should* be most important?

- How do clients' energy levels change when they talk about their most important values? How do they feel about their chosen values? clear and confident? conflicted and concerned? If the latter, what else can they do to clarify their values?

A word of caution is necessary in this phase of prioritizing values. Counselors often ask their clients to rank order the values and decide definitively which is number one, two, and so on. We believe that this is unnecessary and might even get in the way of helping clients determine their most important values. Clients typically hold several values as vitally important to them. Forcing a hierarchy usually feels artificial and adds little to the values clarification process.

MAPPING VALUE PATTERNS

For many career counselors the values process ends with the identification of the top values of the card sort. We suggest two additional steps to help your clients understand their values—mapping values into patterns and then looking for underlying themes. We use the *ValueSearch* Map (Karp & Guterman, 1997c) shown in Figure 7.2 on page 238 and have our clients map out their top 10 or so values, looking for how and where their values cluster. The map is based on Schwartz's research that found that people typically placed specific values into categories.

To find patterns, we have clients read the definitions of the eight categories on the *ValueSearch* Map after writing their own personal definitions. The next step is to highlight or underline each of their top values in the suggested categories if those categories represent their personal definition of the values. If another category feels like a better fit, they simply write the word in that category. "Balance," "spirituality," and "family" are examples of values that people often move to different categories. Our objective is to ensure that the clustering on the map truly reflects clients' personal meaning of their values.

According to our theory, values strongly influence our behavior, decisions, and actions. Therefore, each category can be viewed as representing certain motivational goals. Following is a definition of the eight *ValueSearch* categories and associated motivational goals they represent.

- **Benevolence and Universality.** The motivational goal of benevolence is a desire to preserve and improve the well-being of people with whom one is in close and frequent contact. The motivational goal of universality is an interest in promoting the welfare of all people and of nature. Therefore, the focus of benevolence is much narrower than that of universality. Individuals with a desire to manage a well-functioning team and mentor individuals may have values clustering in the benevolence category. Universality values may be important to those wanting to have an impact on global issues such as homelessness or poverty.

- **Tradition and Security.** The motivational goal of tradition is the commitment to and acceptance of the customs and ideas that one's culture, religion, or society expects of individuals. Security values indicate a desire for consistency and stability. Both categories stress a desire to

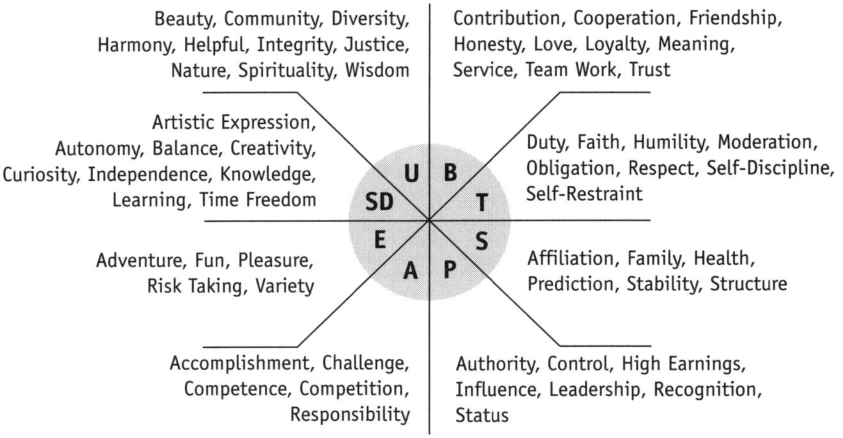

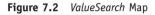

U—Universality
Understanding, appreciation, tolerance, and protection of the welfare of *all* people and of nature.

B—Benevolence
Concern for the protection and enhancement of the welfare of people with whom one is in frequent contact.

T— Tradition
Respect for, commitment to, and acceptance of customs and ideas that one's culture or religion expects of individuals.

S— Security
Desire for safety, harmony, and stability of society, relationships, and self.

P— Power
Attainment of social status, prestige, influence, authority, or leadership of people and resources.

A—Achievement
Desire for personal success or accomplishment. Need to demonstrate competence in everyday life.

E— Excitement
Seek pleasure or sensuous gratification. Enjoy unpredictability and variety in life.

SD—Self-Direction
Pursue independent thought or action. Enjoy the ability to choose, create, and explore.

Source: Copyright © 1999 by Karp & Guterman. Used with permission.

Figure 7.2 *ValueSearch* Map

preserve the status quo and the predictability this provides. However, tradition favors self-restraint to support socially imposed expectations. Security favors self-restraint to protect the self. Some people choose careers based on cultural or familial pressures. One client believed her family would not view her as successful unless she went into one of the few fields approved by them, and thus she became a software engineer. However, after three years of hating her job, she came to career counseling. When clarifying her values, she realized the importance of the tradition category even though it had led her to an inappropriate career decision. This time she chose to use the tradition value but with a different focus—she sought her parents' advice and support but not their belief that only a few career fields were good.

- **Power and Achievement.** The central goal of power values is the attainment of influence, authority, status, or leadership of people and resources. Achievement values indicate a desire for personal success or accomplishment and a need to demonstrate competence in everyday life. For example, a client with achievement values may want to solve complex problems, is motivated by challenge, and loves the feeling of accomplishment from his or her work. This person may not be concerned with the values in the power category, such as authority and status.
- **Self-Direction and Excitement.** The predominant goal of self-direction is independent thought and action. Individuals with values in this category enjoy the ability to choose, create, and explore. We have observed that many entrepreneurs, consultants, artists, and career counselors have values clustering in this category. Excitement values refer to seeking pleasure or sensual gratification. Unpredictability and variety in life seem to be important to people with values in excitement.

Using the *ValueSearch* Map

Most of our clients show definite values patterns. If there is no obvious cluster, we often have them look at the next group of most important values. Usually, they will then see patterns. This clustering gives a greater cohesion to the clients' values, enabling both stronger ownership and deeper understanding of what is most important. Clients tell us that seeing the patterns of their values gives them a clearer picture of what is true for them. It also allows them to see consistencies (those clusters that are close together on the map) and possible areas of values conflict (those clusters that are opposite each other on the map). This helps them integrate knowledge of their values into the entire career development process.

Counselors don't always need a map to find patterns in clients' values. An alternative is to discuss with clients how they see their values clustering and to ask about the areas of consistency or possible conflict. However, we find that having a graphic, such as the *ValueSearch* Map, gives a strong anchor to clients' values patterns. And many clients have told us they believe this mapping is far more meaningful than simply having a list of their top 10 values. We encourage counselors who use other instruments to create their own graphics to help clients see and understand their values patterns.

INTEGRATING VALUES INTO THE CAREER DEVELOPMENT PROCESS

Clients need the next level of identifying connecting themes between their values to enable them to understand the impact values have on their work-life decisions. An effective values clarification process should enable individuals to have a deeper sense of what brings meaning to their lives and how certain career decisions may affect the rest of their lives. Thus, this question becomes, "How can your values be integrated with your next step and bring satisfaction and meaning to your work and life?"

After mapping values and understanding the categories, we help clients look at the underlying themes (Karp & Guterman, 1997c), or "find the hidden meaning of their values." As you can see from Figure 7.3, this is both a simpler and a deeper level of understanding values. It is simpler in that clients can usually identify which of the four themes is most personally meaningful, which provides them with a higher degree of clarity. In fact, our clients are better able to link their values with career possibilities once they understand these themes.

- **Self-Transcendence.** Self-transcendence is a combination of the universality and benevolence categories. This theme indicates a desire to transcend concerns with the self and promote the welfare of others. Typically, people associate these values with careers in the nonprofit sector. However, many other careers are consistent with these values. One client with self-transcendence values worked in e-commerce and believed he was helping people have more free time by shortening the shopping process. Individuals with these types of values will want to consider how they wish to contribute. They may want to find an organization that

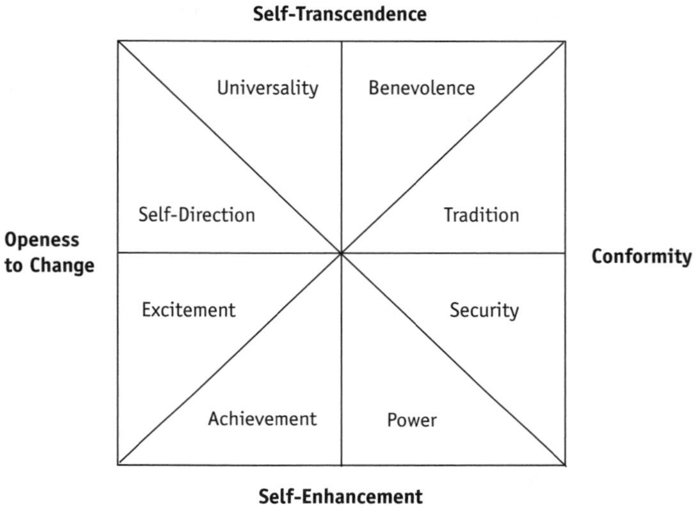

Outer Layer Definitions

Self-Transcendence

Combines universality and benevolence values, which motivate people to transcend selfish concerns and promote the welfare of others and of nature.

Conformity

Combines tradition and security values, leading to a desire to preserve the status quo and the predictability this provides in relationships with other people, institutions, and traditions.

Self-Enhancement

Combines achievement and power values, indicating a desire of individuals to enhance their own personal interests.

Openness to Change

Combines self-direction and excitement values, indicating a desire of individuals to follow their own intellectual and emotional interests in unpredictable and uncertain directions.

Source: Copyright © 1999 by Karp & Guterman. Used with permission.

Figure 7.3 *ValueSearch* Model

mirrors their moral, ethical, and/or spiritual beliefs. Developing a well-functioning team, coaching, and bringing beauty into others' lives through interior design are all examples of ways to integrate these values with various career options.

- **Conformity.** Conformity combines tradition and security values that motivate people to preserve the status quo and the predictability this provides in relationships with other people, organizations, and traditions.

Career counselors should explore the client's feelings around risk taking and change as, many times, they strongly influence the client's ability to engage in the career change process. We have generally observed that individuals with these values want to have a fairly stable work situation. The current need to ensure one's own employability and lack of company loyalty to workers may be extremely difficult for people with these values. Stability and security in today's work environment are difficult to achieve. Also, many companies no longer have position descriptions; there is simply work needing to be done. One might be a project leader on one project and an individual contributor on another. Exploring these business realities with clients who have difficulty with change and lack of security is critical to their ability to find career satisfaction. One strategy is to help them understand that job security lies within and help them create a development plan to ensure their marketability for the future.

- **Self-Enhancement.** People with self-enhancement themes are focused on enhancing their personal interests. Many individuals with these values may want a challenging position where they feel they are accomplishing something tangible. Some of our clients working in start-up companies have values clustering in this area. They are motivated by the challenge and potentially high financial rewards associated with start-up ventures. Financial incentives can be a significant factor to individuals with these values, as can the opportunity for increased levels of responsibility. Career counselors may want to help individuals determine whether they want the emphasis on continuous striving to demonstrate and perfect skills (achievement) or whether they actually want to obtain and keep a specific leadership position or role in an organization (power).

- **Openness to Change.** Openness to change combines self-direction and excitement values, indicating a desire by individuals to follow their own intellectual and emotional interests in unpredictable and uncertain directions. Many creative people fall within this category and counselors should encourage them to explore how they wish to express their creativity. Flexibility may also be an important factor to clients with these values. If clients value fun, pleasure, and adventure (excitement) it is useful to consider what they do during nonworking time for clues about career alternatives.

Working with the Themes

It is important to note that many different career options can satisfy different themes. Making automatic assumptions about which careers are compatible with each theme can eliminate viable possibilities. For example, the engineer in e-commerce with self-transcendence values could have just as easily been satisfied with his career if his values clustered in the self-enhancement area. In this case, the career could express values of challenge and financial rewards. We typically engage our clients in brainstorming exercises to encourage a free flow of ideas about career possibilities.

The four themes help clients understand not only how their values affect their day-to-day decisions, but also how their stance and outlook on life are affected by their values. In this way, the themes enable clients to achieve a much deeper understanding of their values. Again, it is not necessary to use *ValueSearch* to glean these deeper meanings of your clients' values. It does require paying close attention to your client during values work and listening for the deeper themes.

THE IMPACT OF SOCIETAL VALUES ON INDIVIDUAL VALUES

Society often plays a key role in the values we hold. We are taught to believe that some values are "better" than others. This is especially true in contemporary society, as witnessed by the increased coverage of values in the news, within organizations, and even within our government. Values are the hot topic of the new millennium.

Sometimes, this emphasis creates conflicts in individuals. Clients in some settings may be hesitant to claim values of success, power, prestige, or status based on societal pressures. Some of our clients speak of "good" and "bad" values. They describe feelings of anxiety as a result of their perception that, although our society outwardly embraces benevolence or helping types of values, we truly are judged by our success. How financially successful are we? What type of car do we drive? Creating a safe environment in the counseling session or with the group is critical to enable individuals to feel secure in expressing their true values.

As with many facets of career counseling, it is of paramount importance that the counselor be cognizant of how his or her own values influence the client's process. Career counselors can subtly make judgments about the validity or worthiness of values chosen by their clients. For example, "conformity" or "self-restraint" may not be widely held or popular values in Western society. However, one client who had done previous work with values was thrilled to see "conformity" in the process. Conformity accurately expressed her cultural heritage as well as her personal values. Working with clients who hold completely different values requires sensitivity and awareness of our own values.

HELPING INDIVIDUALS WITH VALUE CONFLICTS

Value categories in close proximity tend to be compatible. However, if a client has value clusters on opposite sides of the map, it does not necessarily mean the client is in conflict. For example, a woman from an outplacement firm had values of helping, meaning, and contribution, as well as influence, achievement, power, and competition. She felt her career was perfect. Her values of helping others were expressed through assisting outplaced workers. Values of achievement, success, and power were met by her responsibility to generate new business for the firm.

Once value themes are identified, it becomes apparent how the simultaneous pursuit of incongruent values can lead to feelings of stress and conflict for individuals. Many times, people have incompatible values as a result of a changed life situation. One client, a new father, had values of adventure and risk taking. His dream was to become associated with a start-up company and he had been interviewing with several. However, his wife had quit her job to stay home with their baby and the family needed him to provide a steady income. Ultimately, after exploring his values and considering the needs of the family, he understood the necessity of putting some of his values on hold until a more opportune time.

Confusion or conflict may sometimes arise in those holding values of financial success or achievement who also want balance and/or family time. They may have sacrificed the latter two values in order to attain financial rewards. Consider the high-wage earner who has become accustomed to a certain lifestyle. In fact, the individual's family members have also grown to enjoy the benefits of high income. We have often heard these clients say that they need to earn a certain amount of money but want more balance in their lives.

Balance and lifestyle are values we hear a lot about. Many times, they are the values that create the most tension with clients' other values (as well as other career aspirations). There are no easy answers to this dilemma. External constraints often prevent us from being able to be passionate about our work in every age and stage of life. Often, tradeoffs are required for clients to craft a satisfying career path. One strategy is for career counselors to assist these clients in developing two-tiered career plans—one for the near term that addresses current needs but also provides a bridge to a more ideal work-life situation in the future.

Assisting individuals with identifying value conflicts may result in a better ability to make work-life choices that are compatible with their current situation. For example, some individuals may need to fulfill certain values at work and others in nonwork environments. As a career counselor, you can affect your clients' ability to obtain clarity regarding their values and help them develop strategies to resolve some value conflicts.

A KEY FOR ALL VALUES CLARIFICATION PROCESSES

Exploring clients' perspectives on integrating their values into career decision making is just one piece of the process. Clients continually need to be reminded that many other factors (such as skills, interests, and temperament) must be considered in order to obtain a full view of their criteria. Some clients want to rush to judgment every step of the way, to make their decision and move on to the next step. Resistance to change, fear of the unknown, and issues around transition may underlie these tendencies. Exploring these issues with clients often brings clarity about fears and can lead to developing effective coping strategies.

It is important to remember that values are not just a listing of words, but rather a way that people make sense of the world and how they see themselves in the future. In this way values are deeply connected to aspirations. Values, therefore, must be understood clearly, not only to ensure good decision making, but also to help clients move toward their own meaningful future. Whatever methodology you use, it is vital to take values work to the depths we have suggested.

SUMMARY

Values are becoming increasingly important for individuals and organizations. More people are seeking meaning in their work lives, and more organizations are recognizing that they can harness this need to enhance their growth. Values are the glue that brings the two together. We have described how we see values work, including some methods and our underlying thinking. We encourage you to continue your exploration and thinking about values and to keep the following in mind as you do:

- **Values work is not an absolute process.** There is no one right or best way to get at values. Allow whatever method you use to be open and flexible, and be prepared to try something new if what you are doing isn't working.
- **Resist the temptation to provide answers for your clients.** Don't presume that you know the answers or know what is best. Help your clients develop comfort with not knowing and working through the process. Continue to build your own tolerance for ambiguity.
- **Your own values influence your work with clients.** They influence your assumptions, the way you hear your clients' issues, and how you work. Work on your own clarity and take ownership of your values.
- **Every encounter with a client is an opportunity for learning—for you and the client.** We are here for clients and, at the same time, must always be open to our own growth and development. Keep an open mind and a warm heart and allow your clients to be your teachers.

REFERENCES

Karp, T., & Guterman, M. (1997a). *ValueSearch card deck.* Oakland, CA: ValueSearch.

Karp, T., & Guterman, M. (1997b). *ValueSearch counselor's manual.* Oakland, CA: ValueSearch.

Karp, T., & Guterman, M. (1997c). *ValueSearch profile form.* Oakland, CA: ValueSearch.

Schwartz, S. H., & Bilsky, W. (1987). Toward a psychological structure of human values. *Journal of Personality and Social Psychology, 53,* 550–562.

Schwartz, S. H., and Bilsky, W. (1990). Toward a theory of universal content and structure of values: Extensions and cross-cultural replications. *Journal of Personality and Social Psychology, 58,* 878–891.

Schwartz, S. H. (1992). Universals in the content and structure of values: Theoretical advances and empirical tests in 20 countries. *Advances in Experimental Social Psychology, 25,* 1–65.

8

Multicultural Career Counseling

AWARENESS, KNOWLEDGE, AND SKILLS FOR THE CHANGING FACE OF THE WORKPLACE

Rosie Phillips Bingham

Many career counselors have been trained to counsel in fairly homogeneous settings. The vocational theories and intervention techniques are generally effective in these situations. A challenge arises when the setting becomes more culturally diverse. With the addition of multicultural counseling guidelines, counselors can understand how to work with people from culturally diverse groups. The need for such understanding is increasing. Statistics show that the U.S. workforce and workforces around the world in multinational corporations are becoming more diverse. (See chapter 2 for more on these trends.) The data suggest a complex array of factors that could have dramatic effects on U.S. society. Career counselors can help workers and employers sort through many upcoming decisions to positively manage the change that the dawn of the 21st century is bringing. The challenge is how to put all of the information together in a meaningful way.

This chapter is designed to help individuals become more effective as multicultural career counselors. It describes some of the existing literature that addresses career counseling in a multicultural setting and includes several checklists and culturally appropriate career models. The chapter ends with an exercise designed to help practitioners explore their knowledge about and comfort with working with someone from another culture.

BACKGROUND

During the last several decades, an upsurge of writing on multicultural topics has added significantly to career counseling theories. Each work indicates a need for awareness, knowledge, and skill in working across diverse ethnic/racial groups, and many offer suggestions on how to do so. For example, counselors might increase intercultural awareness by seeing a movie about a specific cultural group, having a conversation with someone from that group, or eating in a restaurant specific to the group. Knowledge can be gained through workshops, classes, or other courses of study. Skills might be enhanced by a supervised practicum or by coleading a group with a counselor who is more experienced in cultural diversity.

A starting point for all counselors is an awareness and understanding of their own and their clients' worldviews, so that they can develop and implement appropriate intervention strategies based on their clients' worldviews. A worldview is the lens through which we see and understand the world around us. It shapes and is shaped by all of the norms, mores, and folk traditions that are held by an identified group, and it is passed on to successive generations. It determines our frame of reference, interests, beliefs, values, and attitudes. Career counseling interventions often seek to measure our interests, values, beliefs, attitudes, and abilities in order to help individuals find satisfying careers. It seems reasonable therefore that career counselors would be interested in worldviews.

Wade Nobles (1976) introduced many counselors to this notion when he described African and European worldviews. The European worldview focuses on the individual, competition, and survival of the fittest, whereas the African worldview is concerned with groupness, cooperation, and survival of the group. Most of the major U.S. ethnic minority groups—Native American, African American, Asian American, and Latin American—have a worldview that focuses on relationships as opposed to the individual. Asian groups include a strong emphasis on the family and a concern for hierarchical relationships, encompassing, for example, a great deference to parents. Judith Katz (1985) provided an extensive discussion of White culture in the United States, which is centered on the individual, survival of the fittest, the nuclear family, the Protestant work ethic, and future time orientation. This worldview is most prevalent in counseling theories and is sometimes measured with interest inventories.

Career counselors work from their own worldviews. If a counselor has a European worldview and is working with a client with a different worldview, then the client's career indecision may mean considerably different things to each party. For example, when Asian Americans seek career counseling because they are undecided about what they want to do, the career counselor operating within a European worldview may not understand that these clients may be really concerned with respecting their parents' wishes. An interest inventory may indicate that the client is interested in becoming a psychologist. The instrument will not show that the client's parents have been promoting an engineering career. If the counselor is not aware of the influence of worldviews, such clients will leave with a great interpretation of their interest inventory but will continue to have the same problem for which they originally sought counseling.

This example may shed some light on the phenomenon of early termination of the counseling process by many ethnic minority clients. Perhaps the client and the counselor are actually seeing the world just differently enough that the two are not accurately communicating. Because ethnic minorities are so important to the workforce, it is essential that career counselors begin to understand how to effectively counsel racial and ethnic minorities. The steps below may provide insight about the place held by worldviews and other cultural variables in the career counseling process.

CAREER ASSESSMENT

Often the most challenging part of the career problem-solving process is the assessment. If an appropriate, thorough, and accurate assessment can be completed, then the intervention is relatively simple and straightforward. The intervention can be creative and culturally sensitive. Bingham and Ward (1997) proposed a four-step model for career assessment, which, although originally designed for women of color, is applicable to any cross-cultural counseling setting (see Figure 8.1). The authors recommend that counselors assess the following:

1. **Cultural variables**–including worldviews, identity development, family, and *structure of opportunity*. Structure of opportunity refers to any

particular barriers, rules (written or unwritten), or laws that influence the opportunities for groups of people to obtain certain jobs. Racism and sexism help determine the structure of opportunity in the United States. For example, it is currently very difficult for a woman to ascend to the presidency of the United States of America, and there are very few representatives from ethnic groups who hold seats in the U.S. legislature. In India, the "untouchables" are often restricted to the lowliest of occupations. Some career options may be closed to some cultural groups or may be very difficult for them to achieve because of the formal and informal design of the society in which they reside.

2. **Gender variables**—including gender-role socialization and the importance given to work and home, families, and relationships.

3. **Efficacy variables**—defined as one's beliefs or self-confidence in one's own ability to succeed in a career, task, academic major, or specific subject (such as math or science).

4. **Traditional career factors**—such as interests, abilities, values, and decision making.

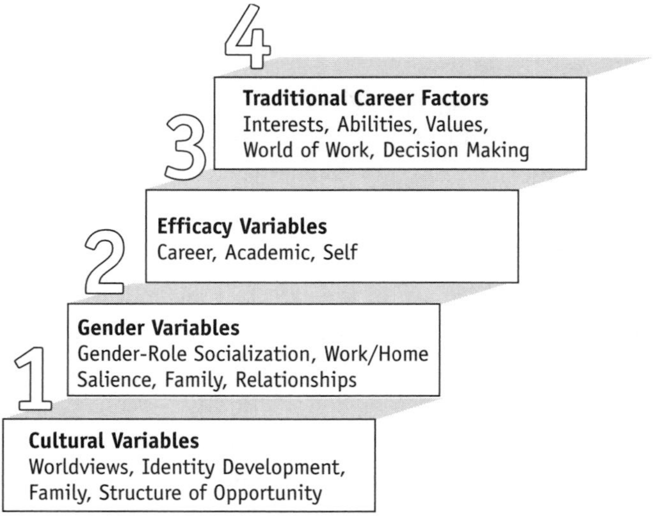

Source: Copyright © 1997 by Rosie Phillips Bingham, University of Memphis. Used with permission.

Figure 8.1 Steps to Multicultural Career Assessment

In a cross-cultural counseling setting, beginning the process with the cultural variables—step 1 in Figure 8.1—may be enough to identify the real issues. Sometimes when a person of color enters into a career counseling relationship, there are issues at play that have little to do with actual indecision about a specific job or career. For example, many African Americans will ask for help from a vocational/career counselor when in fact they need personal counseling. These clients are not comfortable with the notion of seeking professional help for psychological disturbances. Many times these individuals are more likely to seek personal help from a friend or a spiritual helper. In my own practice, I have noticed that some Latin students have been more willing to obtain help with study skills than help for an ailment like depression. Therefore, the career counselor needs to be certain that cultural conditioning has not misdirected the client because career counseling is more acceptable than psychological counseling. At the beginning of the assessment process, the counselor should determine whether the client is there for career issues or for something else. The counselor must develop an intake process, such as a verbal interview or a paper-and-pencil problem checklist, which asks questions about personal as well as career issues. If the client's answers suggest that the issues are mainly psychological or personal, it is important to validate that with the client and then refer the client to an appropriate therapist or conduct psychological counseling, if qualified.

If the client indicates that the matter is career related, then the counselor must determine if cultural variables are interfering with a career decision. If no cultural variables (including gender) are interfering, then it may be wise to proceed to a more traditional career assessment. The key question is, "How does one determine if there are cultural variables?"

Because worldview, identity development, and family are important considerations in the career development and counseling process with racial/ethnic minorities, several protocols were created to help organize the career counseling intake process as well as career interventions. Readers can use these instruments as guidelines to accommodate clients from diverse backgrounds.

A major protocol for organizing the intake process is the *Multicultural Career Counseling Checklist* (MCCC) by Ward and Bingham (1993). It contains 48 items to help the counselor think through issues that might affect a client's career decision. The MCCC includes sections on the client's and counselor's ethnic/racial identities, counselor preparation, exploration and assessment, and negotiation and working consensus. It is shown in Exercise 8.1 and discussed in some detail below. The checklist is not a research-based instrument; it was designed to help counselors organize some of the countless variables when working with clients in all cultural groups. It can be difficult to remember all the idiosyncrasies of all the cultural groups with which a career counselor works. Having a frame of reference for processing data from the client can be useful when a client is culturally different from a counselor. Ward and Bingham recommend that counselors adapt the inventory to suit any ethnic group or gender.

COUNSELOR PREPARATION

The initial phase of any career counseling intervention is counselor preparation. With multicultural clients this includes factoring in multicultural issues. The MCCC is designed for use before counselors begin an intake interview with a potential client. The checklist asks counselors first to identify their racial/ethnic identity and their client's. This starts counselors thinking about possible similarities and differences between them. For example, if the counselor is an African American female and the client is a Nigerian female, it is helpful to be aware that in some Nigerian groups women are discouraged from entering an occupation that would put them in competition with men for jobs (Denga, 1988). If the student wants to be a doctor, and her brother also wants to be one, her family might object. This client might tell the counselor that she is undecided about a career whereas in reality she might feel in conflict with her family's wishes. But, if the same African American counselor is working with a European American woman who wants to be a doctor, she has no reason to expect family conflict about it.

As you think about groups, traits, and tendencies, remember that a client from a particular ethnic/racial group may hold none of the generally ascribed traits. "Think globally; act locally." The general information serves as a basis for a hypothesis, not as a basis for fact. The common worldviews are only a starting point.

In the MCCC preparation section, counselors are reminded to think about the client's culture, cultural identification, ethnic/racial group history, sociopolitical issues (see Katz, 1985, for a discussion of sociopolitical

EXERCISE 8.1

MULTICULTURAL CAREER COUNSELING CHECKLIST

If you have a client of a different ethnicity or race than yours, you may wish to use this checklist as you begin to do the career assessment. The following statements are designed to help you think more thoroughly about the racially or ethnically different client to whom you are about to provide career counseling. Check all the statements that apply.

My racial/ethnic identity ____________________

My client's racial/ethnic identity ____________________

I. *Counselor Preparation*

☐ 1. I am familiar with minimum cross-cultural counseling competencies.

☐ 2. I am aware of my client's cultural identification.

☐ 3. I understand and respect my client's culture.

☐ 4. I am aware of my own worldview and how it was shaped.

☐ 5. I am aware of how my SES influences my ability to empathize with this client.

☐ 6. I am aware of how my political views influence my counseling with a client from this ethnic group.

☐ 7. I have had counseling or other life experiences with different racial/ethnic groups.

☐ 8. I have information about this client's ethnic group's history, local sociopolitical issues, and attitudes toward seeking help.

☐ 9. I know many of the strengths of this client's ethnic group.

☐ 10. I know where I am in my racial identity development.

☐ 11. I know the general stereotypes held about my client's ethnic group.

☐ 12. I am comfortable confronting ethnic minority clients.

☐ 13. I am aware of the importance that the interaction of gender and race/ethnicity has in my client's life.

EXERCISE 8.1 (CONT'D)

II. *Exploring and Assessment*

☐ 1. I understand this client's career questions.

☐ 2. I understand how the client's career questions may be complicated with issues of finance, family, and academics.

☐ 3. The client is presenting racial and/or cultural information with the career questions.

☐ 4. I am aware of the career limitations or obstacles the client associates with race or culture.

☐ 5. I understand what the client's perceived limitations are.

☐ 6. I know the client's perception of the family's ethnocultural identification.

☐ 7. I am aware of the client's perception of the family's support for the client's career.

☐ 8. I know which career the client believes the family wants the client to pursue.

☐ 9. I know whether the client's family's support is important to the client.

☐ 10. I believe that familial obligations are dictating the client's career choices.

☐ 11. I know the extent of exposure to career information and role models the client had in high school and beyond.

☐ 12. I understand the impact the high school experiences (positive or negative) have had on the client's confidence.

☐ 13. I am aware of the client's perception of his or her competence, ability, and self-efficacy.

☐ 14. I believe the client avoids certain work environments because of fears of sexism or racism.

☐ 15. I know the client's stage of racial identity development.

EXERCISE 8.1 (CONT'D)

III. *Negotiations and Working Consensus*

☐ 1. I understand the type of career counseling help the client is seeking (career choice, supplement of family income, professional career, etc.).

☐ 2. The client and I have agreed on the goals for career counseling.

☐ 3. I know how this client's gender role in the family influences the client's career choices.

☐ 4. I am aware of the client's perception of the role of work in the family and in the culture.

☐ 5. I am aware of the client's understanding of the role of children in his or her career plans.

☐ 6. I am aware of the extent of exposure to a variety of career role models the client has had.

☐ 7. I understand the culturally based career conflicts that are generated by exposure to more careers and role models.

☐ 8. I know the client's career aspirations.

☐ 9. I am aware of the level of confidence the client has in his or her ability to obtain his or her aspirations.

☐ 10. I know the client understands the relationship between type of work and educational level.

☐ 11. I am aware of the negative and/or self-defeating thoughts that are obstacles to the client's aspirations and expectations.

☐ 12. I know if the client and I need to renegotiate goals as appropriate after exploring cultural and family issues.

☐ 13. I know the client understands the career exploration process.

☐ 14. I am aware of the client's expectations about the career counseling process.

EXERCISE 8.1 (CONT'D)

☐ 15. I know when it is appropriate to use a traditional career assessment instrument with a client from this ethnic group.

☐ 16. I know which instrument to use with this client.

☐ 17. I am aware of the research support for using the selected instrument with clients of this ethnicity.

☐ 18. I am aware of nontraditional instruments that might be more appropriate for use with clients from this ethnic group.

☐ 19. I am aware of nontraditional approaches to using traditional instruments with clients from this ethnic group.

☐ 20. I am aware of the career strengths the client associates with the client's race or culture.

Source: Ward, C. M., and Bingham, R. P., "Career Assessment of Ethnic Minority Women." Reproduced by special permission of the publisher. Psychological Assessment Resources, Inc., Odessa, FL, from the *Journal of Career Assessment, 1*(3).

influences in counseling), attitudes toward help seeking, strengths, and the interaction of gender and race/ethnicity in the client's life. Counselors are also reminded to think about their own worldview, racial identity development, socioeconomic status, life experiences with the client's ethnic/racial group, personal comfort with confronting ethnic minority clients, and familiarity with cross-cultural counseling competencies.

Part of counselor preparation is a knowledge of racial identity development. The best-known and best-researched theory on this topic explores the racial identity development of Black Americans in the United States. See Cross (1971) and Helms (1990) for an extensive discussion of the model. Based on the work of these writers, others have indicated that most racial/ethnic groups in the United States go through some type of identity development process because of being in a minority group. Atkinson, Morten, and Sue (1983) proposed a minority identity development process that captures the essence of the models for most groups. The developmental models generally include four or five steps (or *statuses*—the term preferred by Helms). Sue et al. (1998) delineate the steps as follows:

- First, ethnic minority individuals wholeheartedly accept the dominant culture. They may be inclined to accept the stereotypes (positive and negative) held by the majority group. These individuals tend to be very positively focused toward the majority group and negatively inclined toward the minority group.
- Next, minority individuals begin to question their majority group frame of reference. They may have encountered discrimination that is clearly a result of their ethnicity and are forced to recognize the place that minority status holds as a determinant of gaining access to a job, partner, or housing.
- Then, minority individuals may become immersed in their culture. They may change their hair, clothing, speech, and even friendship groups in an attempt to be involved only in their own cultural group. They may begin to speak or learn a native language such as Spanish or Yoruba. They may opt to only obtain services from members of their cultural group and may resist any interactions with the majority group. Outwardly these individuals seem to be very in favor of their own group and against the majority group and may be ambivalent about other ethnic groups. Inwardly these individuals are likely to be confused and ambivalent about their ethnicity. As they begin to discover that there is no utopia, even within their own group, and that there are still potential problems with achieving their hopes and dreams, they begin to emerge from this stage.
- Finally, ethnic minority individuals begin to become more accepting of themselves and others, including majority group members. They begin to have a more internally defined sense of self and a greater commitment to a pluralistic society.

The stages are thought to be cyclical. Therefore, individuals may move through them several times depending on their personal development and/or environmental situation.

As ethnic/racial identity development models appeared, Helms (1990), Hardiman (1982), and others began to write about White racial identity development. These writers proposed that Whites develop from having no awareness of themselves as racial beings to feeling anger and guilt about their group as oppressors to blaming the oppressed. Some White individuals will retreat into White culture after they are confronted with race issues. Others will begin to work deliberately, though not in an internalized way, to learn about ethnic minorities. Eventually, however, those who are committed arrive at a state where they begin to fight for a more pluralistic society. Table 8.1 contains a summary of minority and white racial identity development models as described in *Multicultural Counseling Competencies* (Sue et al., 1998).

This model is included to help career counselors understand more about their clients. For example, if a Latina client is at a developmental stage in which she believes that assimilation into White culture is the only way to the "American dream," her career indecision question may really mean, "Can you help me find a career that will guarantee me a way into White society and will save me the difficulty of dealing with cultural customs, skin color, accent, and so on?" Or the Asian client may be rejecting a career because he does not want to be a "model minority."

Another reason for counselors to develop some understanding of identity development is that they and their clients may be in antagonist stages. For example, if a Black client is in the immersion stage, where he or she is hostile to Whites, and the counselor is in a stage where he or she only wants to be involved with other Whites, then counseling is likely to be difficult or impossible. Neither client nor counselor may understand what has happened and, of course, no career decisions can be made.

In order to gather information on clients' identity development, career counselors can ask clients to describe their ethnic or racial identity and how they feel about members of their cultural group. Counselors will need to observe verbal and nonverbal behaviors in order to evaluate clients' responses. If uncomfortable with verbal inquiries, counselors might consider using the assessment instruments developed by Carter and Helms (1992). These instruments can help structure conversations around identity development. It is more important to know whether identity issues are influencing clients' career behavior than it is to name the clients' ethnic identity stage. Clients and counselors can use the information to help clarify the ethnic identity stage and determine an appropriate intervention. Note

Table 8.1. General Racial Identity Development Models

White		Minority	
Pre-exposure/ precontact	Ethnocentric; little awareness of self as a racial being; limited knowledge and understanding of other cultural groups; denial	**Conformity**	Preference for majority group values and norms; antiminority group; denial
Conflict	Encounters inconsistent information or experience; beginning realizations of biases and prejudices; shame, guilt	**Dissonance**	Breakdown in previous system of beliefs; questions rigidly held preference for dominant group values and norms; encounters bias and prejudice; shame, guilt
Prominority and antiracism	Questioning and awareness of racism; anger and shame surrounding Whiteness and oppression	**Resistance and immersion**	Complete rejection of dominant group values and norms; total acceptance of specific ethnic group culture; anger with dominant group; validation of ethnic group
Immersion/ emersion	A "compromise state" between accepting White culture as universal to over-identification with ethnic minorities; an existential state and search for meaning	**Intro-spection**	Questions attitudes and rigid beliefs and behaviors of resistance/immersion state; acceptance of self and ethnic group
Integrative awareness	Development of a non-racist identity; self-acceptance; understanding and appreciation of other ethnic groups; understanding and awareness of socio-political influences regarding race and racism	**Synergetic articulative awareness**	Self-acceptance; transcendent attitude; belief in a pluralistic society; positive acceptance of self, other ethnic minority groups, and majority group

Source: Names of the stages are from Sue et al., 1998.

that clarification, questions, and interventions are more effective if counselors have explored their own identity.

The MCCC also contains sections on exploration and assessment. Again, thinking about these items before seeing the client is useful. Many of these items concern the client's perceptions of family support, familial obligations, self-confidence, and limitations. Other items assess the client's exposure to career information, role models, and high school experiences.

The literature consistently indicates that family interactions are important across most racial/ethnic groups. There may be familial expectations for the client to choose a particular occupation because he or she is the eldest child. Some clients feel enormous pressure to conform to family wishes. Morgan, Guy, Lee, and Cellini (1986) reported that in some Native American families, community, family, and home may be more important to the decision-making process than the job or career. While the MCCC has 15 items in this section, the simplest thing for the career counselor to do is ask the client questions such as these:

- Which career would members of your family want you to have?
- How important are their wishes?
- How important is it to you to do as they wish?

These questions may lead to the information you and the client need to understand and clarify the family's role in the career issue. I have found it necessary on occasion to bring family members into the counseling session, although few career counseling books suggest this option.

The MCCC contains items on role models and exposure to information about the world of work because sometimes individuals of color live in environments where they don't see people doing a wide range of jobs. Page (1999) reported that on the Pine Ridge Indian Reservation the unemployment rate was 73 percent. In 1996, one African American housing project in Memphis, Tennessee, had an unemployment rate of 9 percent. The children in these situations do not see the people they know best going to work. "Take your son or daughter to work" has no meaning in these communities. And, therefore, career day at the local public school will not convey the real essence of what it means to have a career. In these instances, the career counselor may need to be more creative and provide activities such as taking the clients on excursions to the hospital, a courtroom, or the research and development division of the local manufacturing company.

The third section of the MCCC underscores the point that counseling is a collaboration between the client and the career counselor. The career counselor is not expected to keep complete, up-to-date information on every cultural group. Clients are experts on themselves, and the effective counselor is open to the client's expertise as a teacher and cultural informant. An experienced career counselor will know how to facilitate the counseling process through a wealth of career and cultural information.

For example, the counselor may discover that his African American client is in the pre-encounter/dissonance stage of development and does not want to be involved in any careers in which race is a factor. The counselor needs to respect the client's decision. The counselor may despair because he thinks the client would have a richer life if he were more self-accepting. Yet the client is not ready or interested in exploring racial identity development. He just wants information on careers in sales. The goal for counseling is set. At some point the client may renegotiate the career goal, but not now.

One caveat on goal setting is that the counselor must be aware that even negotiating appropriate goals may be difficult because of cultural differences in groups. For example, Asians are more inclined to agree with the counselor because they have a tendency to be polite and to defer to authority figures. Native Americans might engage in silence more than other groups. Personality or cultural traits might make it more difficult to clearly understand the client's goals. In each instance the career counselor must be patient and continue to carefully solicit information rather than provide too much.

The MCCC aids career counselors in reflecting on the type and extent of information needed to do an effective assessment of the cultural issues that might influence client career behavior. If counselors complete the thought process started by the items on this instrument, they will have climbed the first three steps of the career assessment shown in Figure 8.1, on page 250: cultural variables, gender variables, and efficacy variables (belief in one's ability and self). Counselors will then know whether the clients' career issues are solved or step four needs to be implemented.

The MCCC was designed to help counselors organize their thoughts, information, and assessments more thoroughly, but the checklist is quite long. Given the time constraints of many counselors, it might be useful to develop an abbreviated form of the instrument that can stimulate and organize thoughts in a similar but shorter way. An abbreviated version should be used only after career counselors have gained sufficient awareness, knowledge, and skill in the multicultural career counseling area. Figure 8.2 shows an abbreviated form that counselors might find effective.

NONVERBAL CULTURAL ISSUES

Counselors must give serious, in-depth consideration to all facets of culture that can affect career counseling interactions. While the MCCC can help counselors think through numerous issues, additional cultural variables must be considered when the client is in the counselor's presence. For example, time, space, distance, bodily gestures, and eye contact are nonverbal features of interpersonal interaction that are heavily influenced by culture. An interesting exercise would be observing various ethnic group members sharing a meal at a restaurant. Look at pairs to see which ethnic groups tend to sit adjacent to each other and which tend to sit across from each other. There may be observable racial/ethnic differences.

I know about

- ☐ Worldviews
- ☐ Racial/ethnic identity development
- ☐ Multicultural counseling competencies
- ☐ Family role in the client's life
- ☐ Social and economic status of the client
- ☐ The actual career question and possible underlying culturally related questions
- ☐ The agreed-upon goals for counseling
- ☐ Culturally appropriate interventions

Source: Copyright © 1999 by Rosie Phillips Bingham. Used with permission.

Figure 8.2 The Multicultural Career Counseling Quick-Check Form

It is important for career counselors to be especially observant of any signals that indicate that the client may be operating from a different perspective than the counselor's. For example, Euro-Americans and individuals from northern European countries tend to require more distance between conversants than do members of many ethnic groups, particularly those from southern European and North African countries. Because African Americans in the United States close the distance between speakers and will not use as much eye contact, they can be seen sometimes as hostile, inattentive, or insecure.

While a shrug of the shoulder is virtually a universal sign, a handshake is not. In Euro-American culture, a firm handshake is seen as evidence of confidence and acceptance. In some cultures, the same handshake would be viewed as rude and offensive. Some Native American cultures prefer a much softer, limper handshake.

Likewise, in some cultures a direct stare is considered offensive and rude, but in the United States the majority culture may use direct eye contact as a diagnostic sign of psychological health, honesty, and self-confidence. In some Asian cultures, indirect eye contact is a sign of respect. In the same way, a nod of the head in some cultures is merely a sign of politeness and respect for authority. In another culture, that same head-nodding gesture could mean, "Yes, I agree with you." Or it could mean, "I am listening, though not agreeing."

Concepts of time vary almost as much within cultures as between cultures. In the Euro-American culture, a therapy hour usually means 50 minutes. In some cultures, the therapy hour may mean working as long as it takes to finish with the issue at hand. On some college campuses in the United States, professors may arrive up to 15 minutes past the scheduled start time before they are formally considered late, but students are generally expected to be in class at the beginning of the allotted class hour.

These differences in cultural norms around nonverbal behavior imply at least two things for the career counselor. First, the counselor must be observant of the client's behavior and reserve interpretation until the meaning unfolds through the interaction. Second, the career counselor must be aware of the potential need to help clients understand differences between their cultural behavior and that of members of another group, especially if the intervention involves an interaction between two culturally different groups. If a career counselor designs a job-shadowing experience in a large law office in the United States for a career client from India who wears traditional ethnic clothing, the counselor may need to discuss with the client possible reactions from those in the law office.

CLIENT PREPARATION

The above sections on counselor preparation and nonverbal cultural issues have demonstrated a need for the counselor to be very thoughtful and deliberative, and to plan carefully for interacting with the client. Research has shown that it is equally important for the client to get ready for counseling. Clients who know what to expect and who have some understanding about the issues tend to have better outcomes. Therefore it is beneficial for the counselor to have some ways for the client to prepare for counseling. This section explores issues clients might explore before seeing the counselor.

Most career clients seek counseling because they have a question. They often ask if they can take one of "those tests" that will tell them what to do. Counselors repeatedly oblige and provide the clients with a testing instrument. And yet, asking for a test may be the wrong question—resulting in clients' leaving counseling without really knowing what they want to do. Counselors may provide the assessment protocol or interest inventory too early in the counseling process. You may recall from Figure 8.1 that the administration of an inventory is part of the last assessment step.

Clients need to be prepared for career counseling. There are a variety of ways in which this important preparation can occur. For example, a counselor could prepare a short videotape about the career counseling process. This tape would need to be culturally sensitive, cover the most important topics, and be relatively brief. A paper-and-pencil instrument can also help the preparation process.

Ward and Tate (1990), experienced counselors formerly at Georgia State University, found that they were far more effective if they engaged the client in a reflective exercise before beginning the verbal career counseling session. They designed a *Career Counseling Checklist,* modified by Ward and Bingham (1993) and Prigoff (1996), to engage clients in thinking about issues that could influence career choice behaviors. The clients complete the instrument before seeing the counselor. Clients are asked to check items from a list of questions about personality, self-confidence, race/ethnicity, family, career, daydreams, physical abilities, intellectual abilities, fears, insecurities, and the influence of religion. Clients begin to see that making a career decision is more complex than just "taking a test." When counselors use such a checklist as a conversation piece, it can be easier to introduce issues of worldview and identity development. Such instruments help set the clients' expectations about what will be discussed during the counseling session. The checklist can also help the counselor quickly discern whether the client's concern is a career issue or more of a psychological one. Counselors also have reported that when they use the checklist, clients' questions are often answered without administering additional instruments. A good diagnosis often results in a simpler, straightforward intervention.

See Ward and Bingham (1993) for a complete description of the 44-item *Career Counseling Checklist.* Figure 8.3 shows a short checklist covering many of the variables mentioned above. These ten items cover a range

---

Welcome to your career counseling session. You can take this time to talk with a counselor about the work you might want to do. Making a decision about a career can be a complex task and can involve many people. In order to help you and the counselor think through all the factors that might influence your decision, please check as many items as apply to you or about which you might want more information.

- ☐ I have no idea about which career I might want to consider.
- ☐ My family has decided which career is best for me.
- ☐ My race/ethnicity will influence my career decisions.
- ☐ I secretly know and dream about what I want to do.
- ☐ I am afraid that I do not have the ability to do what I want to do.
- ☐ I have prayed about my career.
- ☐ I want a career that will help my race.
- ☐ I have a physical disability that will limit my ability to get certain jobs.
- ☐ I do not have the kind of personality that will fit the career I want.
- ☐ My gender will be a barrier in getting the job I want.

Source: Copyright © 1999 by Rosie Phillips Bingham. Used with permission.

Figure 8.3 Abbreviated Career Counseling Checklist

of topics that can open discussions on factors—especially cultural variables—that might affect clients' career counseling process. Combining such a checklist with the *Multicultural Career Counseling Checklist* will help vocational counselors effectively include cultural variables in the counseling process.

INTERVENTION

When appropriate counselor and client preparations are completed, it is time to focus on career intervention, where the client and the counselor engage each other. Interventions and assessments need to be respectful of culture. Fouad and Bingham (1995) proposed a seven-step Culturally Appropriate Career Counseling Model. These steps will be reviewed only briefly here. The seven-step model includes

1. Establishing rapport and a culturally appropriate relationship
2. Identifying career issues in terms of cognitive, social, emotional, environmental, and/or behavioral issues or external barriers
3. Assessing the impact of cultural variables on career issues
4. Setting a culturally appropriate counseling process and goals
5. Choosing culturally appropriate interventions
6. Helping the client make the decision or cycle back through the process if additional clarification is needed
7. Implementing the career plan with appropriate follow-up

Please note that some of the steps (the third, for example) in this model now ask counselors to assess or solicit information they were asked only to think about during counselor preparation. Now counselors must actively obtain specific information from clients.

The model begins with establishing rapport and a culturally appropriate relationship. Even when the counselor and client are fully prepared, if the counselor is unable to establish a "right" relationship with the client, counseling is likely to fail. For many people of color, the success of any intervention depends on the strength of the relationship established between the client and the counselor from the first contact. Tucker, Vosmik, and

Brady (1999) reported significant differences in medical treatment compliance rates between Black and White patients depending on their relationship with the health care provider. Black patients were significantly more likely to comply with treatment for their own health if they had a strong positive relationship with the provider. Compliance for White patients was not influenced by the relationship with the provider. My colleagues and I have regularly observed this phenomenon in our own clinical practice in psychology. We have generally observed that African American clients tend to value a relationship that appears more friendly and in which they feel especially valued.

Comas-Diaz and Jacobsen (1987) reported that some Latin clients prefer to see counselors as if they were a family member, like an aunt or uncle, while Sue and Sue (1990) stated that many Asian clients expect a more formal authority-based relationship. Martin (1991) indicated that many Native Americans value silence during counseling. The challenge for the career counselor is to provide the appropriate qualities in each relationship and still remain within the boundaries of the counselor role. The importance of the counseling relationship cannot be overstated—the success of the interaction may depend more on the relationship than anything else.

The second step involves identifying career issues in terms of cognitive, social, emotional, environmental, and/or behavioral issues or external barriers. It refers to the need to determine whether the career decision is influenced by the way a client is thinking about the career situation. For example, a client could become very anxious every time he or she thinks of giving a speech in public, yet may need that skill in an occupation. Or a client may face an external issue such as racism or sexism, which could influence his or her opportunities for advancement in a chosen field.

In the third step of this model the counselor will need to look at issues of worldview, ethnic/racial identity development, family, cultural group expectations, and so on. Earlier in this chapter counselors were asked to think about clients' possible worldviews. Now counselors must specifically determine clients' worldviews and their role in the career exploration process. Racial identity, gender role, structure of opportunity, family role expectations, and other factors need to be appropriately explored with clients to determine what role they play in their career decision-making efforts. The earlier preparation by both counselor and client should provide openings to assess these variables.

The fourth step involves setting a culturally appropriate counseling process and goals, and is completed when the client and counselor negotiate and agree on the goals. A careful study of the client's culture and an effective assessment of how the client fits into and reflects that culture will enable the counselor to establish an appropriate counseling process.

The fifth step focuses on choosing culturally appropriate interventions and needs more discussion. If the counselor has completed an accurate and culturally relevant assessment, the intervention should proceed from that assessment. In fact, the intervention should be nearly self-evident. However, some of the most obvious interventions are not the ones typically associated with career counseling. Instead of merely providing a career inventory, the counselor might need to involve a client's family member, church, or other community resource. Take, for example, the instance mentioned earlier, of some Asian families in which the parents tell the children which career to enter. If the client is very conflicted about the career, the counselor might need to involve the family. If the family comes to the counseling session, the counselor must be sensitive to family hierarchy and familial interaction patterns. It might be appropriate to address more comments to the parents than to the client. If the counselor has established an appropriate relationship with the client, then the client will be able to help the counselor understand the family dynamics. In the African American community, many individuals turn to the church for guidance. The counselor might need to ensure that the career decision is consistent with church philosophy. That might mean helping the client involve the church in the career exploration process. Or it might mean that no other individuals need to be involved in the process, but the intervention and decision will need to fit with the dictates of the client's worldview, ethnic/racial identity, and maybe the expectations of one of the client's subgroups.

By the sixth step, clients will have enough information to make a decision or to explore further. Counselors must continue to assess the situation and provide the necessary guidance for clients to determine whether they are ready to make a decision. In the final, seventh step, clients can implement the decision. Counselors should caution clients to be aware of any obstacles or impediments to fully implementing the career decision in order to inoculate clients against some of the potential structural barriers that might exist in the world of work.

Career counselors are cautioned to remember that cultural variables have a differential impact on clients. Some clients will be more tightly woven into the fabric of the family while others will be more concerned with their role, purpose, and obligations to their racial group. Still others will perceive more barriers to their career choices because of racism and sexism. The counselor must assess the strength of each variable and work with the client to decide on appropriate interventions to moderate, ameliorate, or include the factor in the career decision plan.

GAINING EXPERIENCE

Exercise 8.2, on page 270, is a simple nine-step imaging exercise that can help counselors become more effective at cross-cultural career counseling. Periodic practice with exercises like this will help career counselors gain increased awareness and confidence in working across cultures. Exercise 8.2 helps counselors gauge gaps in their knowledge and experience to enable them to devise strategies to fill the gaps. Many writers mentioned in this chapter, including Sue et al. (1998), suggest ways to increase cultural awareness, knowledge, and skills. Willingness, education, time, and supervised practice will ensure a beneficial counseling experience for counselors and clients. But the process begins with counselors' willingness to take a risk and begin to practice cross-cultural/multicultural career counseling.

EXERCISE 8.2

DISCOVERING CULTURAL INFORMATION

Find a comfortable place in which you will not be disturbed. Take a moment to get relaxed, and close your eyes.

1. Imagine an individual with a career concern who is from a different culture than yours. (Focus on the person's physical appearance—height, weight, hair color, language, nonverbal behavior, and so on until you can create a clear image.)
2. Now suspend judgment.
3. Feel a sense of respect and acceptance for the client.
4. Wonder what the career issue might be.
5. Search your mind for what you generally know about the history, sociology, and politics of people from this cultural group.
6. Wonder how what you know about the cultural group influences your behavior with the imagined client.
7. Think about the current local sociopolitical condition of people from the client's cultural group.
8. Now suspend judgment again while you imagine welcoming the client into your office.
9. As you begin the counseling process, prepare to depend on your counseling skills, especially listening. Allow the client to take the lead as much as possible.

Now open your eyes and make notes about your thoughts, impressions, and feelings while doing the exercise. You might be surprised by the amount of information you already have.

Source: Copyright © 1999 by Rosie Phillips Bingham. Used with permission.

REFERENCES

Atkinson, D. R., Morten, G., & Sue, D. W. (1983). *Counseling American minorities* (4th ed.). Madison, WI: Brown.

Bingham, R. P., & Ward, C. M. (1997). Theory into assessment: A model for women of color. *Journal of Career Assessment, 5*(4), 403–418.

Carter, R. T., & Helms, J. E. (1992). The counseling process as defined by relationship types: A test of Helms's interactional model. *Journal of Multicultural Counseling and Development, 20,* 181–201.

Comas-Diaz, L., & Jacobsen, F. M. (1987). Ethnocultural identification in psychotherapy. *Psychiatry, 50,* 232–241.

Cross, W. E. (1971). Negro-to-Black conversion experience: Toward a psychology of Black liberation. *Black World, 20,* 13–27.

Denga, D. I. (1988). Influence of traditional factors on career choice among Nigerian secondary school youth. *Journal of Multicultural Counseling and Development, 16,* 1–15.

Fouad, N. A., & Bingham, R. P. (1995). Career counseling with racial and ethnic minorities. In W. B. Walsh & S. H. Osipow (Eds.), *Handbook of vocational psychology: Theory, research & practice* (2nd ed., pp. 331–366). Mahwah, NJ: Erlbaum.

Hardiman, R. (1982). White identity development: A process-oriented model for describing the racial consciousness of White Americans. *Dissertation Abstracts International, 43,* 104A. (University Microfilms No. 82-10330).

Helms, J. E. (1990). *Black and White racial identity: Theory, research, and practice.* Eastport, CT: Greenwood Press.

Katz, J. H. (1985). The sociopolitical nature of counseling. *Counseling Psychologist, 13,* 615–624.

Martin, W. E., Jr. (1991). Career development and American Indians living on reservations: Cross-cultural factors to consider. *Career Development Quarterly, 39,* 273–283.

Morgan, C. O., Guy, E., Lee, B., & Cellini, H. R. (1986). Rehabilitation services for American Indians: The Navajo experience. *Journal of Rehabilitation, 52*(2), 25–31.

Nobles, W. W. (1976). Extended self: Rethinking the Negro self-concept competencies. *Career Development Quarterly, 40,* 378–386.

Page, S. (1999, July 8). President stops at SD reservation that prosperity passed by. *USA Today,* p. 8A.

Prigoff, G. L. (1996). *A comparison of African American and Caucasian American college students' responses on the Career Checklist for clients.* Paper presented at the annual meeting of the Tennessee Psychological Association, Gatlinburg.

Sue, D. W., Carter, R., Casas, M., Fouad, N. A., Ivey, A. E., Jensen, M., LaFromboise, T., Jeanne, M., Ponterotto, J. G., & Vazquez-Nutall, E. (1998). *Multicultural counseling competencies.* Thousand Oaks, CA: Sage.

Sue, D. W., & Sue, D. (1990). *Counseling the culturally different: Theory & practice.* New York: Wiley.

Tucker, C. M., Vosmik, J. R., & Brady, B. A. (1999). Medication adherence among ethnically diverse pediatric renal transplant patients. Paper presented at the annual meeting of the Southeastern Psychological Association, Savannah, GA.

Ward, C. M. and Bingham, R. P. (1993). Career assessment of ethnic minority women. *Journal of Career Assessment, 1*(3), 246–257.

Ward, C. M. and Tate, G. (1990). *Career Counseling Checklist.* Atlanta: Georgia State University Counseling Center.

9

Developmental Career Counseling

DIFFERENT STAGES, DIFFERENT CHOICES

Judith Grutter

What are clients really asking when they say, "I can't find the right job," or, "Is there a place in this organization that would be a better fit for me?" or, "I used to really like my work, but I'm not challenged anymore. Am I in the wrong career field?" or, "How can I slow down and still advance in the organization?"

Not surprisingly, when our clients ask these questions they are looking for concrete answers. As career development professionals we have become proficient in the shorthand of career assessments, job titles, and computerized "best-fit" systems. These approaches provide us with concrete answers, but are they the right answers? The developmental perspective suggests that questions, although seemingly identical, need to be reframed at different stages of our lives, and that specific responses require a variety of interpretations with reference to the particular life stage of the individual.

For instance, a 24-year-old MBA candidate asks himself, "Is this job the right job for me?" What he's really asking is, "Will I have the opportunity in this job to confirm my career direction, to test out the person I think

I am becoming?" On the other hand, a 45-year-old experienced salesperson asking the same question may really be asking herself, "Will I have the opportunity in this job to develop new skills that will enrich my workday and broaden my future employability?" And a 62-year-old pre-retiree may be asking, "Will this job enable me to develop opportunities for contract employment or meaningful volunteer service after I retire?" The initial question is the same for all three, but, developmentally, how they approach the answers will differ.

As career management professionals, we tend to use a static approach to our clients' questions, focusing on the right match between personality attributes and work requirements. The desired outcome for us and for our clients is *the right choice*. In actuality, looking at career as a lifelong process, rather than as the singular event of choosing an occupation, is often more effective, both for the individual and for the employing organization. The individual benefits from a career path that is guided more by growing and changing internal needs than by the external requirements of the economy, and the organization benefits from greater employee satisfaction and retention. The desirable outcome for both is *a growth process*.

INTRODUCTION

The ideas and strategies explored here are not new. Their roots are in the developmental psychology writings of Buehler (1933) and Ginzberg, Ginsburg, Axelrad, and Hermal (1951), popularized by Donald Super (1953, 1954a, 1954b, 1957). What is new is their application to adult career management programs. Traditionally accepted in college career development settings, the process has long been viewed as too inefficient for organizational applications. A process that involves asking difficult questions and guiding the answers in a meaningful direction may not be as quantifiably measurable as a standardized assessment process that produces specified job titles, personality coding systems, and potential "matches." Qualitatively, however, the process certainly adds value.

I am not suggesting that we discard everything we have learned about assessment and career management, but that we add a new angle to our use of assessments—that we use them to direct client questions rather than to provide artificial answers. Repeat assessments to "get it right" will become less frequent as employees become more self-reliant in their career development.

THE FRAMEWORK

The suggestions that follow incorporate many familiar, standardized assessments and career exploration activities that can be adapted to a variety of settings and aren't dependent on an entirely new career counseling skill set. However, their application to career development may have a new twist for many of us. The role of the career professional in a developmental framework is to move clients away from an expectation of finding the right answer and toward learning a growth process, which ideally will be adapted and refined with increased maturity.

Basic to the career development viewpoint is the concept of *stages*—age-related periods of personal development, professional implementation, and expected outcomes. Table 9.1, on pages 276 and 277, summarizes the career and life stages, with related career development focus, implementation strategies, and desired outcomes. Each stage is addressed more fully in the following sections with client case studies and program applications.

To begin to familiarize yourself with the concepts, consider some of the points related to each of the stages, both in light of your own career development and as they relate to clients with whom you have worked. See Table 9.2, on pages 277 through 279, for career development concepts. As you read them, you might make mental note of your clients who have these issues.

Identity Formation

Career Development Strategies

- Varied experiences
- Role playing
- Unconditional support

It is not surprising that most employer career management programs pay little attention to the years prior to career entry. Appropriately, the major workplace concerns are job performance and productivity. But developmental career counseling begins earlier. If issues from the earlier years are not resolved, they become workplace issues. An understanding of them puts puzzling employee behaviors in perspective and opens the door for growth and improvement.

Table 9.1 Career Development Stages

Stage	Time of Life	Career Development Focus	Strategies	Desired Outcomes
Identity formation	The early years	Discovery of interests and awareness of abilities Possible foreclosure	Varied play and school experiences Role playing Unconditional support	Awareness of unique self Emergence of positive self-concept
Exploration	Middle and high school (ages 12–18)	Initial separation from parents Development of interests and unique abilities Examination of values	Varied play, school, and work experiences Interest and personality assessment Assessment of abilities	Alignment of interests and abilities Preparation for work or additional education
Commitment	Post-high school and college (late teens to early 20s)	Narrowing of interests Interests/values conflicts Focus and commitment Finding a sense of purpose Possible diffusion	Prioritizing and decision-making training Values clarification Examination of interests/values conflicts	Alignment of interests and values Refinement of appropriate skills Initial career decision
Career entry	Post-traditional formal education	Search for congruence Clarifying commitment Securing position	Clarification of purpose Job search techniques Coaching for induction	Initial career position Successful induction

Table 9.1 Career Development Stages (cont'd)

Stage	Time of Life	Career Development Focus	Strategies	Desired Outcomes
Career progression	Mid-20s through 40s	Competition Career adjustment Career satisfaction	Self-promotion Networking Strategic alliances	Clarification of position Promotions or satisfying lateral moves
Career refinement	Late 40s through 50s and 60s	Balance Career change Life/career enrichment Preparation for retirement	Self-assessment (values shift) Evaluation of opportunities Transition	Repacing of lifestyle Job redesign Ultimate congruence
Career disengagement	The retirement years	Deinstitutionalization Role change Personal enrichment	Identity reevaluation Self-assessment (new interests)	Successful deceleration Institutional disengagement New interests

Table 9.2 Appropriate Questions at Career Development Stages

Stage	Questions	Client Issues
Identity formation (pre- and elementary school)	At this stage were they . . . Encouraged to explore anything and everything? Curious to learn? Trying out lots of different skills and roles? Aware that they had personal worth and were valued by others, even when they weren't good at something?	A sense that only one career path was right for them, and it was told to them by others rather than chosen A conviction that failure is never acceptable, and so trying new things is difficult Little sense of individual uniqueness; poor self-concept

Table 9.2 Appropriate Questions at Career Development Stages (cont'd)

Stage	Questions	Client Issues
Exploration (middle and high school)	At this stage were they . . . Discovering that they liked things that their parents didn't like? Finding out that they were good at things they hadn't even thought of before? Struggling with what was right and wrong?	Their aspirations are not in line with their abilities No awareness of the connection between education and career
Commitment (post–high school and college)	At this stage were they . . . Beginning to narrow down their options? Focusing on career plans? Clarifying what was important to them in life and in work?	Inability to commit to a career decision, however temporary What they enjoy doing does not meet their needs
Career entry (post–formal education)	At this stage were they . . . Applying for career-related positions? Looking for work environments that matched their interests and skills? Beginning a career path?	Many "yes, buts": Unable to commit to a position that isn't perfect Doesn't fit in: Superior attitude, many personality conflicts and job assignment misunderstandings
Career progression (mid-20s through 40s)	At this stage were they . . . Setting career goals for the future? Adapting to unexpected realities? Making professional connections and becoming active in their field? Applying for promotions?	Still unsure of career commitment Unable to find work satisfaction Blames others for lack of opportunity

Table 9.2 Appropriate Questions at Career Development Stages (cont'd)

Stage	Questions	Client Issues
Career refinement (late 40s through 50s and 60s)	At this stage were they . . . Reevaluating the role of work in their life? Learning new skills to approach new challenges? Confirming their career direction and evaluating the need for change?	Overworked, plagued by family problems Dissatisfied with what is; not willing to risk change Left behind; won't retrain for advancement
Career dis-engagement (retirement years)	At this stage were they . . . Expanding interests outside of work? Reinvesting in family relationships? Finding ways to continue con-tributing?	Whole life is work; dreads forced retirement Keeps returning to employer functions and activities Blames employer for lack of meaningful retirement

An Example: Steve. Steve knew when he was a little boy that he would go into banking. It was expected of him. His father and two uncles were in banking, and, although they weren't college graduates, they had advanced in their careers and were successful in their work. He had many relatives in mainland China who were in finance, and Steve was expected to carry on the family work tradition. He was barely able to talk when his uncles opened a savings account for him. He was introduced to the bank manager, and a family ritual was started. Every week for 15 years he would go to the bank to deposit his coins, and eventually bills, and ask the bank manager a question about banking that had been carefully rehearsed with his family. He was good with money and began his career in preschool as keeper of the lunch money box. He eventually grew to be treasurer of his high school senior class and naturally chose a college with a fine business school. A bachelor of science in finance led him to a career with a large bank in the Midwest. He started as a teller and progressed rapidly through several branch manager and loan officer training positions. At 30 he was in charge of small-business loans for his branch. Steve was a success. Then the bank was acquired by one of the largest commercial banking institutions in the country. Steve's responsibilities became much more sales oriented than he was used to, and he became nervous and depressed. He was offered the opportunity to return to college to study computer science, but he refused. College did not appeal to him at his age, he said. He was laid off shortly thereafter.

What happened to Steve probably started long before he began his formal career in banking. Most developmentalists agree that the years from birth to adolescence, often referred to as the formative years, are a foundation for the interests, beliefs, and behaviors of later life. The development issue during these years is discovery—of self and of the world. Discovery depends on the opportunity to try out things that are fun. We can develop these into interest patterns and skill sets as we get older.

A potential danger of the identity formation stage is vocational *foreclosure* (Bluestein, Devenis, & Kidney, 1989; Marcia, 1966), experience that is restricted by influences that are out of our control. Some people's experiences are restricted by gender and cultural roles, others (like Steve's) by parental expectations, still others by geographic boundaries. In these cases the individual's interests and skill development are limited to what society makes available to him or her. Ironically, the foreclosed are often very high achievers. Their identity is in their achievements, and, undistracted, their early focus often enables them to reach great heights at a young age. Enjoyment is not their career goal—accomplishment is.

There is nothing wrong with focus and achievement. In fact, the high school student who knows what he or she wants by the tenth grade is every guidance counselor's dream—at least on the surface. But an externally imposed focus that precludes the self-development process can prevent young people from experiencing enjoyment in work. This type of foreclosure can be as dangerous in its subtlety as overt employment discrimination. In either case, the payback in later life can be quite negative. People who lose their lifelong jobs have a narrow range of experience on which to expand. Their identity is their work, and when that is taken away, they have few fallback interests from which to develop alternatives. Steve could very well be experiencing the later-life consequences of a foreclosed career decision. His industry changed, and he was not willing to change with it. He couldn't see any other options.

A key strategy during this time is guided involvement in varied play and school experiences, with the unconditional support of parents and teachers. A seasoned user of the *Strong Interest Inventory® (Strong)* and *Myers-Briggs Type Indicator® (MBTI®)* instruments, I have found their theoretical models to be helpful even at an early age.[1] The *Strong*'s RIASEC framework, based on the work of John Holland, suggests six general categories of interests, shown in Table 9.3.

The MBTI® instrument proposes four dichotomies: two orientations (Extraversion–Introversion and Judging–Perceiving) and two mental functions (Sensing–Intuition and Thinking–Feeling). These are shown in Table 9.4, on page 282.

Table 9.3 Holland's Six Interest Categories (RIASEC)

Category	Description	Childhood Activities
Realistic	Physical	Participating in sports, planting a garden, building model airplanes, playing with Legos
Investigative	Analytical	Doing scientific experiments, solving math problems, studying insects and reptiles, reading
Artistic	Creative	Molding things out of clay, drawing, finger-painting, writing verses, playing a musical instrument, dancing
Social	Helpful	Caring for hurt animals, playing doctor or nurse, playing cooperative games, making friends with new children at school
Enterprising	Persuasive	Setting up a lemonade stand, selling school promotions door-to-door, playing competitive games, convincing friends to do things your way
Conventional	Organized	Collecting stamps or coins, saving money, playing on the computer, organizing your room or play space

Table 9.4 The Four MBTI® Dichotomies

Dichotomy	Description	Childhood Application
Extraversion–Introversion	The source and focus of our energy	Being with others versus being alone
Sensing–Intuition	The way we gather information and explore	Through everyday experiences versus through imagination
Thinking–Feeling	The way we evaluate information to make decisions	Using logic versus what is personally meaningful
Judging–Perceiving	The way we set goals and respond to change	Planful versus spontaneous

From what you know about Steve, you can probably surmise how much exposure he had to the RIASEC categories and the MBTI® dichotomies during his childhood. How might different circumstances have broadened his early experiences?

In the best of all possible worlds, children are encouraged to explore all six of the RIASEC categories through all eight of the MBTI® preferences. Parents do not express opinions about which interests are "good for you" and which interests are "not for *our* child." Schools do not promote some subjects or play activities as being more important than others. In this perfect world, children are encouraged to discover and experience, repeating those things that are fun and rejecting those that are not. They develop patterns of interests and related skills. Likewise, they develop preferences for particular poles of the MBTI® dichotomies. They become aware and appreciative of their own uniqueness, and develop a positive self-concept to guide them through the next stage.[2]

Most public education systems have career education programs in place that are designed to implement the identity formation developmental tasks throughout the school years. The more support we give to these programs and activities, the better chance our children will have to succeed later, both in and out of the workplace.

Exploration

Career Development Strategies

- Varied play, school, and work experiences
- Interest, personality, and ability assessment

Middle and high school (ages 12–18) is a time for *exploration*. The career development focus of this stage is the extension of the interests and abilities discovered in early childhood into play activities, school subjects, part-time work experiences, and volunteer service activities. As an identity is shaped that is separate from the parents, values begin to emerge as major determinants of behavior.

Assessment begins to play an important role during this time, as evidence of maturing interest patterns and personality preferences. The standardized measurement of abilities is included in most academic programs and can be a valuable strategy for broadening awareness. Had Steve had the opportunity to thoroughly explore early measures of his abilities, he might have discovered some beyond those that had been prescribed for him by his family and culture.

The desired outcome during the exploration stage is not a career decision, but the evaluation of six important elements of career development in preparation for work or additional education:

1. **Prior exposure to a wide range of interests.** The young person who has not had the opportunity to enjoy a variety of experiences is likely to foreclose into a career field by default, often missing an opportunity for career satisfaction just from lack of awareness. Ask about experience and knowledge in each of the RIASEC interest categories if you are interpreting interest inventories for people in this age group and find profiles that are undifferentiated and/or flat. Perhaps it is because they have little knowledge of most or all of those categories. A good strategy is to first describe the groupings and then to provide systematic experiences in each category such as job shadowing, activities or classes at school, after-school activities, information to read, people to talk to, or web sites to visit. The newly acquired knowledge may add depth to the interest profiles and provide a foundation of information for future decision making.

2. **Alignment of natural tendencies and interests.** The pairing of the MBTI® instrument with interest assessments can be particularly helpful at this stage if we consider the inborn nature of MBTI® preferences and the socialized nature of interests. MBTI® results represent a genetic imprint of preferences, while interests are often what we've experienced and enjoyed. If you find that the MBTI® mental functions—the core of type—are not in alignment with logically related RIASEC interests (for example, NF + Conventional or ST + Artistic), it may be that the young person is developing a unique pattern of interests for his or her personality type, which will need special encouragement as he or she gets older. Or such combinations may signal that the young person's natural inclinations have not been encouraged. In such cases further exploration of the RIASEC categories can be beneficial.

3. **Identification of Sensing–Intuition preference for perception.** One way to make the exploration process personally meaningful is to key into the young person's MBTI® preference for Sensing or Intuition. This preferred way of gathering information will guide experience and the development of interests, as the young person's identity core is formed. Without this, the later application of the Thinking–Feeling judgment preference will have only limited experience for evaluation.

4. **Alignment of interests and abilities.** We sometimes find that young people express interests in areas in which their ability is minimal: the young man who wants to be an astronaut but has little ability in math or science, for example, or the young woman who imagines herself a writer but who is reading way below grade level. When this happens, they are setting themselves up for possible later disappointments. Such setbacks can be avoided early by helping them to develop the appropriate skills, or by gently redirecting their interests if the required skills are unattainable. The opposite often occurs as well, when children develop skills in areas in which they find no enjoyment. These skills may later be necessary requirements of a job, but they may not be the best foundation of career choice.

5. **Readiness for career decision making.** Career decision making is often required of children in middle and high school by parents who are well meaning and want their children to be ahead of the game, and by school

programs that enforce the declaration of a college major or vocational training prior to or during the last year of high school. Such a "tracking" system can be damaging to young people who are not ready. Students are ready for career decision making when their interests focus and stabilize and when they have come to that point through their own choices and not by foreclosure.

6. **Adequate preparation for work or further education.** School-based interest and ability testing at this age may suggest education and training potential in various fields. For students who will enter the workforce directly after high school, early training can ensure a skilled entry rather than the necessity of taking just any available job. Others might be considering highly technical career fields that require an early start in math and the sciences. And others will be entering colleges and universities that have specific entrance requirements and for which early guidance is critical.

Ultimately, varied experiences and wisely used assessments will help bring about an alignment of interests and abilities and an adequate preparation for the next stage, without which the young person may flounder into adulthood.

Commitment

Career Development Strategies

- Prioritizing and decision-making training
- Values clarification
- Examination of interests/values conflicts

The major career development focus during the first years after high school (late teens to early 20s) is in direct contrast to the previous stage of exploration, which encouraged widening horizons. This is the time for narrowing interests, resolving apparent interests/values conflicts, finding a sense of direction and purpose, and preliminary career commitment. Some will face these issues in their first full-time jobs; others will face them in college. Young people who develop a sense of purpose early have an internal basis for directing their lives. Those who don't have a sense of purpose seem to struggle with direction much longer because they have nothing to hang it on. It's the difference between having a "mission in life"—and seeing how work relates to that mission—and just having a job. It may be idealistic to think that 18-year-olds can address this issue, but those who can seem to become much more career self-reliant later. The danger at this stage is that commitment issues will not be faced at all, resulting in career *diffusion* (Bluestein, Devenis, & Kidney, 1989; Marcia, 1966).

Diffusion is indecisiveness—the inability to make decisions, the opposite of the foreclosed decision making that we saw in Steve. Indecisive may be differentiated from undecided in that the undecided person can be taught the principles of decision making, personalize them, and apply them. The indecisive person is less likely to be able to make even tentative commitments. Laura is like this. The only child of a southern California, entertainment industry family, Laura was raised with all of the advantages money could buy. Her early career questions were consistently met with "anything that makes you happy, dear," and everything made her happy. She was good at everything, too, which didn't make it any easier. She saw college as a continuation of high school, collecting experiences and experimenting with majors. Her choices were based more on "this feels good so I'll give it a try" than "if I choose this, the consequences will be that." Laura majored in liberal studies and graduated from college with many more credits than were required and with almost a perfect academic record. Then she considered teaching, advertising, acting, psychology, and graduate school, but nothing was just right. Hoping that she would stumble onto something at work that would give her life direction, she took a job as an administrative assistant for a law firm. Within a month she was restless. She started telling her coworkers how they could do their jobs better and let her supervisor know that she could do his job better, too. Laura wasn't long for the law firm and continued a similar pattern through six positions in four years.

Without resolution, diffusion may produce adults in the workplace who, like Laura, have no career direction. They don't decide at all, showing indecision rather than undecidedness. They are an interesting dilemma in today's workplace because they are initially successful, and then they set themselves up for failure. Their lack of focus often impedes their progress through college and formal training. They often are very bright, but without the formal education to match their ability level, they may be forced to settle for employment beneath their potential. They often express a superior attitude and lack of tolerance for people's differences. They change jobs frequently, searching for the answer from others rather than from within themselves. Unfortunately, the answer for diffuse adults is not usually found in the workplace. It comes from within a well-developed identity core and accompanying sense of life's purpose that begins in these early stages and is constantly refined throughout life.

Career development strategies during the commitment stage involve decision making. Developing and applying the MBTI® judgment function, a preference for Thinking or Feeling as the favorite way of evaluating and prioritizing information and experience, is crucial. With the development of this function, the identity core is formed—the pairing of our preferences for perception and judgment that are the basis of our interests, values, potential abilities, and resulting career direction. With our perception and judgment functions in place, we can use our preferred Sensing or Intuition to acquire additional information and experience as needed, and our Thinking or Feeling to try out new experiences and evaluate them against what we need to be happy—our internal value system. We can use our preferences for exploration and commitment.

An Example: Jeff. Jeff is an ENFJ who is a junior in college, majoring in business. He is preparing for graduate work in finance. Jeff's father is a bank president, and his mother is a real estate broker. His family tends to measure success by income, and Jeff has learned to do the same. At the same time, he has always been drawn to the arts. He is a talented writer and has a passion for lithography. His grandfather was a printer, and Jeff has enjoyed restoring and classifying his large collection of antique prints. He is experiencing some conflict between his love of the arts and his desire for income—the frequent interests/values conflict of those who discover that their interests are not in high-paying career fields. Jeff's RIASEC interests are equally high in Artistic and Enterprising. He is clear in his preferences for Intuition and Feeling (NF), representing an identity core that seeks fulfillment in creativity and self-expression. In the battle between his core values and his Enterprising interests, his core values are winning. Jeff is realizing that he probably would not be happy in the corporate world of competition and bottom-line results. He is now considering graduate work in arts management.

Jeff is at the stage when finding a sense of purpose in life is critical to identifying career direction. In his case, as with most, clarifying his values through an understanding of his MBTI® type and comparing that information with his interest inventory results of Artistic and Enterprising pointed out the conflict. He was then able to bring his interests and his values more in line with each other and begin to investigate possible combinations of his skills to refine his individuality. The desired outcome of commitment to an initial career decision has been achieved. He may or may not continue toward his specific goal of arts management, but he has determined his direction, and he will not be intimidated by the journey. He has found that "decisions are easy when you know what you believe in."[3]

Career Entry

Career Development Strategies

- Clarification of purpose
- Job search techniques
- Coaching for induction

At this stage the primary career development focus is securing and succeeding in one's first professional position. If the commitment issues of the previous stage have been resolved, the young adult is now ready to search for a good fit between his or her sense of purpose, personality, and skills and the mission of the employing organization and requirements of the job. The career counselor's role is to add extensive work knowledge to the self-knowledge acquired earlier, and to teach job search and *induction* strategies—survival strategies for the first few months on the job (Tiedeman & O'Hara, 1963). The desired outcome is an initial career position that reflects the characteristics of the job seeker and a successful induction period that leads to a satisfying future.

The most interesting challenge of teaching job search strategies is convincing new job seekers that specification opens more doors than generalization. The more specific they can be about who they are, what they want, and what they're good at, the more likely it is that employers will be interested. The "whatever job you have available" approach falls on deaf ears in most employing organizations. Generally employers are not career counselors. They expect applicants to know themselves, so they can evaluate the fit with their culture and specific position descriptions. The same RIASEC and MBTI® models that were discussed earlier can now be applied to

- The search for congruence
- The self-promotion/application process
- Induction

The Search for Congruence. Searching for an employer and an entry position that are a good fit is one way in which individuals clarify their sense of purpose.

- What is life all about for me?
- What are my special talents and gifts?
- How does work fit into what I want from my life?
- How can the mission of this or that employer help me fulfill my sense of purpose?
- How can this or that job allow me to use and develop my skills and abilities?

An important career development strategy during this time of questioning is to teach the client information-gathering skills and how to generate options. Researching employers through reading, Internet investigation, and interviewing are skills that will be called on repeatedly in the later stages of career development. If they are learned and sharpened now, future transitions will be that much easier.

Equipped with the guidelines suggested in Tables 9.5 and 9.6, on pages 290 and 291, respectively, job seekers can be coached to evaluate what's written about employers and the tone of their interviews as they evaluate positions and organizations, promote themselves in résumés and interviews, and begin their first professional position.

Given these guidelines, options need to be evaluated against the individual's personality characteristics and can be focused around the MBTI®/RIASEC profile of the work environment. If our client Jeff were considering a position, we would validate his choice and ask a clarifying question to probe and test his career commitment. We might say, "Yes, that is an interesting possibility. How will it encourage your need to make a difference in people's lives (NF), and allow you to apply your writing and photographic (Artistic) interests?"

The Self-Promotion Application Process. Once an organizational fit is found and potential entry positions are identified, the next strategy is to frame the application process in the language and style of the employer. The same MBTI® and RIASEC frameworks that are used to evaluate individuals and organizations are also helpful to use as key words in the résumé

Table 9.5 Using *Strong* Results to Match Job Seeker Strengths with Professional Positions

RIASEC Category	Work Environment Descriptors	Emphasize in Résumé and Interviews
Realistic manufacturing/ industrial	Working primarily with machines and tools in manufacturing/ industrial or outdoor settings that are product driven, organized, structured, and clear in lines of authority	Tangible results, getting things done
Investigative research oriented/ scientific	Working primarily with information in research oriented, scientific, or academic settings that are unstructured and task oriented	New ideas, research, scientific evidence
Artistic creative and/or aesthetic	Working primarily with imagination and creativity in artistic and creative settings that are self-expressive, nonconforming, flexible, and unstructured	New ways of doing things, aesthetic beauty
Social service oriented/ helpful	Working primarily with people in settings that provide services to improve the welfare of others, which are collaborative, supportive, cooperative, and helpful	Benefit to others, personal meaning
Enterprising profit oriented/ helpful	Working primarily with people in business-oriented settings that are profit making, entrepreneurial, competitive, and fast paced	Profit and gain, bottom-line results
Conventional data/detail oriented	Working primarily with information, in data-oriented settings that are structured, organized, predictable, accurate, and hierarchical	Accuracy, organization, company policy

Source: Modified and reproduced by special permission of the publisher, Consulting Psychologists Press, Inc., from *Where Do I Go Next? Using Your Strong Results to Manage Your Career* by Fred Borgen and Judith Grutter.

Table 9.6 Using MBTI® Results to Match Job Seeker Strengths with Professional Positions

MBTI® Core	Organizational Purpose	Emphasize in Résumé and Interviews
ST	Using information for bottom-line results	Efficient, practical solutions
SF	Providing practical services to others	Service
NF	Encouraging others to grow and develop	Relationships
NT	Theoretical problem solving, analysis, and design	Strategies

development and interviewing stages of the self-promotion process (see Tables 9.5 and 9.6). Framing the client's uniqueness in the language and style of the employer is a very subtle coaching process. The focus of the organization needs to become the focus of the initial client contact, to be shaped and refined as the relationship progresses into employment.

Induction. Just as important to career development as finding a good fit is succeeding once a potential fit is found. Every employer has certain expectations of its employees, certain rules of conduct. Sometimes these are written down, sometimes they aren't. Successful induction is a very delicate process, in which a balance is reached between employer expectations and individual uniqueness. Unlike the military connotation of induction, most employing organizations do not want all of their employees to behave in exactly the same way. It is more likely that the individual and the organization will affect each other in important ways, as the individual adapts and the organization changes as a result of their new relationship. The first career position is the foundation of the career journey that will follow. The insights acquired in this stage will have future benefits as well.

An Example: Sara. Consider, for instance, the case of Sara. Sara is fresh out of college with a brand-new MBA and all the energy in the world. She did everything right all the way through school—good grades, a variety of extracurricular activities, leadership roles, meaningful employment, and a thick file of networking contacts. Wanting to find the perfect career "fit," she took all of the career assessments that her college had to offer. Consistent with her test results, she majored in business, polished it off with her graduate degree, received 11 job offers during on-campus interviews, and chose the one that paid the best. Sara thought she had it made. At 25 she was assistant director of human resources for a large insurance company and had her advancement steps all planned out. Six months into the job, Sara's boss called her into his office for her probationary performance review. The review was awful! Whereas Sara thought she was doing her job well above the standards set by her employer, the review suggested that she was not working as "part of the team." She was perceived as having a superior attitude and not contributing her share. Sara was despondent. What she had felt sure was the perfect career track wasn't even close. Now she had to start all over.

Sara is a good example of inadequate preparation for induction. With all of her planning, self-confidence, and achievements, no one had told her that the employment game has very specific rules, which are much subtler than superior job performance. In the large insurance company where she worked, being perceived as a team player was much more important than exceeding the production standards set by her supervisor. Her mistake was jumping in too fast and not taking the time to absorb the unwritten standards of her new environment. She did not see that in this particular human resources department, change happened by consensus, not by mandate. Each member of the department was involved in the day-to-day operations of the company, as well as in the program planning for the year. Sara changed old ways and implemented new ideas too fast, and her colleagues were not buying in. Before long they were not even interested and began to look for ways to sabotage her good intentions.

Sara's drive was so great that she neglected a very important first step: building internal relationships and support. She was so excited about her own potential that she failed to notice that most of the important decision making in her department happened during informal discussion times—Monday morning post-weekend exchanges, Wednesday bag lunches that had unofficially become an expectation, Friday afternoon debriefings over a glass of wine after work. She missed a Saturday picnic and softball game because she had work to catch up on at the office. She wasn't picking up on the politics of the organization—the real sources of power and authority. What Sara missed was that in this particular insurance company, camaraderie—loyalty to each other—was a requirement for acceptance and advancement. It didn't matter that she was exceptionally competent and turned out more work in a week than her predecessor had in a month. What mattered was that she was perceived as being aloof, having a superior attitude, and not "fitting in."

In her initial dejection over her performance review, Sara's first thought was that she had made the wrong choice; she had joined an organization that was not congruent with her personality. She was a leader, not a follower, and she would go someplace where that was appreciated and rewarded. Fortunately for Sara, her supervisor was willing to mentor her through the steps of induction, first backtracking a bit to rebuild some bridges, and then moving ahead to develop the relationships in the company that would ensure the success of the programs she had been hired to develop. Sara won't be likely to forget her induction lesson. If and when she moves to another organization, she will remember the steps:

- **Wait.** Hold back a little at first and see how the game is played.
- **Watch.** Watch how successful people do things, and use them as models for behavior.
- **Listen.** Be where informal conversations are taking place, and listen for clues to the unwritten rules of organizational politics.
- **Act (slowly).** Once acceptance is gained, gently assert your individuality. Your contributions are more likely to be recognized if you wait, watch, and listen before acting, and both you and the employer will benefit.

Induction may take some patience. The higher the level of the position, the longer it takes to fit in. A general rule of thumb is one month of induction time for each year of formal training required for the job. But your patience will be rewarded with the opportunity to grow and advance in your career field. Table 9.7, on page 295, offers some induction tips that might be helpful at career entry.

Sara missed on two bases. Her insurance company was a Conventional industry leader, sure of the accuracy of its procedures, traditional in its approaches, and slow to accept change. She was hired to effect change and set about it too soon. Her human resources department was a team. They worked and played together. She did neither. She gained neither friendship nor respect, and she almost lost out. Fortunately, she had a wise mentor who had seen it all before, and who was willing to coach her along the path to success. When induction is successful, the groundwork is established for the promotions or satisfying lateral moves that are typical of career progression–the next stage of career development.

Career Progression

Career Development Strategies
- Self-promotion
- Networking
- Strategic alliances

The career middle years, from the mid-20s through the 40s, are a time for striving, succeeding, and proving. There tends to be a competitive quality to our actions, as we position ourselves for promotion and advancement or appropriate lateral moves. The major focus of this period is career adjustment–modifying our original goals to reflect our growing maturity–and career satisfaction–feeling a sense of purpose in our work. With these issues resolved, our career position and direction are clearer and our career development moves forward.

An Example: Sam. Now consider Sam, a sales supervisor for a large marine manufacturer. Sam was lucky from the start. He always loved his work. He joined the military right after high school and was ready to go to work as soon as his tour of duty was finished. College wasn't for him. He loved the water and found a job selling marine parts and service contracts for a well-established company. He was good at it and was quickly promoted to larger territories and positions of increasing responsibility. Two years ago he became restless and, at 35, thought he needed a career change. He took a sales position with a major competitor with the opportunity for larger and more frequent commissions. The money was good, and for a while it felt like his restlessness was over. But now he's bored. He just isn't as happy with his work as he was when he was younger and is beginning to wonder if he may have been in the wrong job all along. At this point,

Table 9.7 Matching New Employee Behavior to RIASEC Organizational Expectation

Type of Organization/ Department	Induction Expectation	Examples
Realistic	Physical participation	Joining the softball league
Investigative	Exchange of ideas	Publishing with a senior colleague
Artistic	Honoring individuality	Discussing others' creative interests
Social	Friendly cooperation	Being a team player, at and outside of work
Enterprising	Amicable competition	Participating in sales challenges
Conventional	Following procedures	Recognizing traditional ways of doing things

Sam hears that the human resources department is starting a career exploration workshop series for employees who want to increase their potential for advancement. The workshop includes various self-assessments and information about all of the career tracks in the company. He is curious and signs up. The workshop assessments indicate that he is a good fit for his work and should be happy. He is dejected. What else could be wrong?

Sam is a good example of someone who is experiencing career adjustment issues typical of this stage. His love for the water lured him into a sales career that capitalized on his outgoing, competitive nature. He positioned himself well, building contacts while in the military that eventually led him to interviews and satisfying employment. He used his induction time well, too. Unlike the planful Sara, he instinctively knew how to promote himself with those who counted and form the alliances that would position him for advancement. When the time came, the right people recognized his achievements, and he was rewarded with promotions. At the same time, Sam was promoting himself to others in the marine business as well, making sure that he was visible to those who could help him in the future. He liked his work and produced well for his employer, but he was clear about what he wanted for himself. He needed to feel that his work was challenging, varied, and fun, and he needed to be recognized for his efforts with large commissions and bonuses. He was ready to move in any direction that best met those needs. When the time came for a change, he knew whom to call.

Eventually advancement for Sam meant changing employers. And for a while his new position fulfilled his desire for excitement. But when the newness wore off, he found himself looking around again. He was changing as he matured, and his work wasn't changing with him. He needed to adjust his career aspirations and clarify what he wanted for his future.

The career exploration seminar was puzzling to Sam at first. His assessment results indicated a good fit for what he was doing: high Enterprising/Realistic interests and clear MBTI® preferences for ESTP. Sam's restlessness came from his vision for the future. He couldn't see himself moving faster and faster, selling more and more, for the rest of his life. Career exploration activities that focused on values clarification seemed to be leading in another direction. Just as important to him as playfulness and financial reward were challenge and independence.

Sam was a hard worker and produced well. His employer did not want to lose him. In the career exploration seminar they explored several options within the company, including territory expansion and sales management. Eventually Sam was brought in on discussions of the development of a completely new line of marine products for a territory that had never been approached by the industry. He relished those meetings and spent many hours of his own time researching marketing and geographic considerations. He formulated start-up plans and provided valuable input to the management team.

When the green light came, Sam was ready. He was on his own now, with the responsibility of hiring the right people, making the right contacts, and establishing his company's new product line in a new territory. He was excited by the challenge of having to forge his own way and looked forward to even greater financial rewards than he had received in direct sales. He was even beginning to form some plans for 10 years down the road—perhaps owning his own business. Sam was successfully clarifying his position in his field and adjusting his career direction to maximize his satisfaction.

Specific career progression strategies differ from workplace to workplace, but Sam's techniques of networking, self-promotion, and forming strategic alliances are critical to their success. The techniques came to Sam's personality naturally, without a great deal of awareness and practice. It isn't as easy for clients whose personalities aren't a natural fit for the work environment they have chosen. But appropriate advancement strategies can be coached, without the client giving up his or her unique style—frequently even capitalizing on their differences. Consider some of the strategies in Tables 9.8 and 9.9, on pages 298 and 299, respectively, based on the RIASEC and MBTI® concepts we applied to the previous stages.

Career Refinement

Career Development Strategies

- Self-assessment (values shift)
- Evaluation of opportunities
- Transition

In contrast to the career progression stage of career development which tends to be active and assertive, the career refinement stage is often more reflective. These are the mature years—the late 40s through the 50s and 60s. The tasks of this stage are more oriented toward life balance than toward career achievement. The goal is to refine our work so that we get it just right, rather than folllow the competitive achievement urges of the previous stage. And, if it isn't right, this is perhaps the last chance for change—a transition to a field in which we might find satisfaction for our last years in the workplace.

This is a career stage that is often overlooked by employer programs that profess to focus on employee development. Such programs emphasize the *best fit* of career entry and subsequent advancement, using matches between assessment results and organizational position descriptions as a major tool. At this stage in the employee's career development, however, the questions are more subtle:

Table 9.8 Appropriate Self-Promotion Strategies in Organizations/Departments of Different RIASEC Categories

Organization/Department's RIASEC Category	Self-Promotion Strategies
Realistic (production, engineering, facilities maintenance)	Exceed production quotas, prepare accountability statements, present timelines and plans
Investigative (research and development, MIS, long-range planning, quality control)	Coauthor publications with senior researchers, develop new systems, present long-range visions with practical applications
Artistic (advertising, public relations, communications)	Write and speak with aesthetic flair, recognize others' creative contributions, express new ways of doing things
Social (HR, customer service, employee assistance, training and development)	Participate on committees, cooperate with others on group projects, arrange social functions
Enterprising (organizational development, sales, marketing)	Exceed sales quotas, participate in strategic planning discussions, speak at business professional meetings and organizations
Conventional (finance, accounting, operations, administration)	Author financial reports, written summaries, and recommendations for procedural improvement

- How can I make my work more rewarding?
- My values are changing. Are there other areas of my life that need attention?
- What can I do now to prepare for the time when I am no longer formally employed?
- Is it too late for me to really find my niche?

It is more important now than ever for employers to invest in career development programs that are geared to life enrichment and balance

Table 9.9 Appropriate Self-Promotion Strategies in Organizations with Different MBTI Cores

Organization/Department's MBTI Core	Self-Promotion Strategies
ST (applied science, business administration, banking, law enforcement)	Emphasize facts, efficiency, practical solutions
SF (community service/ nonprofit, health care, teaching, office support)	Emphasize facts, service, communication
NF (psychology, graphic arts and design, health care, teaching, religious organizations)	Emphasize ideas, relationships, responsiveness to personal needs
NT (theoretical science, research, technology development, law, engineering, management)	Emphasize ideas, strategies, logical problem solving

issues. Usually workers are no longer satisfied with the typical financial rewards of career advancement and achievement. These workers are looking for meaning and purpose, and paid employment is only one of their sources. Often we hear from people in this stage that they would rather have time than money—time for family, for leisure, for potential retirement interests. But, then, when time is given to them, they are frequently directionless. If career professionals can provide them with some direction for adding breadth to their lives—at work and outside of work—both they and their employing organizations will benefit from their rejuvenation and increased motivation.

An Example: Tom. Tom is an engineer—always has been and was sure that he always would be. His father and grandfather were both engineers, and he knew when he was in elementary school that engineering was where he was headed. When he first got out of college, engineering jobs were scarce, but Tom had been smart. During his college internships he had developed an aerospace specialty that was unique, and he found a job in his specialization. Almost 30 years later, he is watching his company downsize to accommodate a diminishing market in his area of expertise. He is being asked to do more work as his department is reduced in size, and, what's worse, his work is becoming more and more routine. He feels that his job is fairly safe, as he has seniority in his field and he is a highly valued employee. But that isn't enough anymore. He feels desperate. His career seems over, and he is barely 50.

Tom's scenario is not uncommon in the career refinement stage. He is actually facing most of the questions typical of this stage. He is ready to refine his work, but two elements are missing: earlier mastery of the tasks of career exploration and workforce availability. As a result he is facing layoff and has no suitable alternatives. Up to now his work has been his life. He has few interests that are not work related. But, even without the pending layoff, his job has lost its excitement. He was considering a change but had no idea how to go about it at his age. If he were to relocate and remain with his employer, he would have only a few years left until retirement anyway, and what then?

Tom's employer had instituted an internal outplacement program for its employees who were being downsized. Their training and development department wanted to implement a small pilot program for those who were remaining with the company as well, and Tom was the perfect candidate. Reluctant to participate at first, Tom found in the program the information and the strategies to make his life more fulfilling both at work and outside of work.

The program Tom participated in is built on self-assessment and the evaluation of opportunities, with an anticipated result of transition or enrichment. Transition would be either in or out of the organization. Enrichment would be either job redesign or some other life role enhancement. The core is the familiar RIASEC and MBTI® models, plus a thorough assessment of emerging life values as well. Program logistics typically include an overview of career exploration, group interpretation of assessments, small-group follow-ups, and individualized action planning.

Tom is a good example of how the program works. Although hesitant at first, he was reassured during the first orientation session that the assessment results would be completely confidential and that he would have ample opportunity to discuss the results with a career professional. At this meeting he was able to define his goal of staying with his present employer, but redefine his function in some way that would be more challenging. He took the *Strong* and MBTI® instruments online in the organization's learning center, and took a *Values Checklist* with him to complete at home that evening. The checklist was difficult, but finally he was able to narrow the list of 56 down to 10 and prioritize them. It was particularly challenging for Tom to consider values not related to his work, and he found it interesting that "more time with family" and "developing physical strength" were rated almost as high as "work competence" and "financial reward."

The group interpretation of the assessments was interesting for Tom. He was able to predict his RIASEC code and MBTI® type even before he saw his results and was not surprised at his Investigative/Realistic, INTJ profile. What did surprise him was evidence from the *Strong* assessment of moderate interest in Social/helping activities. Tom's response was a predicted "if only there were time," but he left the group meeting with a great deal to think about.

The final group session was held the following evening after work. The facilitator had identified a group of six men and women with expressed interest in career/life enrichment and arranged for them to meet around an informal supper. The focus of this meeting was on occupational similarities and the basic interests represented by the *Strong* instrument and on identifying emerging, type-related interests that tend to develop as people mature. This latter technique emphasizes the other preferences (not in the type) and their growing importance in an individual's life, for example, STs' growing interest in their NF side.

Tom's need to understand theoretical and technical principles for problem solving was evident in his INTJ type. More interesting, however, was the group discussion that evolved around the development of NT types—emerging SF interests in later life. He recognized an interest in providing practical services to others and helping people with information and resources that his current design job never left time for. Combined with this were the *Strong* basic interests in teaching and religious activities—an interesting complement to his expected mechanical activities, mathematics, and science. Athletics was also high for him—an interest that he hadn't pursued since high school. Tom's occupational similarity on the *Strong* instrument was with scientific and technical occupations, but also with athletic trainer and physical education teacher—more evidence of his growing awareness of his interests.

In the individual meeting with the career professional that followed, Tom was able to seriously evaluate his *Strong* and MBTI® results along with his top values of work competence, financial reward, more time with family, and developing physical strength. Two ideas came to him: (1) the possibility of remaining in his current position but delegating more of the routine work to his staff to make time for a few hours a week in human relations work—either recruiting or employee development; and (2) spending less of his off-work time reading technical journals to make time for some other interests. He thought of replacing some of his indoor treadmill time with real running, to participate in a community run scheduled the following month. Also interesting was the idea of co-teaching a Sunday school class with his wife or playing on the church softball team.

Tom's life is enriched, and his attitude toward work has improved. But by expanding his self-awareness, he has generated options for the next stage of career development as well.

Career Disengagement

Career Development Strategies

- Identity reevaluation
- Self-assessment (new interests)

The retirement years are not usually the subject of career development programs in the workplace, but, like the childhood years, they have ramifications throughout the life span. The anticipation of retirement often affects employee work attitude and performance for years preceding the actual event.

An Example: Barbara. Barbara is a 63-year-old corporate accountant who has been considering retirement for several years. She does not have to work for financial reasons, but she isn't sure what else she would do. She is divorced, her children are grown, and she enjoys her professional identity and status. She would like to either continue working in her field on a part-time basis or contribute her services to a worthwhile organization. Her daughter chided her in a recent conversation, "Mom, you're too old for career counseling. You should be happy that you don't have to work." Barbara is frustrated and confused about what lies ahead. Her frustration and concern are impeding her ability to do her work, and she senses that others think it's time for her to retire.

People who find intrinsic satisfaction in their work and who find congruence with their work environments are apt to continue in similar environments after retirement. In contrast, people who work primarily to meet extrinsic needs and who don't hold work enjoyment as a high value tend to look for new and different things to do. If people are happy in what they have been doing, they are drawn to retirement activities in the same areas—the retired teacher who volunteers in an elementary school, for instance, or seeks other ways to help in her community, or the engineer who enjoys his new handyman role in his condominium complex. However, people who work in office or routine jobs for many years, with no inherent satisfaction, might look to the arts, outdoor activities, or helping others for retirement enjoyment—the postal worker who has always wanted to travel to Europe and see great works of art, or the office worker who is volunteering in a daycare center, or the bookkeeper who is learning to ski at 65.

What is the role of the workplace in preparing employees for the career disengagement tasks of deinstitutionalization, change of role, and personal enrichment? Is it the responsibility of the workplace to ensure successful deceleration and institutional disengagement? If, as employers, we are to accept our commitment to the betterment of society as a whole, it is. And if we want to capitalize on the wisdom and special gifts of our older workers, it is.

During the 60s and 70s, the individual often experiences a reevaluation of identity as roles change and formal employment is left behind. Combined with the anticipation of employment freedom is the fear of loss. "Who am I if not an employee?" is a question often heard in retirement counseling sessions. If the tasks of career refinement have been mastered, and life enrichment and balance have been achieved, the disengagement process is apt to be easier. Tom, for instance, will more likely be ready to face these issues now that he is discovering interests outside of his work. Barbara may find reassurance, too, if she is able to take advantage of the guidance that is made available to her.

Organizations do not typically devote hours of work time to career exploration for its preretirees, but other options may be possible:

- **After-work or weekend seminars and retreats.** A time for older workers to come together to discuss mutual retirement concerns: The agenda might be formal, to include professionals representing financial planning, the Social Security Administration, health insurance and Medicare, volunteerism, travel and leisure, and part-time employment.

Or it might be informal, just to get concerns out in the open for future program planning.

- **A retirement mentoring program.** Prior retirees are often the best source of information for those who are looking ahead. Pairing current older workers with those who have left formal employment during the last few years and who have similar interests will benefit both. The retiree will feel useful and honored. The worker will feel more reassured and hopeful.

- **Brown bag seminars.** A regular program of lunchtime speakers and resources is often helpful to those who are anticipating retirement. Presenting panels of successful volunteers, hobbyists, part-time workers, and world travelers will attract interest and open the door to further discussion and opportunities for assistance.

- **Part-time employment.** A resource file of part-time employment opportunities for older workers will be appreciated by anyone who needs to continue working or who is restless without paid employment. Part-time contract positions with the current employer are also a possibility with many organizations and could be made available to those who are planning to decelerate. Barbara researched this option and found that her employer was very open to the idea of a contract position. With this knowledge, she began to look forward to the future.

- **Personality assessment.** The same assessment tools that are helpful in other stages of career development are helpful here as well. Offering group interpretations that target disengagement issues can be beneficial to many. Assessments can be helpful for suggesting leisure, volunteer, and part-time employment possibilities as well as assisting with identity issues and overall life satisfaction. Were Barbara to avail herself of this option, she might find that there is something she would enjoy doing more than the "maintenance work" she has been doing since her divorce.

Any option that promotes successful work deceleration and disengagement from the employing institution is likely to be reassuring to workers who are crossing the threshold to this last stage of their work lives. It may also promote a sense of positive anticipation among workers who are looking ahead, as they see their predecessors make successful transitions.

SUMMARY

Career development counseling requires a commitment to the right of all workers to lead the fullest and most productive lives possible—not just upper management or salaried; not just outplaced or downsized. A developmental approach encourages employability through self-reliance, contributing to a healthy workforce, economy, and society. But it is not a commitment to be entered into lightly. It will always be easier to offer "one size fits all" career programs to our employees and hope that if we toss enough information out, some of it will stick. Hopefully the issues raised here will encourage more to consider the individual developmental needs of our children, young adults, established workers, and retirees.

REFERENCES

Bluestein, D. L., Devenis, L. E., & Kidney, B. A. (1989). Relationship between the identity formation process and career development. *Journal of Counseling Psychology, 36*(2), 196–202.

Buehler, C. (1933). *Der menschliche Lebenslauf als psychologisches problem (The human life course as a psychological subject).* Leipzig: Hirzel.

Ginzberg, E., Ginsburg, S. W., Axelrad, S., & Hermal, J. (1951). *Occupational choice: An approach to a general theory.* New York: Columbia University Press.

Holland, J. L. (1958). A personality inventory employing occupational titles. *Journal of Applied Psychology, 42,* 336–342.

Holland, J. L. (1959). A theory of vocational choice. *Journal of Counseling Psychology, 6,* 35–45.

Holland, J. L. (1994). *The self-directed search.* Odessa, FL: Psychological Assessment Resources.

Marcia, J. E. (1966). Development and validation of ego-identity status. *Journal of Personality and Social Psychology, 3,* 551–558.

Myers-Briggs Type Indicator. (1998). Palo Alto, CA: Consulting Psychologists Press.

Strong Interest Inventory of the Strong Vocational Interests Blanks. (1994). Palo Alto, CA: Consulting Psychologists Press.

Super, D. E. (1953). A theory of vocational development. *American Psychologist, 8,* 185–190.

Super, D. E. (1954a). Guidance: Manpower utilization or human development? *Personnel and Guidance Journal, 33,* 8–14.

Super, D. E. (1954b). Career patterns as a basis for vocational counseling. *Journal of Counseling Psychology, 1,* 12–20.

Super, D. E. (1957). *The psychology of careers.* New York: Harper & Row.

Super, D. E. (1994). A life-span, life-space perspective on congruence. In M. L. Savickas & R. W. Lent (Eds.), *Convergence in career development theories* (pp. 63–74). Palo Alto, CA: Consulting Psychologists Press.

Tiedeman, D. V., & O'Hara, R. P. (1963). *Career development: Choice and adjustment.* New York: College Entrance Examination Board.

NOTES

[1]For further discussion of the *Strong Interest Inventory®* and *Myers-Briggs Type Indicator®* instruments, see chapter 10.
[2]For further discussion of the importance of the early years in the development of the individual, see Mary McCaulley (1992). Roads to the mountaintop—pathways to individuation. *Bulletin of Psychological Type, 15*(4), 12–14.
[3]Attributed to Walt Disney.

10

Using the Strong Interest Inventory® and Myers-Briggs Type Indicator® Instruments Together

THE WHOLE IS GREATER THAN THE SUM OF ITS PARTS

Jean M. Kummerow

Aren't there some tests that will tell me what I should be? This is a frequent refrain voiced by many clients seeking a job or career change. In this world of rapid change and resulting uncertainty, there is a longing for the alleged certainty of "test results" and the hope that a specific job or career is out there just waiting to be discovered. The bottom-line answer is that nothing brings certainty, but some inventories will help the exploration for life work through identifying patterns in the client's personality and interests.

This chapter will examine two of the most widely used assessments in career counseling: the *Myers-Briggs Type Indicator*® (MBTI®) and the *Strong Interest Inventory*® *(Strong)* instruments. The focus of this chapter is on integrating the two instruments with the view that using the two together provides far more information than using them separately. A series of client exercises at the end of the chapter provides step-by-step integration methods.

Instruments are used often in the career counseling process because they are a systematic and efficient means of gathering and summarizing data. Both the MBTI® and *Strong* inventories give information on personality style and interests, although the MBTI® instrument emphasizes the former and the *Strong* instrument, the latter. The MBTI® assessment focuses on the question "Who am I?" while the *Strong* assessment helps answer the question "What do I want to do?" Both instruments are oriented toward the positive, yet they provide an objective view of clients. They may confirm what clients already know about themselves as well as point to new directions, thus giving clients options to consider. In other words, they may save time and supply some good information, but they do not give the answers.

Note: When discussing these instruments with clients, it is best to avoid using the word *test* because that implies a right or wrong. Both instruments are value-free and point to normal patterns of personality differences. Neither measures abilities.

THE TWO INSTRUMENTS

Strong Interest Inventory® Instrument

The *Strong* instrument is an empirically based measure of vocational interests. It provides an assessment of the client's interests by comparing that person's interests with those of satisfied people employed in a variety of occupations. It is based on a wide variety of familiar occupational tasks and day-to-day activities. It consists of five sections:

- 6 General Occupational Themes based on John Holland's theory of vocational types (RIASEC)
- 25 Basic Interest Scales of common activities also organized by RIASEC codes
- 211 Occupational Scales (with RIASEC codes) comparing interests to those of individuals successfully employed in the occupation
- 4 Personal Style Scales identifying work, learning, leadership, and risk-taking styles
- 3 types of Validity Measures, including total responses, infrequent responses, and summary of item responses

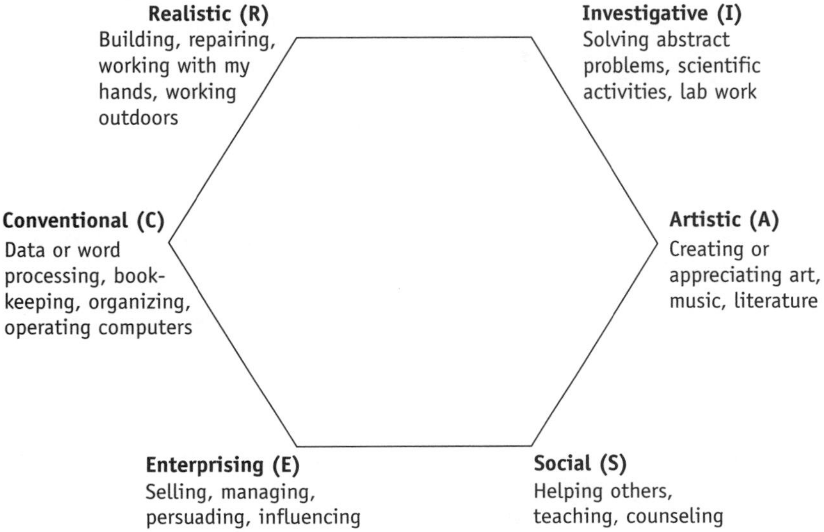

Source: Reproduced by special permission of the publisher, Consulting Psychologists Press, Inc., from *MBTI Manual* by Isabel Briggs Myers, Mary H. McCaulley, Naomi L. Quenk, and Allen L. Hammer.

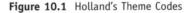

Figure 10.1 Holland's Theme Codes

The first three sets of scales are organized around Holland's theme codes and thus help describe personality as well as occupational interests. These General Occupational Themes or Holland codes are shown in Figure 10.1. According to the theory, the themes that are adjacent to each other on the hexagon have the most in common. Those that are opposite each other have very different interest patterns. They create more challenges for those with such codes since it is often difficult to incorporate such widely varying patterns into one job or career. For example, the creative process (Artistic) is rarely organized (Conventional).

Most people identify several themes as descriptive of their interests; the order of the codes reflects the order of importance in their career interests. Scores from the *Strong*'s General Occupational Themes are ranked with the highest one as the first code. Clients are invited to arrange the codes in whatever order is most meaningful to them. For example, my code is SECA, indicating that I most enjoy helping people (Social) and do so through running my own consulting business (Enterprising), organizing whatever I can (Conventional), and creatively putting together different ways of helping (Artistic). I like having those four codes involved in my work daily, but all in service of the first theme—Social. I even have a bit of Investigative, with rare forays into research. But don't ask me to run any machines—Realistic isn't my thing.

The instrument and its results are generally easy to comprehend since many of the *Strong* assessment's categories and job titles fit into our everyday understanding of the terms. It requires an eighth-grade reading level (age 14) and usually 25 to 40 minutes to complete. The current version was revised in 1994 and contains 317 questions. It may be taken in paper-and-pencil or online versions, including via the Internet.

Some basic *Strong* resources useful to career counselors include *Strong Interest Inventory: Applications and Technical Guide* (Harmon, Hansen, Borgen, & Hammer, 1994) and *Where Do I Go Next?: Using Your Strong Results to Manage your Career* (Borgen & Grutter, 1995). *Real People, Real Jobs* (Montross, Leibowitz, & Shinkman, 1995) offers portraits of workers in each of the Holland codes. There are also training manuals with *Strong* materials for use in corporate settings (Hirsh, 1995), colleges and universities (Prince, 1995), and high schools (Rumpel & Lecertua, 1996b). An introductory video is also available (Consulting Psychologists Press, 1995). The *Strong* is scored only by computer with report options including a basic six-page profile; an Interpretive Report (Hammer & Grutter, 1994); a Professional Report (Hammer, 1994), based on occupations requiring a university degree; and a high school version (Rumpel & Lecertua, 1996a).

Myers-Briggs Type Indicator® Instrument

The MBTI® instrument is based on Carl Jung's theory of behavior patterns related to how individuals perceive information and make decisions. Four dichotomies are described, each with two poles, or preferences. While all people possess some measure of all eight preferences, one pole in each dichotomy typically is preferred. The four dichotomies describe

- How an individual gains energy
  Extraversion (E): an external, outside world focus
  Introversion (I): an internal, inward world focus

- How an individual perceives information and gathers data
  Sensing (S): through attention to the details and what is
  Intuition (N): through attention to the big picture and what might be

- How decisions get made
  Thinking (T): through objective, logical analysis
  Feeling (F): through subjective, person-centered values

- Lifestyle
  Judging (J): seeking closure, often through quick decisions
  Perceiving (P): seeking options and continued exploration

The MBTI® Step I is the resulting four-letter type; there are thus 16 unique personality or psychological types. The focus of the MBTI® instrument is on broad personality categories, not on specific career interests. However, it appears that similar types (usually those with the same middle letters or function pairs of ST, SF, NF, or NT) are often attracted to similar careers. Nevertheless, all 16 types end up in every career, although each type may emphasize different aspects of a particular job.

The MBTI® assessment tool requires a seventh-grade reading level (age 13) and approximately 25 to 40 minutes to complete. The standard form is Form M, with 93 items, published in 1998. Forms F, G, J, and K also may be used to identify the Step I type.

Levels of Interpreting Type. Hammer (1994) has identified three levels of type interpretation, with a fourth added by Kummerow (1998). These approaches can be helpful in navigating the career development process.

The Static Approach provides a core understanding of each of the preferences, the preference combinations, and the 16 types.

- The common characteristics of each preference and type are emphasized.

- Individual differences within type are ignored.

- This approach helps us understand our clients' personalities and the trends in job selection by type.

For example, these descriptions use the Static Approach: Extraverted types typically want variety, activity, and opportunities to interact with people in their work. NFs are often attracted to occupations in the arts, writing, and counseling. A core component of INFPs is their drive to live their values.

The Dynamic Approach suggests that there is a theoretical interplay between the preferences within the type; not all are used equally.

- According to the model, each type has a dominant or lead function with an auxiliary function for balance; one relates to how information is perceived and the other to how decisions are made.
- Each type has a preferred way of showing the dominant and auxiliary functions—that is, with one Extraverted (outward) and the other Introverted (inward).
- A formula determines the dynamics for each type—that is, the order of "importance" of the type's preference and whether that preference is primarily extraverted or introverted. For example, an INFP's dominant or preferred function is Introverted Feeling (core values), the auxiliary or second function is Extraverted Intuition (possibilities), the tertiary or third function is Sensing (details), and the fourth or inferior and least preferred function is Extraverted Thinking (logic).
- The fourth function may provide a clue as to typical stress reactions of the type. For example, a dominant Intuitive type may focus on unimportant facts when under pressure and obsess about seemingly irrelevant details.
- To be well developed according to this model means being able to use both Perceiving (data-gathering) and Judging (decision-making) skills as well as accessing both the outside (Extraverting) and the inside (Introverting) worlds. Thus the dominant and auxiliary functions are readily available, and the third and fourth functions are incorporated as needed. Good type development does not mean using all functions equally well.
- This approach is useful in assessing how a person is functioning in the use of his or her type, particularly with career exploration and decision-making processes. For example, these three uses are possible:

1. Identifying activities that are likely to be important and interesting to clients. Are clients able to use their dominant functions in their work? Are dominant Thinking types free to use their logic, dominant

Intuitive types free to create possibilities, dominant Feeling types free to focus on their values, dominant Sensing types free to get grounded in reality?

2. Ascertaining how clients are using their type, including issues of balance (access to all "letters") and imbalance (overemphasis on just one to the exclusion of the others). For example, are they extraverting both their dominant and auxiliary functions? One needs to be extraverted and the other introverted so that there is both reflection and action. Are they relying only on their dominant function and thus missing the balancing nature of the auxiliary–that is, making decisions with no information (all Judging with either Thinking or Feeling) or gathering lots of information but making no decisions (all Perceiving with either Sensing or Intuition)?
3. Improving decision making through the use of all four functions. People are generally most effective if they tap all four functions: gathering information (S), generating alternatives (N), analyzing the alternatives (T), and noting what's of value (F).

The Developmental Approach posits that each type may have a different path to development given that all functions cannot be equally well developed and utilized. A natural unfolding occurs over the life span and theoretically follows the order of the type dynamics. People may have the same type but be in a different stage of life and thus be comfortably accessing different aspects of their personality. See chapter 9 for more on this.

- There may be an "ideal" order to type development: first the dominant (perhaps by age 12), then the auxiliary (perhaps in the teen years), next the tertiary (perhaps in early adulthood), and last the fourth function (perhaps in midlife). Integrating the functions is a task in the latter half of life.

- When development of a function has been skipped, problems may arise. For example, a Feeling person in a Thinking family and work environment may never have learned to trust his or her Feeling function in decision making. This person may be torn continually between head and heart, always second-guessing decisions.

- There will also be certain times in an individual's life when a function may take on more salience than it did previously; for example, in midlife the third and fourth functions tend to demand more attention, leading to a midlife career transition for some individuals. For Thinking types, this may mean more interest in developing people (utilizing their preference for Feeling) than earlier in their careers. Helping clients integrate their understanding of this process may be particularly beneficial.

The Behavioral Approach utilizes the MBTI® Step II (from Form K or J only). Step II recognizes that the expression of type may be individualized for each person. Each of the four dichotomies has five facets or subscales that help show the unique expression of a person's type. This personalization can guide an individualized career development process. However, the focus of this chapter is Step I; for more on Step II see Kummerow and Quenk, 1992; Mitchell, 1999; and Saunders, 1989.

Best-Fit Type. With the MBTI® instrument it is important to determine and work with the *best-fit type*—the type that most fully describes the client's personality. This is likely to be the same as the reported type approximately 65 to 80 percent of the time. The best-fit type is determined through a verification process such as the one described in the *MBTI Manual* (1998)—a process that encourages clients to question their results and search for the type that most accurately portrays them. *Type Clarification: Finding the Fit* (Carr, 1997) also offers excellent techniques for working with clients who are having difficulty identifying their best-fit type. Some suggested descriptions for clients to use in verifying their best-fit types include *Introduction to Type®* (Myers, 1998), *Introduction to Type® in Organizations* (Hirsh & Kummerow, 1998), and *LIFETypes* (Hirsh & Kummerow, 1989).

For further reading on applications of MBTI to career counseling, see the *MBTI Manual* (1998), particularly Chapter 12 by Kummerow; *MBTI Applications* Chapter 3, (Hammer, 1996); *Introduction to Type and Careers* (Hammer, 1993); and *MBTI Career Report Manual* (Hammer & Macdaid, 1992). The MBTI® instrument is available in self-scorable, template-scorable, and computer-scorable versions, including via the Internet. Among the computer-scorable versions, the following are available: a basic profile, an interpretive report, an interpretive report for organizations (Hirsh & Kummerow, 1998), and an interpretive report for careers (Hammer & Macdaid, 1992).

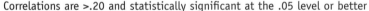

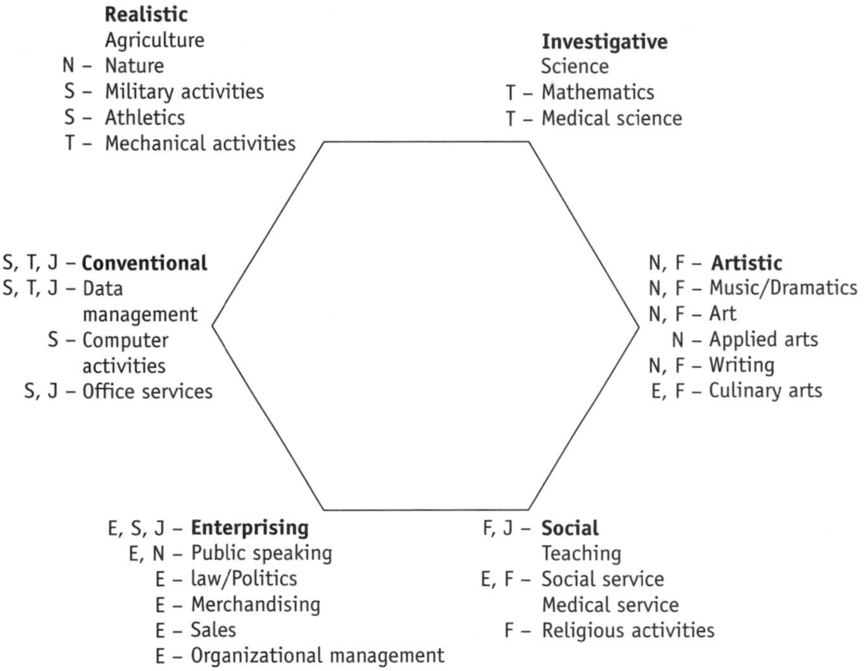

Correlations are >.20 and statistically significant at the .05 level or better

Source: Myers & McCaulley, *Manual,* 1985; Hammer & Kummerow, *Strong and MBTI Career Development Guide* (rev. ed.), 1996.

Figure 10.2 Statistical Relationship Between MBTI® and *Strong Interest Inventory®* Results in Samples of Adults

STATISTICAL RELATIONSHIPS

Correlational data between the two instruments has been gathered for over 25 years on samples of students and adults. The results correlate in the expected directions but the numbers are generally low, indicating that the two instruments have their own distinct contributions. Student samples have more statistically significant correlations between the two instruments than the adult samples. However, since interests tend to stabilize for people in their mid-20s, only data on adult samples will be presented here, as it is believed these are the more stable and enduring relationships. Figure 10.2 indicates correlations at or above .20 from several sources. The strongest correlation in these data is between S–N and Artistic at .48.

The statistical patterns are the clearest in the following areas: Artistic interests with the MBTI® poles of Intuition and Feeling; Social interests with the Feeling pole; Enterprising interests with the Extraversion pole; and Conventional interests with the Sensing and Judging poles.

CAREER COUNSELING USING THE TWO INSTRUMENTS

The process of career counseling is complex; Waterman (see chapter 5 in this volume) suggests this process involves (1) understanding career realities, (2) self-assessment, (3) setting priorities, and (4) acting and keeping the process moving. The *Strong* and MBTI® instruments are particularly well suited to the self-assessment step. However, both instruments also can be helpful guidelines to the third step—clients' priorities, and to the fourth step, keeping the process moving. It seems appropriate that clients' priorities be congruent with who they are (personality) and what they like to do (interests). The instruments' results may help clients identify some of what their priorities might be and may serve as useful filters with which to check priorities. For example, I have a priority to be involved in my community as a volunteer (Social), but also one to support my family financially. I can use my ESTJ personality to organize my time efficiently so that I can do both.

Acting and keeping the process moving is also part of Waterman's career counseling process. Obviously, this process can have its ups and downs—there are exciting times, such as when an "aha" insight occurs as to why one just didn't like that job in XYZ, but it can also be draining when nothing seems to go right. At these times, using *Strong* and MBTI® results can keep the energy high and the process moving. It may not so much be a matter of integrating the results at this point, but rather focusing clients on their natural inclinations in either personality or interests to get them reenergized.

For example, an ENFP client who has been doing Internet research on possible companies to target may find herself worn out by so much introverted activity. She may need to turn to her preferred Extraverted side and invite friends to go on a walk in the woods with her (if nature is high) or to go with her to a play (if music/dramatics is high). An ISFJ individual found interviewing was quite stressful. She decided to plan for what she could and got together with a small group of friends to help her generate "what if" questions (to assist with her less-preferred Intuition). She then concentrated by herself (using her Introversion) on coming up with answers and practiced them with her career counselor (using her Sensing Judging to plan and prepare). She rewarded herself for her hard work by cooking a special meal for her family (high culinary arts).

Type can be particularly helpful in understanding the process a client may use in exploring careers and identifying predictable pitfalls and ways out. For example, an ENTP client may keep generating more alternative careers to explore (using dominant Intuition) and end up going in circles, with the possibilities delaying any action. This client may tune into his judging side (Thinking) and make a "parking lot" for the less promising jobs–they are parked there, but not gone forever. Then the focus can be on learning about a few jobs and careers in greater depth to make some decisions and move forward.

Several workbooks are available to help clients integrate the results of these two instruments in different phases of the career development process. Kummerow and Hammer (1995) have a series of exercises walking clients through self-assessment phases and prioritizing job titles to pursue; they also acknowledge likely obstacles clients may encounter based on their personality and interests, and suggest ways to stay motivated. Grutter (1998a, 1998b, 1998c) also offers explicit exercises helping clients self-assess; design strategies to enrich, transition, or advance in their careers; and develop plans to keep enriching their lives in the future.

Skilled counselors use results from both instruments in all phases of career counseling, including adjusting their own styles to create better communication with their clients (for example, allowing more silence in sessions with clients who prefer Introversion). They can also help clients take advantage of their personality preferences to find techniques that work well for them and to understand which tasks might be more difficult. The bulk of this chapter, however, will be involved with the self-assessment portion of career development counseling and will include assessing personality, preferred activities, and possible job titles.

INTEGRATING PERSONALITY DESCRIPTIONS

Both the *Strong* and MBTI® instruments include personality descriptions in their results with the addition of Holland's themes to the *Strong* instrument in 1972. (Please note that the terms *Holland themes, Holland codes, General Occupational Theme [GOT] Codes,* and *RIASEC* are interchangeable in this chapter.) The meshing of the personality components from the two instruments helps provide a more accurate and inclusive description of an individual than either instrument provides alone. Exercise 10.1 is designed to help that integration of personality descriptors occur. Several examples follow that illustrate the use of the two instruments' personality components. These include

- A family with the same Holland theme but different MBTI® types
- Two people with the same occupation (training manager) and Holland themes (AS) but different MBTI® types
- Six people all of the same personality type (INFP) but each with a different Holland theme

Examples of "Personality" Level Integration

Same Interests, Different Types. Cindy, Mac, and Joan are a mother, father, and daughter who share more than a common gene pool and family environment—they all score as Enterprising on the *Strong*. However, they differ in their psychological types, and that shows up in their career paths as well. Cindy, an ENFP with an Enterprising-Social code, is in her mid-50s and has worked as a journalist and fundraiser as well as a homemaker and community volunteer. She can organize events and people like no one else, persuading others to get excited about helping the arts organization, church, school, or wherever she is involved. She has just finished law school and is entering the legal profession; she sees the law as a way to proactively help people. She is interested in small-business consulting as well as estate planning (wills and trusts)—both fields include Enterprising activities.

Mac is an ISTJ with an Enterprising-Conventional code. In his mid-50s, he has been a naval officer and a manager in a computer hardware company, and now he is an in-house computer consultant in a large business organization. His role is to help people at all levels utilize their personal computers. He has always loved to take charge, and his off-hours are often spent as a referee at various sporting events—he is decisive in those roles. When he was downsized several years ago and without work for months, he was able to referee even more to fulfill his needs for being in charge of something. It was important for him psychologically to have his Enterprising acknowledged, even if it was in a volunteer setting. At present, he has developed a large network of people in his organization—from custodians to executives—who can help him get the answers for the people who need them. He uses his influence daily.

Their daughter, Joan, is an ESTJ with an Enterprising-Conventional code. She is in her mid-20s with a university degree in art history; she spent some time studying in Italy. Her career goal is to work in the wine industry, preferably as a buyer and preferably allowing her to make many return trips to Italy. She has taken a position as an assistant chef in a restaurant to learn more about wine and also to learn the business aspects of running a restaurant. However, she would rather be making decisions now, instead of being in the training mode.

All three like to lead and persuade others—components of their Enterprising personalities. (We won't ask how this works in their family dynamics.) But they use their Enterprising in different ways through the incorporation of their second Holland codes and of their different psychological types.

Same Occupation and Interests, Different Types. Taking another perspective, consider how two people in the same career field have used their types and Holland codes in their work. Both have Artistic-Social codes, but Patricia is an ESTJ and Carlotta, an ENFP. Both are in the training and development function in human resources and both want to find the best ways to train the employees of their organizations. Carlotta (ENFP) likes finding new ways of educating the staff she works with; she is constantly scouting for the latest trends, for cutting-edge people to learn from and bring in-house, and for creative ways to present information. Her focus is on new possibilities. Patricia (ESTJ) wants to find programs that work, document them, and deliver them consistently. She is always on the lookout for new and better training programs. She has particularly enjoyed supporting the compensation and benefits area, not only because of its structured nature, but also because it allows her to create and implement new packages that help people. Her focus is on finding and maintaining a logical structure for her creative endeavors.

Same Type, Different Interests. In a more complicated example, note in Table 10.1 how six individuals, all INFPS, may choose different careers and may approach their work differently as a result of differing Holland codes. As INFPs, they have much in common. They are focused on their internal values. They have a creative bent and enjoy looking for new ideas and

Table 10.1 Personality Relationships Between INFP and the Six RIASEC Codes

Holland Code	How the Two Combine in an INFP Individual
Realistic (Doers*) Practical, handy, common sense, making/repairing things, reliable, outdoorsy, "get to it" attitude	Nick is a rehabilitation counselor whose clients are injured construction workers. His ideal is to help them get back to work—to "doing" as quickly as possible. He also is very handy himself, always remodeling his home or helping his neighbors with their building projects. He is curious about the way things work, including the way his clients think and act.
Investigative (Thinkers*) Analytical, curious, explorative, independent, searching, asking "why," wanting to understand	Pamela works as a social science researcher. Her ideal is to discover as much information as she can from many sources, pull together disparate views, and recommend programs that can then be developed to meet people's needs. In the past she had not valued her analytical skills to really dig into issues and figure out sensitive ways to write about different viewpoints. She had put herself down as a "people pleaser." Now she sees how valuable this is.
Artistic (Creators*) Creative, original, independent, unconventional, seeking the unusual, spontaneous, unstructured, flexible, seeking beauty	Deb is a librarian. When she worked in a small branch library, she loved getting to know the idiosyncrasies of each patron and indulging them. She now heads the library's training department. Her ideal is to create a community of learners, both staff and patrons, who have no boundaries on their learning. When she was first in her job, she started by focusing on the needs of new librarians, empathizing with all they do. She then developed programs to help them get what they need.
Social (Helpers*) Nurturing, caregiver, do-gooders, helpers, cooperative, enablers, teachers, supportive, friendly, compassionate	Sue is a special education teacher who works with emotionally disturbed teenagers. Her ideal is to help students learn ways to manage their own emotions and find a place in their community. She takes a personal interest in each student's background. Those without families are invited into hers. Her caregiving also spills over to her family, neighbors, and friends; she is always doing something "nice" for someone.

Table 10.1 Personality Relationships Between INFP and the Six RIASEC Codes (cont'd)

Holland Code	How the Two Combine in an INFP Individual
Enterprising (Persuaders*) Convincing, persuading, political, influencing, leading, decision maker, opportunity driven, risk taking, recognition seeking	John is a community volunteer now that he's retired from teaching. His ideal is to lead community committees through the morass of political issues to a common purpose. For example, one committee he chairs recommends grants and loans from tax revenue dollars. He keeps focused on the purpose of the committee—to stimulate economic development (not to be a social service program). At times he comments on the low status and lack of recognition volunteers get for their work, but mostly his sense of purpose carries him through these times.
Conventional (Organizers*) Organized, attentive to detail, stable, orderly, practical, efficient, no surprises, reliable, plan in advance	Bert is a tax accountant who loves handling the particularly difficult returns where he can be somewhat "creative" and also concentrate in-depth. His ideal is to organize his practice to fit his style and to identify the guiding principles in the tax laws to make his clients happy. He recently left a large firm to set up his own business in the small town where he grew up. While recognizing the possible lack of variety in the new business, he hopes his additional free time will make up for this and allow him the variety he also enjoys.

Source: * The one-word descriptions for the RIASEC codes are from Grutter, *Making It in Today's Organizations,* 1998a. The word lists for each code were generated by workshop participants of that code in several countries.

possibilities. They get to know people slowly and find places for each person to make contributions. Their gentle style belies their determined quest for the ideal. The six examples illustrate how different Holland codes have affected six INFPs, resulting in a variety of career choices despite the commonalities of personality described above.

You'll note the most "natural" overlap between INFP and the two Holland themes of Artistic (creativity) and Social (helping others). Data indicate that these are the two most common codes for INFPs (Hammer & Kummerow, 1996). Where the two relate, it's easier to find a fit. Where they differ, the clients have had to work harder to create a niche for themselves, but each of these individuals has been able to do so with satisfactory results.

INTEGRATING TASKS IDENTIFIED IN EACH INSTRUMENT

In addition to personality information, each instrument can also be interpreted based on specific activities or tasks inherent in its scales. Clients are encouraged to focus on their scale results and the underlying tasks associated with each. (See Grutter, 1998a, 1998b, 1998c for more on this focus; she first suggested this technique.) These tasks might also be preferred activities, skills and/or abilities, depending on the client. The *Strong* instrument has four sets of scales that identify possible tasks: General Occupational Themes, Basic Interest Scales, Occupational Scales, and Personal Style Scales. The MBTI® instrument also suggests a number of tasks based on the preferences, on different combinations of preferences, or on whole types. For all clients, of course, it will be necessary to further translate these tasks into actual skills and abilities. A client, for example, may score high on Artistic and enjoy the task of creating art objects, but may have no real skill or ability in doing so, and thus may be unable to earn a living in an Artistic field. Be sure to inquire about skills levels of clients.

Tasks Based on MBTI® Results

There are three exercises at the end of the chapter for clients to use to identify preferred work tasks from their MBTI® results. They are based on

- The eight preferences (Exercise 10.2)
- The four function pairs (Exercise 10.3)
- The 16 types (Exercise 10.4)

In addition to the tasks suggested in each of the exercises, there are other descriptions of these three combinations in books such as *Introduction to Type* (Myers, 1998), *Introduction to Type in Organizations* (Hirsh & Kummerow, 1998), and *LIFETypes* (Hirsh & Kummerow, 1989). Each description can be combed for work tasks associated with type, and clients are invited to note those in addition to the ones identified in the exercises.

Tasks Identified by the *Strong* Instrument

The *Strong* instrument offers four types of scales that identify tasks or activities. Clients are invited to identify activities or tasks associated with their high scores on the following scales. Please note that for clients with very few high scores, it works to lower the "cut" scores to the average ranges for these exercises.

- General Occupational Themes in Exercise 10.5
- Basic Interest Scales in Exercise 10.6
- Occupational Scales in Exercise 10.7
- Personal Style Scales (look at both poles here)

–Work Style in Exercise 10.8

–Learning Environment in Exercise 10.9

–Leadership Style in Exercise 10.10

–Risk taking/Adventure in Exercise 10.11

Occupational Scales Tasks. The Occupational Scales essentially refer to job titles, and from any job title it is easy to go further and identify what people in that job do–that is, what their typical work activities are. Exercise 10.7 is about identifying the typical tasks associated with the occupations on which clients scored in the "similar" ranges. Useful resources are the descriptions of the *Strong*'s occupational scales such as in Appendix A of the *Strong Interest Inventory Applications and Technical Guide* (Harmon, Hansen, Borgen, & Hammer, 1994) or on the *Strong* Interpretive Report (Hammer & Grutter, 1994). Job descriptions are also available on Internet sites, such as America's Job Bank at **www.ajb.org**, and from resources such as the *O*Net Dictionary of Occupational Titles* (Farr, 1998). Clients simply read the job description, noting the words and phrases–particularly those with "action" verbs–that appeal to them. (Grutter, who first wrote of this technique, describes it in her publications; she further advises clients to create their own ideal job descriptions based on the appealing words.)

As an illustration, read the occupational descriptions below for guidance counselor and human resources director (from Appendix A of the *Strong Interest Inventory Applications and Technical Guide*; used with permission). These occupations likely encompass much of what readers of this chapter do for a living. Which of the tasks mentioned appeal to you? Are you incorporating them into your work?

- **Guidance counselor.** Counsels individuals and provides group educational and vocational guidance services. Collects and organizes information about individuals through records, tests, interviews, and professional sources to appraise their interests, aptitudes, abilities, and personality characteristics for vocational and educational planning. Studies occupational, educational, and economic information to aid clients in making and carrying out objectives. Assists individuals to understand and overcome social and emotional problems. Engages in research and follow-up activities to evaluate counseling techniques. May teach classes.

- **Human resources director.** Plans and carries out policies relating to all phases of personnel activities. Organizes recruitment, selection, and training procedures. Confers with company and union officials to establish pensions and insurance plans, workers' compensation policies, and similar functions. Studies personnel records and supervisors' reports for information such as educational background to determine personnel suitable for promotions or transfers. May act as liaison between management and labor.

Examples of Personality and Interest Results Integration

Several examples are included to illustrate how personality and interest results are integrated. Exercise 10.12 provides a place to summarize results.

Client Examples Integrating MBTI® Type with General Occupational Themes (GOT) & Basic Interest Scales (BIS) Tasks. Raol, an ISTP with Realistic-Investigative codes, is a rehabilitation services department manager in a hospital. He is tired of it and wants something different. He focused on his Basic Interest Scales to identify the activities he most enjoys: agriculture, nature, mechanical activities, medical science, merchandising, and sales. His ISTP nature indicates that perhaps hands-on activities, including troubleshooting of a technical nature, may appeal. His Realistic-Investigative code suggests he likes tangible projects where some research is needed. He used this knowledge to design a special projects position still within the hospital setting (incorporating his high medical science BIS). The hospital is expanding its facilities, and he's in charge of the project. He gets to meet with the architects, engineers, builders, hospital administrators, politicians, and community members, and help sell them on making the project happen. He's excited about the variety of the next few years as he shepherds the project through. When this position ends, he sees the possibility of a consulting job assessing rehabilitation departments. He enjoys camping, fishing, and gardening in his avocational time (see agriculture and nature); when he is least satisfied with his work at least his hobbies bring him satisfaction.

Liz is an ENFP with an Artistic-Social-Enterprising code. While she currently works as a bookstore manager, her ultimate goal is to start up her own business teaching people to use natural plant substances (herbs, aromatherapy) to help alleviate physical and mental concerns. She has taken many classes in these areas, reads extensively, and uses her "remedies" on her family and friends. She has developed a newsletter for a gardening store to teach people about this field. Her high Basic Interest Scales are nature, art, applied arts, culinary arts, teaching, and social service. In pursuing her dream, she has found a creative path to include all of them.

Client Examples Integrating Type and Occupational Scales Tasks. Herman, an ISFJ with Conventional-Social interests, was a bank manager laid off in a merger. The banker description included many tasks he liked and was good at, such as "Directs bank's monetary programs . . . in accordance with banking principles and legislation. Coordinates program activities and evaluates operating practices to ensure efficient operations. . . . Reviews financial and operating statements." He also loved learning with an Academic pole style (see discussion of this scale below). His fine-tuned sense of detail, part of his ISFJ type, also was important to him. He decided to attend graduate school to study higher education administration and now consults with colleges and universities on financial matters, a nice blending of his interests, preferences, and experience.

Stephen, an INFJ with Social-Artistic interests, is a research and development manager. His results were dissimilar to those in that occupation, but were similar to psychologists, college professors, and guidance counselors. In reading all of these descriptions, he realized why he disliked his current role. He couldn't find any tasks he enjoyed in the descriptions! But he liked many of the activities suggested in the other three, one of which included researching, but with a focus on people, not things. He has enrolled in a counseling program and hopes eventually to work in employee assistance, preferably in a high-tech company. He believes his background as a technical manager can help him build relationships quickly with the people seeking his help.

Chad, an INTJ with a Conventional code, is a public administrator. His government department is undergoing cutbacks. He likes what he is doing, as confirmed by his enjoyment of the job tasks on the jobs he scored similar to. He is now searching for a similar position (and there are many) that require those same activities, such as directing, coordinating, developing and administering budgets, and preparing reports.

Paul, an ESFJ with Enterprising-Social interests, has a doctorate in counseling and works with Native Americans, advising them on educational and career opportunities. He took the *Strong* assessment as part of a workshop to learn more about interpreting the instrument. The job titles hair stylist, travel agent, and flight attendant came out high on his list of similar occupations and almost personally invalidated the inventory for him. His career certainly hadn't gone in those directions, nor could he imagine himself doing those occupations. But when he read the task descriptions emphasizing the service elements of those jobs and saw in his ESFJ description how often service to others was mentioned, his results all fell into place. It was service to people that was important, and he was doing it through his work.

Personal Style Scales Tasks. The Personal Style scales describe four important elements related to a client's work. Combining client results on these four scales with particular MBTI® preferences (based on their statistical relationship) leads to specific activity preferences of clients. These combinations are as follows:

- Work Style: who (with people) or what (with data, ideas, or things) you want to work with, combined with Extraversion–Introversion (Exercise 10.8)
- Learning Environment: how you like to learn, in academic or hands-on settings, combined with Sensing–Intuition (Exercise 10.9)
- Leadership Style: how you prefer to lead, by example or through directing others, combined with Extraversion–Introversion (Exercise 10.10)
- Risk taking/Adventure: how much risk you are willing to take and your combination of Intuition Perceiving (NP) or Sensing Perceiving (SP) or Intuition Judging (NJ) or Sensing Judging (SJ) (Exercise 10.11)

While specific results may be expected based on statistical correlates, other combinations do occur and these are particularly illuminating to clients. Questions to help clients understand their scores are included in each exercise.

Pulling Task Information Together. Exercise 10.12 encourages the client to review all the information from Exercises 10.2 through 10.11 and look for patterns. Clients are invited to look beyond the preferred activities for actual skills. Complementary and contradictory information is sought, and compromises may need to be made.

INTEGRATING JOB TITLE INFORMATION

While the focus in career counseling has moved from concentrating on job titles to identifying lifelong skills and personality characteristics, there is still a place for noting job titles that fit with skills and personality. This is partly because clients want and need something concrete. And employers still list job titles. The *Strong and MBTI Career Development Workbook* (Kummerow & Hammer, 1995) and the *Strong* and MBTI® Career Report (Grutter & Hammer, 1996) both have systems to identify job title and check the match between the two instruments.

There are two steps to utilizing the job title information from both instruments:

1. Generate possible job titles.
   - Identify the client's *Strong* Occupational Scales with "high" scores along with the RIASEC code of each occupation.
   - Take those RIASEC codes and search for other occupations with the same codes.
   - For the MBTI® type, identify jobs highly attractive to that type.
2. Prioritize job titles to explore.
   - Place top priority on jobs that appear high on both *Strong* and MBTI® results.
   - Explore the high ones from either instrument that are not mentioned on the other one.

- If desired, explore jobs that appear high on one instrument but not the other.
- If desired, examine jobs that appear low on one or both instruments for what is appealing about them.

Generating Possible Job Titles

The first step involves identifying, on the *Strong* instrument, all job titles with a score of 40 or higher (that is, in the similar range or higher), as well as the RIASEC codes attached to each of those occupations. For those RIASEC codes, find additional job titles with the same codes from resources such as Appendix A and Appendix B in the *Strong Interest Inventory Applications and Technical Guide,* (Harmon, Hansen, Borgen, & Hammer, 1994), *Where Do I Go Next?* (Borgen & Grutter, 1995) and *The Dictionary of Holland Occupational Codes* (Gottfredson & Holland, 1996).

This step continues with the generation of job titles from MBTI® results. While the research on linking job titles with psychological type is not as well developed as that for the *Strong* assessment, there are several starting points. Table 12.9 in the *MBTI Manual* (Myers., McCaulley, Quenk, & Hammer, 1998) offers some general trends. Both Myers and McCaulley's *Manual* (1985) and the *MBTI Career Report Manual* by Hammer and Macdaid (1992) reported, for 208 occupations (based on samples of convenience), the attractiveness of that occupation to each of the 16 types. Generally the types listed in the top 50 for that occupation are attractive to members of that type. The *Myers-Briggs Type Indicator Atlas of Type Tables* (Macdaid, McCaulley, & Kainz, 1986) also offers similar data.

Prioritizing Job Titles

Several levels of priorities are possible based on the instrument results. Both instruments may encourage or discourage further exploration of job titles, or they may differ in their results. On the *Strong* assessment, "encourage" is defined as any occupation in the "similar" ranges, and on the MBTI® assessment, as an occupation that attracts more people of that type than one would expect given the percentage of that type in the general population. The "discourage" definition is based on dissimilar scores on Occupational Scales on the *Strong* instrument and on low attractiveness for the MBTI®

type. (See the sections on career data and self-selection ratios in chapter 12 of the 1998 *MBTI Manual* for more on this topic.) Any occupations that appear "high" on both instruments can be considered excellent possibilities. Focusing job search efforts on these occupations first is advised. These jobs are most likely to fit both the personality and the interests of the client.

Because the number of job titles generated from either instrument is limited and their overlap is only 59 occupations, it is possible to have jobs highlighted on one instrument but not even mentioned on the other. Gathering more information about the tasks involved in the jobs may help a client decide whether or not to pursue a particular occupation. Utilizing the task approach from Exercises 10.2 through 10.12. may help with that decision.

It is possible to have a job title suggested by one instrument but discouraged by the other instrument. On the *Strong* assessment this would mean Occupational Scales scores in the "dissimilar" ranges. On the MBTI® assessment, it would generally be the occupational titles in the bottom 50 of the lists from the 1985 *Manual* or the *MBTI Career Report Manual.* Exploring tasks related to particular jobs and then identifying how the client might adapt the job or his or her personality for a better fit may be most appropriate. It may take more work on the client's part to reconcile the two, but it certainly can be done. Reviewing the personality in Exercises 10.1 through 10.12 and the task focus is likely to be especially helpful here.

For example, an ESTP who scored "similar" on the librarian scale found that that occupation was not highly attractive to her type. After some creative brainstorming and considering a variety of possibilities, she found a position where she can specialize. She identifies technological solutions for her library system and often assists others in learning the technology in a hands-on way—a position she finds very satisfying.

For some clients, the desired occupations are low on all lists. When that occurs, you need to check out the client's motivations for the identified positions—is there a specific family expectation? Does it fit with a monetary value? As an ESTJ psychologist (with a midrange score on psychologist and very low attractiveness for my psychological type), this is my pattern. Family values of helping people and an enjoyment of academics led me to a Ph.D. in psychology. However, I do not practice psychology in the usual way; I've had to create a niche—testing, training, and writing practical guides.

To help clients identify specific job titles to explore, see Exercise 10.13. It utilizes *Strong* job titles, Holland codes, and MBTI® results. Exercise 10.14 is designed to help clients prioritize and examine specific job titles. You'll note the process does not stop with identifying a job title, but encourages further investigation of each title. The second client example below shows how Exercises 10.13 and 10.14 helped in her job title exploration.

Client Examples

Sometimes the process of looking at job titles also helps people understand prior decisions. Mark is a hospital administrator with an ENTJ, Social-Artistic-Enterprising code. He scored "very similar" to both English teacher and nursing home administrator. He loved his first job, as an English teacher. However, all of his friends were in Enterprising jobs and gave him a hard time. He decided to show them (ENTJs like challenges) and pursued a degree in hospital administration. His new job as a hospital administrator allows him to continue helping people (Social theme) and taps his ENTJ personality type to take charge of systems. He gets to be creative in how he manages his hospital, and he still brings in literary references to explain his points. Mark had never fully understood why he was so bothered by his friends' reactions to his first career in teaching, until he began to analyze his Holland codes and the occupational titles on which he scored "similar." He understood where he was different from and similar to those friends.

Unlike Mark, Marty's focus is on attempting to understand a possible future path, not a past decision. Marty is a 20-year-old woman with a year and a half of college credits. She is having difficulty with college work and has been diagnosed with a learning disability; she had wanted to major in elementary education, but she simply could not handle the college-level work required. Her work experience includes teacher's aide with special education students, nanny, and parks and recreation program assistant. Her type is ESFP. See Table 10.2 for her job title search based on her *Strong* and MBTI® results.

When Marty looked at her list, she quickly eliminated any occupations that required a college degree since this is not her focus at present. Perhaps in the future this will be possible. She also eliminated any jobs that would keep her confined to an office. Her ESFP nature is to be out and about with people and to be always on the move. Her high Basic Interest Scales include

Table 10.2 Marty's Job Title Search

Job Title	Holland Code	SII	Similar Code*	"High" Attraction for ESFP
Emergency Medical Technician	RCI	✓		N/A
Police Officer	RE	✓		High
Radiological Technologist	RIS	✓		High
Audiologist	IS	✓		N/A
Childcare Provider	S	✓		High
Community Service Organization Director	SE	✓		N/A
Elementary School Teacher	S	✓		High
Teacher's Aide	S		✓	High
Nurse, LPN	SCE	✓		
Occupational Therapist	SAR	✓		
Parks and Recreation Coordinator	SE	✓		N/A
Physical Education Teacher	SRC	✓		N/A
Physical Therapist	SIR	✓		
Special Education Teacher	SE	✓		
Speech Pathologist	SA	✓		N/A
Dental Hygienist	EIS	✓		High
Flight Attendant	EAS	✓		N/A
Florist	EAC	✓		N/A
Hair Stylist	EC	✓		High
Housekeeping & Maintenance Supervisor	ECS	✓		N/A
Athletic Equipment Custodian	EC		✓	N/A
Optician	ECR	✓		N/A
Banker	CE	✓		
Dental Assistant	CSE	✓		High
Farmer	CSE	✓		
Medical Records Technician	C	✓		N/A
Military Enlisted Personnel	CRE	✓		N/A
Paralegal	CE	✓		N/A
Small Business Owner	CE	✓		N/A

Note: N/A means the job title was not available on MBTI® occupational lists.

*"Similiar code" means an occupation with a Holland code similar to job titles suggested by the *Strong* Occupational Scales.

agriculture, athletics, and medical service, also an indication of her more active nature and her desire to be outdoors at least some of the time. Her Holland code is Social; she enjoys helping people. She felt these two instruments, with a few additional job titles suggested as a "Similiar Code" in Appendix A of the *Strong Applications and Technical Guide*, generated enough job titles for her. She is currently working as a nanny (she scored "similar" on childcare worker) in charge of four children, including infant twins. She is always taking them out to different activities. She is also enrolled in emergency medical technician (EMT) training and loves the hands-on learning (which fits with her practical pole Learning Environment score); the academic/theoretical components continue to be difficult for her. Her risk taking/ adventure score is toward the take chances pole, something that may happen in EMT work. She is looking forward to following the path toward the EMT field, and being a nanny currently affords her the income and the time for the training. She found the job title search reassuring, and it fit well with her personality and the tasks she most enjoys.

RESOURCES COMBINING THE TWO INSTRUMENTS

There are several resources describing various combinations of the two theories and instruments. The *Strong and MBTI Career Development Guide* (Hammer & Kummerow, 1996) describes using the two instruments with statistical and case data illustrations. There is also a companion workbook for clients (Kummerow & Hammer, 1995). Grutter and Hammer (1996) have written a computerized report, the *Strong* and MBTI® Career Report, that combines results from the two instruments. (Note: The decision rules explaining the report are in Hammer and Kummerow, 1996.) Grutter offers a professional's binder (coauthored with S. L. Lund, 2000) and three client workbooks combining the instruments, each as a different career development focus: career enrichment (1998a), career advancement (1998b), and career transition (1998c).

Other resources that draw on both instruments include *Starting Out, Starting Over* (Peterson, 1995), which offers some suggestions on utilizing the interests and personality type along with values and skills. *Reinventing Yourself* (Davis & Handschin, 1998) includes four circles of life: work, play, learning, and relationships. The authors believe your personality may naturally draw you toward one circle more than another. They further suggest that temperament (another personality typology, which uses the same preference codes as the MBTI® instrument) may help predict which circle you find most attractive. They see the SJ drawn more toward work, NT toward learning, NF toward relationships, and SP toward play. Using the Holland codes, those who score high on the Realistic and Conventional themes may be drawn more toward work, the Investigatives toward learning, the Socials and Enterprisings toward relationships, and the Artistics toward play. Since all four circles are important to each person, Davis and Handschin offer suggestions on how to adapt your own style to each circle.

THE WHOLE IS GREATER THAN THE SUM OF ITS PARTS

The MBTI® and *Strong Interest Inventory* instruments are two sophisticated and popular tools for helping clients understand themselves better—their personalities, preferred tasks, and possible job titles. Through integrating the results of both instruments you can help clients identify more options and gain greater self-understanding than is possible using either one alone. However, it is important to remember that there are many more variables besides personality and interests that make up the "whole" person. Other chapters in this book provide in-depth information on some of those other factors.

The following quotes by David McCord and Abraham Maslow, respectively, provide interesting perspectives on careers and life. Please make the latter quote gender inclusive as you read it.

> "Life is the garment we continually alter, but which never seems to fit."

> "A musician must make music, an artist must paint, a poet must write, if he is to be ultimately at peace with himself. What a man can be, he must be."

Skillful use of these instruments together can help clients understand the alterations they might have to make (or accept), or find comfort with the fit as it is.

EXERCISE 10.1

PERSONALITY DESCRIPTIONS

Use your MBTI® type and Holland code to answer the following:

- Which words and phrases best fit you from your MBTI® type description? (Use the whole type description, not simply the preferences, from sources such as *Introduction to Type, Introduction to Type in Organizations, LIFETypes.*)

____

____

____

- Which words and phrases fit you from your General Occupational Theme code? You may use as many of the RIASEC codes as you think fit. (Use the Holland code descriptions from your *Strong* results or from *Where Do I Go Next?)*

____

____

____

- Where do the two descriptions seem to overlap?

____

____

- Where do the two descriptions seem to contradict each other?

____

____

- How do those contradictions affect the way you do your work? Do you see yourself making compromises? How?

____

____

- In what ways can you see yourself adapting your personality in what you do?

____

____

EXERCISE 10.2

MBTI® PREFERENCES

Check the activity next to your preference results. Does it appeal to you? Look for other resources describing the preferences and how they appear in work situations and communication styles (such as those in *Introduction to Type®*, *Introduction to Type® in Organizations*, and *LIFETypes*). Add those tasks that most appeal to you on the lines below.

Do you prefer to engage in activities . . .

with others (E)?	or	alone (I)?
that pay attention to reality and the details (S)?	or	that focus on the big picture and possibilities (N)?
where logic and problem solving are the focus (T)?	or	where people and values are the focus (F)?
that are organized and goal oriented (J)?	or	that are spontaneous and process oriented (P)?

EXERCISE 10.3

MBTI® FUNCTION PAIR COMBINATIONS

For the middle two letters in your type, note the activity associated with it. Does it fit what you like to do? Find the combinations described in resources such as *Introduction to Type®* and *Introduction to Type® in Organizations*. Add any additional tasks/activities that appeal to you in the space below.

ST Finding efficient methods and procedures to get the work done

SF Focusing on customer service, helping people meet their needs

NF Generating ways to help people grow, develop, and communicate

NT Discovering cutting-edge theories and strategies

EXERCISE 10.4

MBTI® WHOLE TYPE (STEP I TYPE)

Find your type and read the list of activities those who share your type often enjoy. Do they appeal to you? Read any descriptions of your type and add more tasks that appeal to you.

ISTJ Working consistently to get things done on time Carefully managing detail Analyzing information logically Honoring and meeting commitments Using standard operating procedures comfortably	**ISFJ** Working to serve others' needs Noticing people's practical needs Being patient and responsible with detail and routine Following through consistently Using traditional procedures conscientiously	**INFJ** Providing insights to serve people Utilizing a quiet, intense course of action Focusing on their ideals Creating ways to make inspirations real Following through on commitments	**INTJ** Providing theoretical insights Organizing ideas into plans Acting strongly and forcefully in their own field Removing obstacles to goal attainment Pushing people to understand entire complex system
ISTP Acting as troubleshooters Keeping relevant information in their heads Finding practical, logical ways to overcome obstacles Handling crises calmly Using technical expertise	**ISFP** Responding to each person's practical needs Working to ensure others' well-being Bringing joy to their work Using cooperation to bring people and tasks together Offering praise, support, and loyalty	**INFP** Encouraging others to act on their ideals Drawing people together around a common purpose Seeking new ideas and possibilities Encouraging all to uphold values Pursuing unique solutions to issues	**INTP** Applying logic, analysis, and critical thinking Concentrating on core issues Tackling intricate problems Adding both short- and long-range intellectual insight Working independently

EXERCISE 10.4 (CONT'D)

ESTP	ESFP	ENFP	ENTP
Taking a realistic, direct approach Negotiating to move things along Keeping things lively and happening Taking calculated risks Noticing and remembering factual information	Enthusiastically cooperating with others Treating people generously Putting people at ease Focusing on practical needs Offering action, excitement, and fun	Initiating change Focusing on possibilities for people Enthusing others with high energy Praising people Using creativity and imagination especially for start-ups	Providing new ways to do things Viewing limitations as challenges Taking initiative and spurring others on Finding conceptual frameworks Encouraging independence
ESTJ	**ESFJ**	**ENFJ**	**ENTJ**
Organizing as much as possible Following through in a step-by-step manner Monitoring tasks to see if they are done correctly Using logic to decide quickly Pointing out and correcting flaws in advance	Keeping people well informed Focusing on a service orientation Cooperating with and pleasing others Completing tasks in a timely, accurate, and responsible way Respecting rules and authority	Encouraging others' development Communicating values Facilitating Bringing matters to conclusions Encouraging broad participation and cooperation	Developing well thought out plans Providing logical structure Designing strategies Taking charge quickly and doing what it takes Dealing directly with problems

Source: Modified and reproduced by special permission of the publisher, Consulting Psychologists Press, Inc., from *Introduction to Type in Organizations* by Sandra Krebs Hirsh and Jean M. Kummerow.

EXERCISE 10.5

GENERAL OCCUPATIONAL THEMES (GOT) TASKS

Which groups of tasks appeal to you the most? Do they fit your high scores? What patterns do you notice?

- Realistic—do you enjoy tasks where you are
  - outdoors?
  - building and/or repairing things?
  - working with tools?
- Investigative—do you enjoy tasks that involve
  - scientific and mathematical pursuits?
  - conducting research studies?
  - solving abstract, complex problems?
- Artistic—do you enjoy tasks that include
  - creating something original?
  - art, writing, music, theater (either appreciating or producing)?
  - being unstructured?
- Social—do you enjoy tasks that allow for
  - helping and caring for people?
  - working cooperatively in groups?
  - teaching others?
- Enterprising—do you enjoy tasks where you are
  - leading others?
  - persuading and selling them on your views?
  - managing people?
- Conventional—do you enjoy tasks that include
  - managing data?
  - being organized and accurate?
  - respecting the known ways of doing things?

EXERCISE 10.6

BASIC INTEREST SCALES (BIS) TASKS

Check your "high" scores on the BIS scales against this list. Do you agree these tasks are enjoyable? Are you incorporating these activities in your work? In your avocational pursuits? Look for any patterns–the scales are grouped according to the RIASEC code with which they are most closely associated.

- Agriculture–working with your hands, out of doors, in activities such as raising animals or gardening
- Nature–being out of doors enjoying the beauty of nature
- Military activities–participating in structured activities of a military nature
- Athletics–participating actively or passively in a variety of athletic endeavors
- Mechanical activities–using large or small tools

- Science–researching, especially in the physical sciences
- Mathematics–working with numbers
- Medical science–learning about the biological sciences

- Music/Dramatic–creating or enjoying a variety of musical and theater events
- Art–creating or enjoying visual arts and appreciating art for art's sake
- Applied arts–creating or enjoying the graphic arts and ways to put art to work
- Writing–creating or enjoying the written word
- Culinary arts–cooking and entertaining

- Teaching–instructing young people (under the age of 18)
- Social service–working one on one with people to help them understand and overcome problems, especially in the interpersonal realm
- Medical service–providing medical assistance to people in need
- Religious activities–focusing on religious/spiritual needs with organized activities

EXERCISE 10.6 (CONT'D)

- Public speaking—espousing your views in public
- Law/Politics—paying attention to public policy and process
- Merchandising—serving customers and filling orders
- Sales—cold calling on customers and winning orders
- Organizational management—leading and managing people

- Data management—managing and organizing data
- Computer activities—using the computer
- Office services—doing activities, such as word processing and filing, for a smooth-running office

EXERCISE 10.7

OCCUPATIONAL SCALES (OS) TASKS

Have clients read through the descriptions of their most similar Occupational Scales and highlight or make note of the phrases that attract them. An alternative to this is to simply note the verbs that appeal. Then look for patterns.

____

____

____

____

____

____

EXERCISE 10.8

WORK STYLE

Using your score on Work Style and your preference for Extraversion or Introversion, see if the patterns described below fit for you. How does your current work setting meet your work style?

Work with people (>55): Do you prefer to work with people, often in group settings, where talking things through is encouraged?

- For Extraverted types, this is often the pattern. They enjoy focusing their work on people, perhaps working in teams, and they gain energy from talking things through and interacting with others.
- Introverts who score in this category, while drawn toward people and enjoying working with them, find the focus on the outside world draining and need to make sure they have alone time to reenergize. They often prefer one-on-one interactions or small groups where they can get to know people in-depth.

Work with data (<45): Do you prefer working with data, ideas, and things, in an independent fashion?

- Introverted types often have this pattern. They find a comfort in controlling their own time, using their energy to tune into the data they find interesting and important. They are invigorated by their quiet time.
- Extraverts who score in this category find they need to be around activity (like having a window to the outside where they can always see what's going on or working at their laptops in a high-traffic area of the library), but concentrating on data or ideas.

Do you prefer a combination of the two (45–55), with both needed for balance?

- Both Introverts and Extraverts report a need for quiet and for activities with people. If they have too much of one activity, they feel it! Extraverts often want to discuss their activities with people more than the Introverts prefer.

EXERCISE 10.9

LEARNING ENVIRONMENT

Using your scores on the Learning Environment Scale and your preference for Sensing or Intuition, find your pattern below. Does it describe you? Can you identify learning environments that are conducive to your style?

Academic pole (>55): Do you prefer to learn for the sake of learning, like reading on your own, and in a variety of formal and informal settings?

- Intuitive types often score in this category. They may enjoy being in school for long periods of time, taking a variety of courses, and/or reading a variety of books simply for enjoyment. Learning anything new is fun whether or not it will ever be applied. They often enjoy learning theories and focusing on new possibilities.
- Sensing types in this category also enjoy learning, but usually have a practical purpose in mind or know they will find a practical use soon for what it is that they are learning. They like to eventually apply what they have learned or at least tie the new learning to things they already know about.

Practical pole (<45): Do you prefer to learn with the goal of developing a practical skill through hands-on activities and shorter, focused courses?

- Sensing types score more often in this category and find they like to key in on specific areas of interest—they know how they will apply that learning quickly to their work. They are disappointed if no practical applications are readily apparent.
- Intuitive types who score on the practical pole often prefer short courses that include hands-on activities. They don't need to be able to use the information immediately. Once they've mastered the information, they like to move on to something new and different.

Do you prefer a mix (45–55) of learning activities and motivations for learning?

- Those in this category describe a variety of learning styles and reasons for learning as comfortable for them. Intuitive types want to see the big picture, whereas Sensing types want enough detail to become grounded in the subject.

EXERCISE 10.10

LEADERSHIP STYLE

Combine your score on Leadership Style with your preference for Extraversion or Introversion. Does the description fit for you? Are you able to lead in a way that is comfortable for you?

Direct others (>55): Do you prefer to make your opinions known to others and do you feel comfortable directing their activities?

- Extraverts often score here and find that with their preference for talking things out, their opinions are available for all to hear. They typically are comfortable commenting on a variety of topics and will take charge quickly, especially if there is a void in leadership.
- Introverts who score here find themselves directing others only in their areas of expertise—they are clear and forthright in those specific situations. However, they have no need to express their opinions when outside of their interests or expertise.

Lead by example (<45): Do you prefer to lead by example, letting others observe your style and figure out for themselves what to do?

- Introverts seem more comfortable with this style of leadership. They often say that the right way is obvious to them and assume it is obvious to others. By showing others the right ways to do things through modeling they demonstrate their leadership.
- Extraverts who like to lead by example want to be with others and attempt to have others join them. They find doing things together is more enjoyable than directing people.

Do you prefer a mix (45–55) of leadership styles depending on the situation?

- While both styles of leadership are possible for Introverts and Extraverts, and both begin by leading by example, the Extraverts will move more quickly into directing.

EXERCISE 10.11

RISK TAKING/ADVENTURE

Combine your Risk-taking/Adventure score with the second and fourth letters of your type. Read your description and identify how your style affects your work.

Take chances (>55): Do you prefer to take chances and have an element of physical, financial, and/or social risk in your life?

- Intuitive Perceiving (NP) types tend to score this way, often following an interesting new possibility with less interest in the practicalities of the situation.

Play it safe (<45): Do you prefer to play it safe and cautiously undertake new endeavors, especially if they involve some physical risk?

- Sensing Judging types (SJ) tend to fall more often in this category, wanting to understand up front as many risks as they can and to gather information on how to overcome them before moving to action. They often need to develop options, such as a Plan A, Plan B, and Plan C, before moving to action.

Do you prefer to take a few chances but not lead your life "on the edge" (45–55)?

- Sensing Perceiving types (SP) may take risks in the moment, but keep the big things in their lives intact, such as a home and a relationship.
- Intuitive Judging types (NJ) may take risks, but only after much thought, so that the risk fits with an internal vision of what is right for their situation.

EXERCISE 10.12

INTEGRATING THE TASKS FROM EACH INSTRUMENT

Review the tasks you've indicated you enjoy from Exercises 10.2 through 10.11. You'll have information on the following from the *Strong* and MBTI® instruments:

- General Occupational Themes
- Basic Interest Scales
- Occupational Scales
- Personal Style Scales
- MBTI® Preferences
- MBTI® Type

Answer the following questions to help you identify patterns and define possible actions.

Do these activities also represent skills and abilities?

Where do these pieces of information fit together and reinforce each other?

Where do they seem at odds and contradictory?

How can you reconcile the differences? Remember to consider both your work and home lives—perhaps you can concentrate on one at work and one at home.

Where do you need to make compromises?

Can you make short- and long-term plans regarding where and for how long the compromises are necessary?

Can you alter the way you do your job to fit better with your personality or with your interests?

Review the cases in this chapter to see how others have made compromises.

EXERCISE 10.13

IDENTIFYING JOB TITLES TO EXPLORE

List job titles suggested by scores in the "similar" ranges on the *Strong Interest Inventory®* instrument. Put a check mark in the column titled "Encouraged" on *Strong* Assessment for each title. Note the Holland code for each job title. Check resources such as the Appendices in the *Strong Interest Inventory Applications and Technical Guide* to find occupations with the same Holland codes; note those job titles in the table. Next, for each of those job titles check MBTI® resources (such as the *MBTI Career Report Manual)* to see if those with the same type as the client are often attracted to that occupation. Place a check mark in the "Encouraged" on MBTI® Assessment column for all those in which this is the case. Now add any additional occupations from MBTI® data that are attractive to people of the client's type. These are the jobs to prioritize in Exercise 10.14.

Job Title	Holland Code	"Encouraged" on Strong Assessment	"Encouraged" on MBTI® Assessment

EXERCISE 10.14

PRIORITIZING AND EXPLORING JOB TITLES

Which job titles are suggested by both the *Strong* and MBTI® assessments?

- What additional information do you need about the job in question?
- How can you explore that job?
- What additional skills would you need to develop to be ready for a job on this list?

Which job titles are on one but not the other? Answer the same questions as above.

Which job titles are interesting to you but are discouraged by the instrument results?

- Why are you interested in that job?
- What do you need to learn about that job?
- Is there a possible niche within the occupation or one you could create that would allow you to "be yourself"?

REFERENCES

Borgen, F., & Grutter, J. (1995). *Where do I go next? Using your Strong results to manage your career.* Palo Alto, CA: Consulting Psychologists Press.

Carr, S. (1997). *Type clarification: Finding the fit.* Oxford, England: Oxford Psychologists Press.

Consulting Psychologists Press. (1995). *Exploring career options with the Strong Interest Inventory* (video). Palo Alto, CA: Consulting Psychologists Press.

Davis, S., & Handschin, B. (1998). *Reinventing yourself: Life planning after 50 using the Strong and the MBTI.* Palo Alto, CA: Consulting Psychologists Press.

Farr, J. M. (1998). *The O*Net dictionary of occupational titles.* Washington, DC: U.S. Department of Labor.

Gottfredson, G. D., & Holland, J. L. (1996). *Dictionary of Holland Occupational Codes* (3rd ed.). Odessa, FL: Psychological Assessment Resources.

Grutter, J. (1998a). *Making it in today's organizations: Career advancement using the Strong and the MBTI.* Palo Alto, CA: Consulting Psychologists Press.

Grutter, J. (1998b). *Making it in today's organizations: Career enrichment using the Strong and the MBTI.* Palo Alto, CA: Consulting Psychologists Press.

Grutter, J. (1998c). *Making it beyond today's organizations: Career transition using the Strong and the MBTI.* Palo Alto, CA: Consulting Psychologists Press.

Grutter, J., & Hammer, A. L. (1996). The Strong and MBTI career report. Palo Alto, CA: Consulting Psychologists Press.

Grutter, J., & Lund, S. L. (2000). *Making it in today's organizations using the Strong and MBTI* (professional's binder). Palo Alto, CA: Consulting Psychologists Press.

Hammer, A. L. (1994). Strong Interest Inventory: Professional report. Palo Alto, CA: Consulting Psychologists Press.

Hammer, A. L. (1996). Career management and counseling. In A. L. Hammer (Ed.), *MBTI applications* (pp. 31–54). Palo Alto, CA: Consulting Psychologists Press.

Hammer, A. L., & Grutter, J. (1994). Strong Interest Inventory: Interpretive report. Palo Alto, CA: Consulting Psychologists Press.

Hammer, A. L., & Kummerow, J. M. (1992). *Strong and MBTI career development guide.* Palo Alto, CA: Consulting Psychologists Press.

Hammer, A. L., & Kummerow, J. M. (1996). *Strong and MBTI career development guide* (rev. ed.). Palo Alto, CA: Consulting Psychologists Press.

Hammer, A. L., & Macdaid, G. P. (1992). *MBTI career report manual.* Palo Alto, CA: Consulting Psychologists Press.

Hammer, A. L., & Macdaid, G. P. (1994). MBTI career report. Palo Alto, CA: Consulting Psychologists Press.

Harmon, L. W., Hansen, J.-I. C., Borgen, F. H., & Hammer, A. L. (1994). *Strong Interest Inventory applications and technical guide.* Palo Alto, CA: Consulting Psychologists Press.

Hirsh, S. K. (1995). *Strong Interest Inventory resource: Strategies for group and individual interpretations in business and organizational settings.* Palo Alto, CA: Consulting Psychologists Press.

Hirsh, S. K., & Kummerow, J. M. (1989). *LIFETypes.* New York: Warner Books.

Hirsh, S. K., & Kummerow, J. M. (1998). *Introduction to type in organizations* (3rd ed.). Palo Alto, CA: Consulting Psychologists Press.

Hirsh, S. K., & Kummerow, J. M. (1998). MBTI Interpretive Report for Organizations, Form M. Palo Alto, CA: Consulting Psychologists Press.

Kummerow, J. M. (1998). Uses of type in career counseling. In I. B. Myers, M. H. McCaulley, N. L. Quenk, & A. L. Hammer (Eds.), *MBTI manual: A guide to the development and use of the Myers-Briggs Type Indicator* (3rd ed., pp. 285–324). Palo Alto, CA: Consulting Psychologists Press.

Kummerow, J. M., & Hammer, A. L. (1995). *Strong and MBTI career development workbook.* Palo Alto, CA: Consulting Psychologists Press.

Kummerow, J. M., & Quenk, N. L. (1992). *Interpretive guide for the MBTI expanded analysis report.* Palo Alto, CA: Consulting Psychologists Press.

Macdaid, G. P., McCaulley, M. H., & Kainz, R. I. (1986). *Myers-Briggs Type Indicator atlas of type tables.* Gainesville, FL: Center for Applications of Psychological Type.

Mitchell, W. (1999). *MBTI Step II: A description of the subscales.* Palo Alto, CA: Consulting Psychologists Press.

Montross, D. H., Leibowitz, Z. B., & Shinkman, C. J. (1995). *Real people, real jobs.* Palo Alto, CA: Davies-Black.

Myers, I. B. (1998). *Introduction to type* (6th ed.). Palo Alto, CA: Consulting Psychologists Press.

Myers, I. B., & McCaulley, M. H. (1985). *Manual: A guide to the development and use of the Myers-Briggs Type Indicator.* (2nd ed.). Palo Alto, CA: Consulting Psychologists Press.

Myers, I. B., McCaulley, M. H., Quenk, N. L., & Hammer, A. L. (1998). MBTI *manual: A guide to the development and use of the Myers-Briggs Type Indicator* (3rd ed.). Palo Alto, CA: Consulting Psychologists Press.

Peterson, L. (1995). *Starting out, starting over.* Palo Alto, CA: Davies-Black.

Prince, J. P. (1995). *Strong Interest Inventory resource: Strategies for group and individual interpretations in college settings* (3rd ed.). Palo Alto, CA: Consulting Psychologists Press.

Rumpel, S. K., & Lecertua, K. (1996a). *Strong Interest Inventory: High school edition.* Palo Alto, CA: Consulting Psychologists Press.

Rumpel, S. K., & Lecertua, K. (1996b). *Strong Interest Inventory resource: Strategies for group interpretations in high school settings.* Palo Alto, CA: Consulting Psychologists Press.

Saunders, D. (1989). *The expanded analysis report manual.* Palo Alto, CA: Consulting Psychologists Press.

About the Contributors

1 The Changing World of Work: Preparing Yourself for the Road Ahead

Wayne F. Cascio, Ph.D., is professor of management and international business at the University of Colorado at Denver. He is past president of both the Human Resources Division of the Academy of Management and the Society for Industrial and Organizational Psychology. His research interests include personnel selection, training, performance management, and the economic impact of human resources activities. He has consulted with over 150 organizations on six continents.

Cascio has authored and edited numerous journal articles and book chapters as well as five texts in human resource management: *Managing Human Resources: Productivity, Quality of Work Life, Profits* (5th ed.), *Applied Psychology in Human Resource Management* (5th ed.), *Costing Human Resources: The Financial Impact of Behavior in Organizations* (4th ed.), *HR Planning, Employment, and Placement*, and *Human Resource Management: An Information Systems Approach.* Current editorial board memberships include *Human Performance, Asia-Pacific HRM,* and *Organizational Dynamics.* Cascio is a recipient of the Distinguished Faculty and Distinguished Career awards from the Human Resources Division of the Academy of Management and the Bemis award for excellence in HRM from the International Personnel Management Association's Assessment Council. He received his B.A. degree in psychology from Holy Cross College, his M.A. degree in experimental psychology from Emory University, and his Ph.D. degree in industrial and organizational psychology from the University of Rochester.

2 Planning for the 21st-Century Workforce: Key Trends That Will Shape the Employment and Career Landscape

Andrea Saveri, M.A., is a director of the Emerging Technologies Program at the Institute for the Future (IFTF) in Menlo Park, California, where she has worked since the late 1980s. Her work focuses on identifying the long-term demographic, social, and technological trends that shape the transformation of work, the workplace, and household life. In particular, she examines the underlying factors and unarticulated needs and desires that shape the diffusion and adoption of information and communications technologies at home and at work.

Saveri is interested in describing the dynamic reinvention of technology, the social institutions of work and household life, the evolving set of alternative work relationships (such as flexible staffing, contracting, and outsourcing), the emerging forms of the virtual office, and the consequences for businesses and other organizations, and has presented her work internationally. She holds a B.A. degree in Hispanic studies from Harvard University and an M.A. degree in Latin American studies from the University of California, Berkeley.

Rod Falcon, M.A., is a research manager at IFTF. He conducts research in emerging technologies and health care, and manages large-scale projects across IFTF. His current focus is on understanding information and communications technology in a global context, including the enabling effects of technology on economies, organizations, and communities. He also pursues research in the areas of globalization, the future of work, and aging policy—with an emphasis on California and the broader Pacific Rim.

Before joining IFTF, Falcon worked as a health policy analyst for the Kaiser Family Foundation. He holds a B.A. degree in American history and ethnic studies from the University of California, Berkeley, and an M.A. degree in public policy from U.C. Berkeley's Goldman School of Public Policy.

We want to thank all our colleagues at IFTF, who challenged and supported us as we developed our ideas about the future workforce and workplace and who continue to stimulate our thinking.

3 A New Deal for a Learning Economy: Jobs and Careers in Postindustrial Society

Stephen A. Herzenberg, Ph.D., is executive director of the Keystone Research Center, a think tank headquartered in Harrisburg, Pennsylvania. Prior to joining Keystone, he taught at Rutgers University and held project director and research positions at the U.S. Congressional Office of Technology Assessment and the U.S. Department of Labor (DOL). While at DOL, he was an assistant to the chief negotiator of the labor side agreement of the North American Free Trade Agreement.

Herzenberg has published in academic and policy books and journals on topics that include the organization of work, the auto industry, international labor standards, and labor unions. He is coauthor of *New Rules for a New Economy: Employment and Opportunity in Postindustrial America.* He holds a B.A. degree in mechanical engineering from Harvard University and a Ph.D. degree in economics from MIT.

John A. Alic, Ph.D., is a consultant in Washington, D.C., and an adjunct faculty member at the Johns Hopkins School of Advanced International Studies. From 1979 until 1995, he was a member of the staff of the U.S. Congressional Office of Technology Assessment (OTA) where he directed studies dealing primarily with international trade and competition. Before joining OTA, Alic taught at Wichita State University and at the University of Maryland.

Alic is coauthor of *New Rules for a New Economy,* and *Beyond Spinoff: Military and Commercial Technologies in a Changing World.* He received his B.M.E. degree in mechanical engineering from Cornell University, his M.S. degree in mechanical engineering from Stanford University, and his Ph.D. degree in materials science and engineering from the University of Maryland.

Howard Wial, J.D., Ph.D., is senior fellow at the Keystone Research Center. He has taught economics, industrial relations, and law at several colleges and universities, including Swarthmore, Brown, and Rutgers, and has been a public policy analyst at the U.S. Department of Labor and the U.S. Congressional Office of Technology Assessment. Coauthor of *New Rules* *for a New Economy*, Wial has published articles in social science journals, law reviews, and books on such topics as youth employment, immigration, job stability, labor unions, and labor and employment law. He holds an A.B. degree in economics from the University of Michigan, a J.D. degree from the Yale University Law School, and a Ph.D. degree in economics from MIT.

4 Integrative Life Planning: A New Worldview for Career Professionals

L. Sunny Hansen, Ph.D., is professor emeritus of counseling and student personnel psychology at the University of Minnesota in Minneapolis. Compelled by a lifelong interest in social issues of justice and equality, she founded and now directs BORN FREE, a federally funded program to expand career options for both women and men. A former high school English teacher and counselor, Hansen has written and lectured throughout the world on aspects of counseling and career development. Her publications are in the areas of multicultural counseling, definitions of career education, eliminating sex stereotyping in school, gender roles, career development education, and more.

Hansen created a nationally disseminated television course on career development and planning. Her major recent work is her book *Integrative Life Planning: Critical Tasks for Career Development and Changing Life Patterns*, which is the basis for her chapter in this volume. She is past president of both the American Counseling Association (ACA) and the National Career Development Association (NCDA). She is a recipient of the Eminent Career Award from NCDA, the Distinguished Mentor Award from the Association for Counselor Education and Supervision and the Professional Development Award from ACA. She holds a B.S. degree in English and journalism, an M.A. degree in curriculum and instruction, and a Ph.D. degree in counseling and guidance, all from the College of Education at the University of Minnesota.

5 Informed Opportunism: Career and Life Planning for the New Millennium

Judith A. Waterman, M.A., is founder and CEO of the Career Management Group and a founding director of MindSteps, Inc., now eProNet, a web-based career management firm. Her main purpose in both endeavors is to help individuals find their most natural, satisfying, and rewarding career/life choices—and, in turn, promote productivity for their employers.

Waterman is the author of several self-assessment computer programs and numerous publications. Among these are the landmark *Harvard Business Review* article "Toward a Career Resilient Workforce" (coauthored with Betsy Collard) and *Introduction to the FIRO-B*™, a definitive interpretation of one of the more commonly used personal development instruments. She has a passion for the environment and is a member of the World Wild Life's Marine Leadership Committee. She holds a B.M.E. degree in music and education from the University of Colorado, studied psychotherapy at Cairnmiller Instituite in Melbourne, Australia, and received her M.A. degree in counseling education from San Jose State University.

Special thanks to those who were interviewed for this chapter and/or its predecessor in the first edition: Albert Bandura, Richard Bolles, Howard Figler, Robin Holt, John Krumboltz, Lili Pratt, Mary Lynn Pulley, and David Ransom.

6 Beyond Balance to Life Quality: The Integration of Work and Life

Betsy Collard, M.A., is Director of Alumni Volunteer Relations at the Stanford University Alumni Association in Palo Alto, California. Previously, she served for 20 years as Director of Program and Innovation at the Career Action Center in Cupertino, California, where her responsibilities included the development of the center's programs and services for individuals and organizations. Having served as a consultant on a wide range of issues relating to career self-reliance and workforce resilience, she is coauthor of the *Harvard Business Review* article "Toward a Career Resilient Workforce" and author of *The High-Tech Career Book.*

Collard has worked for the state of California as a career consultant and served as a dean at Stanford University and the University of California, Santa Cruz. She received her B.A. degree in literature from Scripps College, her M.A. degree in counseling from Stanford University, and an honorary doctoral degree from Golden Gate University in recognition of her contributions to the field of career development.

H. B. Gelatt, Ed.D., author of *Creative Decision Making: Using Positive Uncertainty,* is a nationally known speaker, writer, and consultant on the subjects of career development, futures thinking, decision making, and counseling. He received the Professional Resource Award from the Career Planning and Adult Development Network for "outstanding service as a resource to the career development profession" as well as the Lifetime Achievement in Career Development Award from the California Career Development Association. Gelatt's current passion is bringing to awareness the powerful role internalized beliefs play in our daily decisions and in creating our futures. He received his B.A. degree in psychology from California State University, San Jose, and his M.A. and Ed.D. degrees in counseling psychology from Stanford University.

7 Values: A Key to Meaningful Work

Mark Guterman, M.A., is president of G & G Associates, a consulting firm specializing in teaching people and organizations how to thrive at work in the 21st century. He is the author of *Common Sense for Uncommon Times: The Power of Balance in Work, Family, and Personal Life* and coauthor of *ValueSearch,* and he has created a number of training and development programs used extensively by groups and organizations.

Guterman has worked with a wide variety of large and small organizations, including many in the high-tech industry. He teaches in John F. Kennedy University's M.A. program in career development and is a frequent speaker to organizations and conferences throughout the world. He received his B.A. degree in history and political science from the University of California, Los Angeles, and his M.A. degree in counseling from Sonoma State University.

Terry Karp, M.A., is coauthor of *ValueSearch* and has a private career management practice in Oakland, California, offering counseling and coaching services to individuals. Additionally, she provides team building workshops as well as management training classes for a variety of organizations in the high-tech industry. She also assists organizations with candidate selection throughout the recruitment process. She managed an executive search firm specializing in high-tech and finance for 10 years prior to getting involved with career development. Karp holds a B.A degree in psychology from the University of Wisconsin at Madison and an M.A. degree in career development from the John F. Kennedy University School of Management in Walnut Creek, California.

8 Multicultural Career Counseling: Awareness, Knowledge, and Skills for the Changing Face of the Workplace

Rosie Phillips Bingham, Ph.D., ABPP, is a licensed and board certified psychologist. She is currently Assistant Vice President for Student Development at the University of Memphis in Memphis, Tennessee, and adjunct professor in the Department of Counseling, Educational Psychology, and Research. She has written numerous articles and book chapters in the area of multicultural career counseling. She is coeditor of the book *Career Counseling with African Americans* and is currently on the editorial board of the *Journal of Career Assessment*, the *Journal of Counseling Psychology*, and the *Journal of College Student Development*. She received her B.A. degree in sociology and secondary education from Elmhurst College (Illinois) and both her M.A degree in counseling and guidance and her Ph.D. degree in counseling psychology from the Ohio State University.

I am grateful to Ms. Jeanett Ballentine for her unwavering patience in typing and retyping the manuscript. And thank you, Ms. Roshunda Williams, for helping with charts and tables as we began using a new computer. And, of course, thanks to my son, Akil Davis, and husband, John Davis, for their constant support.

9 Developmental Career Counseling: Different Stages, Different Choices

Judith Grutter, M.S., has been a career development program consultant and trainer for over three decades and is currently a principal with G/S Consultants in South Lake Tahoe, California. A National Certified Career Counselor, she developed and for several years coordinated the graduate programs in career counseling at California State University, Northridge (CSUN). She is on the adjunct faculty of CSUN and of the John F. Kennedy University School of Management, and she is a member of the MBTI® qualifying faculty of the Association for Psychological Type.

Grutter is a recognized authority on the uses of assessment in career counseling and consulting. She is coauthor of the *Strong Interest Inventory®* Interpretive Report, the Strong/MBTI® Career Report, *Where do I Go Next? Using Your Strong Results to Manage Your Career,* and author of a facilitator's guide and series of workbooks titled *Making It in Today's Organizations Using the Strong and the MBTI.* A past president of the California Career Development Association, she is a recipient of the National Career Development Association's Award for Excellence in Career Development and of the California Career Development Association's first Practitioner of the Year Award, which is named in her honor. She received her B.A. degree in English from Syracuse University and her M.S. degree in counseling from California State University, Los Angeles.

10 Using the Strong Interest Inventory® and Myers-Briggs Type Indicator® Instruments Together: The Whole Is Greater than the Sum of Its Parts

Jean M. Kummerow, Ph.D., LP, is a psychologist, consultant, trainer, and author in St. Paul, Minnesota, and an international expert in training professionals to use psychological instruments, such as the *Myers-Briggs Type Indicator®* (MBTI®), the MBTI® Step II, and the *Strong Interest Inventory®*. She is on the faculty of the Association for Psychological Type. She applies psychological principles in career counseling, leadership development and coaching, and team development. She is the staff psychologist to the Blandin Foundation's Community Leadership program, training leaders from rural Minnesota to build communities. Kummerow is author or coauthor of several publications including the best-selling *Introduction to Type® in Organizations, LIFETypes,* and *WORKTypes,* as well as the *Strong and MBTI Career Development Guide* and *Workbook,* MBTI Step II Expanded Interpretive Report, and the chapter on career counseling in the 1998 *MBTI Manual.* She is on the editorial board of the *Journal for Psychological Type* and served as the editor of the first edition of *New Directions in Career Planning and the Workplace.* She received her A.B. degree in sociology from Grinnell College in Iowa and her M.A. and Ph.D. degrees in counseling and student personnel psychology from the University of Minnesota.

It has been my pleasure to work with the contributors to this volume and to learn from them—collegiality and education are both important to me, and this crew was stellar in offering both. They were also great in putting up with my sense of humor. Finally, I appreciated their grace when they accepted my feedback and their wisdom when they gently rejected it.

In addition, I'd like to acknowledge the contributions of Peggy Alexander, Deb Bouchareb, Catherine Fitzgerald, Sally Power, Kari Sandven, and Julie Sellergren, who helped identify what was absolutely right about the chapters and what could be better, as well as Jill Anderson-Wilson of Davies-Black, who worked hard to keep the project on track. As usual, Lee Langhammer Law of Davies-Black provided encouragement, enthusiasm, and wisdom, each at just the right time.

Index